# THE HUMBERSIDE REGION

SERIES EDITOR: David M. Smith

*Associate Professor of Geography, University of Florida*

THE NORTH WEST   David M. Smith

*Associate Professor of Geography, University of Florida*

THE NORTH EAST   John House

*Professor of Geography, University of Newcastle upon Tyne*

THE HUMBERSIDE   Peter Lewis and Philip N. Jones
REGION

*Lecturers in Geography, University of Hull*

IN PREPARATION
SOUTH WALES   Graham Humphreys

*Lecturer in Geography, University College of Swansea*

THE WEST   P. A. Wood
MIDLANDS

*Lecturer in Geography, University College, London*

A GEOGRAPHY OF   David Heal
STEEL IN POST
WAR BRITAIN   *Lecturer in Geography, University College of Wales, Aberystwyth*

# Industrial Britain

# THE HUMBERSIDE REGION

## Peter Lewis & Philip N. Jones

David & Charles : Newton Abbot

ISBN 0 7153 4897 3

*For Rosemary and Jean*

Set in eleven point Times, two points leaded and printed in Great Britain by Clarke Doble & Brendon Limited Plymouth for David & Charles (Publishers) Limited South Devon House Newton Abbot Devon

# Contents

# List of Illustrations

## *Plates*

## Figures in Text

# Preface

THERE IS CONSIDERABLE public awareness concerning the nation's economic health; an awareness fed by news media on a diet of Gross National Product, gold reserves and trade balance. The modern diet is no more palatable than the older fare for the same problems: problems seen in a factory closing, a job lost and a new income source to be found. The problem is one of enormous complexity, and emphasises among other things the interrelationships between different sectors of the economy. The commonly prescribed remedy suggests different doses of regional economic planning: more a faith than an exact science. At best planning can mean reducing the error in what remains an essentially trial and error system of general economic growth. It cannot mean a certain route to a given result. The desired result is the introduction of new business enterprises giving sustained regional growth contributing to sustained national growth. If Humberside is to grow, its growth must be in the national interest and this implies that it must not occur at the expense of other areas that could achieve at least the same level of growth with less input of capital. This seems very simple, but is in reality immensely complex.

This study attempts to discuss the attributes of the region recognised by industrialists under a trial and error system. Those factors that have been selected persistently and those that have been emphasised by recent industrial growth are discussed in particular, because they may continue to provide the elements for growth which are more advantageously available in this region and which, because of this, are attractive to business enterprise. Undertakings that depend on these factors ought to be more strongly encouraged than those for which this region offers no such advantage. We provide a general background to the region, discussing its extent, its location relative to other regions and its links to other areas. We discuss the Humber as a barrier to internal movement, a stimulus for urban growth and as the medium for the established trading contacts with other regions.

9

We examine recent changes in employment opportunities because the people, whose job decisions make the region what it is, are in some way the blood of the region and a blood count reveals the symptoms of health and malaise. We describe the industries and analyse their structure with reference to national patterns. We then confine our attention to a discussion of industrial groupings in the main centres, and conclude by an analysis of movement potential for the region. The book contains precise data on industry, its employment, its size and its location. This data is used thoroughly, but the authors have been aware of the dangers of trying to say more than the data allows, and for ease of presentation the statistical framework of analysis is omitted from the text. For most of the maps depicting industrial distributions, the national Ordnance Survey kilometre grid system has been adopted as the framework for data mapping, measurement and analysis.

In a region with so little written about it, this book provides facts on industry, comparisons with national trends, and enough general local background to distinguish Humberside from other regions and epitomise much of its distinctiveness. But it also uses information and conceptual frameworks that link it with other works such as those of Johnson and Perloff, and in this sense the book is a plea for constructive work of a comparative nature so that the understanding of economic geography can become more exact. Economic geography can never be wholly deductive because the problems ramify too widely to be contained within the framework of one discipline, but studies of this kind should be able to contribute something to this general field of inquiry as well as to the knowledge of a particular region.

# 1

# Background to Humberside

**The Structure for Growth**

HUMBERSIDE is a nascent industrial area. The challenge of assessing its potential for growth in the context of Britain's future industrial structure provides the interest and the problem of this neglected region. There are in effect two regions of Humberside, one north of the estuary and one south. The estuary has given the principal towns and industries their essential character, and it provides a common element of present industrial growth. The Humber is a wide river and the only bridge is at Goole, on the extreme western edge of Humberside; thus there is practically no contact between north and south and each region has its own pattern of spatial organisation, focused on the estuary and oriented along it. Neither region justifies the term *industrial,* because both are typified by pastoral landscapes, with broad fields and a chalk spine of rolling hills. Bold decisions are needed by industrialists or government to invest the capital necessary to transform this region from an almost rural backwater to a central position in the industrial Britain of the next century. Such decisions are being made by the management of large firms and the national strategy for industrial development includes Humberside in an important way. Such decisions are encouraging because they imply that Humberside is judged to have certain advantages for some industries and that, in the strategy for the sustained or accelerated development of Britain in the next century, this peripheral area will be integrated more closely with national growth. Such integration involves improving the infrastructure of the region and making fuller use of the qualities of the local environment. Contemporary industrial investment is attracted because the region has some comparative resource advantages that are likely to be augmented by the provision of an improved infrastructure.

Such changes take a long time, and ideally each element of change would be a successive part of an ordered series, but this is not possible because the industrial pattern at any future time cannot be known. It is important, however, that decisions relate to an anticipated pattern of development, that they are consecutive, and that they are rooted in a thorough survey of existing conditions. In other words there must be reasons for priorities. There is vigorous regional competition for the available public and private investment and it is the spatial pattern of this investment that is reflected in regional growth and industrial vitality. The density of investment in industry over the country varies with time to the extent that businessmen judge that their industrial needs can be met by the resources of particular points. The needs and their regional provision are changing so that the bases of industrial location are not constant. The present pattern of industry in the country reflects successive reinterpretations of regional resources over the past century and a half. This pattern is also changing, and the needs of industry in the next century are likely to be different from those of today. Regions do not have a permanent ability to satisfy these changing needs. The development of even one region is complex because many factors are implied whose precise future interdependence cannot be certainly anticipated. In regions where the rate of economic growth is slight, investment may have to precede greater economic vigour, and a careful assessment of national economic currents is imperative to ensure that regional development is in harmony with national development. This study of industrial Humberside faces the problem of anticipating some of the future needs of industrial development and of isolating those assets which are judged to be of persistent usefulness. In this chapter we shall consider some aspects of the functional organisation of Humberside and review its environment, resources and population changes.

*Changing the Region's Space Relations*

One of the most important features of Humberside is a position on the edge of the principal centres of economic activity in the nation. It seems useful to summarise the reasons why the area did not benefit from earlier periods of industrial expansion.

Industrial patterns change as the locational needs of industry change. The neglected areas of one period of industrial development often possess latent advantages whose recognition or reappraisal depends on more advanced technologies and on the changed circumstances of general patterns of trade. In some ways it is ironic that the comparative neglect of Humberside as a focus of industrial development in the nineteenth century is a principal reason for its suitability for development as an urban and manufacturing centre of the late twentieth century. Rising living standards are creating more sophisticated demands

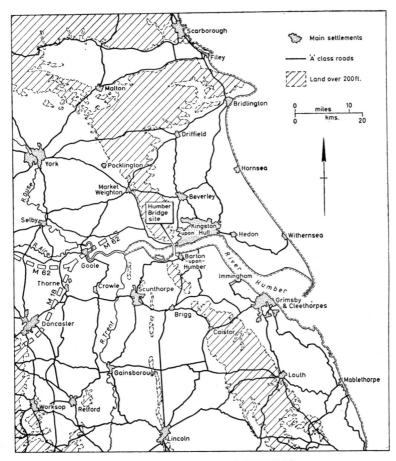

Fig 1.  THE REGIONAL SETTING

The salient geographical features of the region are shown; its relief, rivers and routeways. The area shown is substantially greater than the Humberside region, so that the position of Hull and Grimsby relative to the principal towns of other regions can be judged. Scheduled motorway routes are drawn, and so is the site of the Humber Bridge

for housing and recreation which, with contemporary industrial developments, place a heavy premium upon space. Humberside is uncongested, whereas land for development in the traditional industrial areas is restricted and expensive.

Both features are a legacy of the late eighteenth century and the early nineteenth century, which gave rise to the established industrial regions of Britain. The extensive industrialisation typical of the development of the coalfields did not occur in Humberside, although ripples of it were discernible in the early growth stages of the Scunthorpe iron industry, and the foundation of Hull's industrial structure was laid during this period. Humberside also missed the attendant problems of a shabby environment, of derelict land and of abandoned factories which now prove a great disadvantage in these older industrial areas. Instead, the raw materials imported for Lancashire and West Riding industries stimulated the growth of the Humber ports and encouraged those trade links with other countries which now are so important to general industrial prosperity. This emphasis on overseas trade links rather than on the establishment of more vigorous connections with the rest of the country is reflected in the poor communications that continue to isolate the area from the main-stream of economic activity. This remoteness could continue to inhibit industrial development and a closer analysis of this problem is given in Chapter 6.

As industrial development proceeded, the large and rapidly-growing towns became the new focuses for manufacturing, and during the first half of the twentieth century a new bias emerged in the distribution of industry as it was increasingly associated with the large centres of London, Birmingham and Manchester.[1] These areas apparently provide convenient locations for markets, labour and materials, and offer important services and urbanisation economies. The proliferation of new industries has occurred particularly in the South-East and the Midlands.[2] Once more Humberside did not share in this growth as fully as many other areas, and its effective distance and isolation from the main areas of expansion became the epitome of its disadvantage.

Since 1945 a considerable amount of government legislation has been directed towards redressing the imbalance in industrial growth entailed by the progressive focusing of national industrial and economic expansion, first on the coalfields, and subsequently in the Midlands and South-East, but the tendency has not been altered radically. There is, today, an explicit awareness of the need to see industrial growth and economic development in national terms, and to refer the claims of each region to this context. This point is made in *Humberside—a Feasibility Study*.[3] Any encouragement given to fostering accelerated industrial growth in Humberside must be given in full recognition of the needs of other regions such as Severnside, the Development Areas and the Intermediate Areas. Enthusiastic support for expanded industrial and urban development in Humberside must also be related to the advantages of other regions.

> England in the latter half of the twentieth century abhors a vacuum and the situation behind the Humber is no longer described as a lack of hinterland, but as ample space for development. The Humber offers plenty of undeveloped land around reasonably deep water within reasonable distance (by today's standards) of large centres of population, and there are few such places left in England.
>
> (*The Times*, 26 April 1965)

Professor J. H. James, when chief planner at the Ministry of Housing and Local Government, suggested in 1961 that the strategy of major industrial growth in Great Britain had to be oriented towards our main ports, and particularly to the deep-water estuaries, where raw materials for capital intensive industries such as oil refining and chemicals could be assembled and processed cheaply.[4] And it is in such developments, together with the modernised dock systems, that the quickening pace of industrial development on Humberside is seen.

The greatest investment in these industries since the war has been along Thamesside, Southampton Water, Teesside, Severnside, Milford Haven and the Firth of Forth. Humberside is the deep-water estuary in southern Britain that has had the least development, retains relatively the most room for expansion, and yet is close to the main urban areas of the Midlands and the North, with a short sea-crossing to Britain's fastest growing export markets in Europe. Analogies have been made with Antwerp or Rotterdam-Europoort, but suggestions for such development on the Humber must be made with clear notions of the hinterland for such massive trade. The tonnage of the Humber ports' trade in 1967 was nearly twenty-one million tons, and this is only one-seventh of the tonnage handled by Rotterdam-Europoort in the same year. The creation of a deep-water terminal on this scale implies substantial changes to the estuary, and these changes need major finance. The suggestion to develop Foulness was taken up with alacrity by a consortium of London businessmen; support for a similar scheme on Humberside may have to come from the government, because it is unlikely in this case that private investment will be attracted to a peripheral area in competition with a metropolitan location. An important start to a consideration of some of the technical problems, as distinct from the fiscal problems, is seen in the Humber Estuary Model. The feasibility of creating industrial sites along the

Humber by confining the channel will be able to be evaluated; similar schemes for making use of the river and its water can also be simulated so that some of the effects of interfering with this waterway will be known in advance. This is essential to physical planning, but it is equally indicative of the high level of local initiative; an important feature of regional development.

The rate of development since 1945 has been modest and a considerable acceleration is required before the region can be thought to have acquired the generative vitality of growth that Rostow calls the 'take-off point'.[5] From 1953 to 1967 the expansion of employment was about eighteen per cent, larger than the Great Britain average of eleven per cent, but much of this growth occurred in the service sector, and was dominated by a very marked rise in female rather than male employees. Throughout the period, the unemployment rate for men north of the Humber has remained considerably above the national average, as has that for females south of the river.[6] In fact, the post-war growth record has in many respects been disappointing and unbalanced, especially when measured in terms of indices such as population growth and population migration. From 1951 to 1965 the administrative areas comprising the North Humberside sub-region[7] increased in total population by only 28,000 to 467,000 and concurrently lost 18,000 people by migration to the rest of the country. South Humberside's performance was much better by comparison, the population expanding by 40,000 to about 300,000; but even so the migration gain was only 6,000 people in fifteen years.

The estuary is the basic resource of the area, but it is not enough to assure the future development of the region. The industries attracted to it tend to be capital intensive and do not create a large number of jobs. This is a persistent feature of the region's industries and is related to its urban structure. There has been no substantial development of towns and those that have grown up have restricted central place functions and there is only slight contact with other towns because of their relative isolation. Their service sectors are under-developed, services are not widely exchanged and the region's towns are not integrated to any real extent with the national urban hierarchy. The towns are specialised centres supporting one or more primary resource activity. Humberside has no general industrial cachet; rather Hull and Grimsby are associated with fishing, and Scunthorpe with iron foundries. The regional industrial structure reflects this in the heavy dominance of first and second stage resource using industries producing goods for non-final markets (Chapter 4). These markets lie

outside the region and the accumulation of more resource-based industries is unlikely to engender the development of a major industrial
region capable of self-sustaining growth.

The evidence of the past half-century or so indicates that sustained
economic growth is associated with a major, central city that organises
the regional space, giving it unity and dynamism. Reasonable inferences are that without such polarisation the assets of Humberside
will not be efficiently used, and that the area can most effectively
develop as such a city-region, with the complex economic and social
amalgam that is implicit in that concept. Under such inferences the
status of Hull is particularly significant, as it is by far the largest town,
has the greatest industrial diversity, and dominates employment in
manufacturing and in service industries. It is the obvious focus of
economic growth in the region.

Although Hull is the largest city, with the widest array of city
functions, it cannot claim to unite the Humberside region. South
Humberside is scarcely a part of its hinterland, so that the growth of
Hull through the expansion of its services has been artificially stunted
and its hinterland confined to the northern side of the estuary. Hull
can only assume a metropolitan function and structure when a Humber
bridge allows unrestricted communication between north and south
banks; conversely both North and South Humberside will only enjoy
the higher-quality social and other facilities of a larger city when the
total population to be served by Hull has risen substantially above the
present level.

The proposed Humber bridge must not be seen as a prestige symbol.
Its principal importance is as the physical expression of the functional
unity of both sides of the Humber. Without this there seems no chance
of developing the sort of urban matrix which can engender diverse
industrial growth and support the range of services required. It may
be true that many of the physical advantages of the estuary can be
satisfactorily developed without connecting north and south Humberside. This view has local advocates, but it may well reflect the long
history of separate development of the two halves. There is also a
strong belief that each sub-region should be more efficiently connected
to the principal routeways of England, as this will stimulate trade.
So long as each sub-region remains at its present level of development,
such links will encourage the export function of Humberside, whereas
the need is to expand regional demand. The global evidence seems to
suggest that full industrial development depends upon a network of
closely-linked urban activities, and any increase in the access to Hull

B

of South Humberside would be to that area's advantage. The advantage would be proportional to Hull's increased metropolitan stature.

Exchange and movement are basic to growth. A connection across the Humber would immediately make possible a new pattern of economic circulation which would be superimposed on the existing patterns of movement parallel to the river. There are two distinct patterns of movement, which are complementary, not competitive. Both are essential to sustained growth, but each has a separate function. It is unfortunate if one has to be preferred to the other. The effect upon potential accessibility of improving east-west links will be far slighter than that of creating a north-south link. If the effective distance between Hull and Grimsby is reduced by construction of a bridge, then the amount of contact will be increased and suddenly the smaller places will share a new opportunity for growth. Under a general hypothesis that the amount of interaction between places is directly proportional to the product of the population and inversely with the square of the distance separating them, then the amount of interaction induced by a bridge should be at least increased by nine times. Hull would become much nearer to the small villages along the southern bank of the Humber. There is no real question of Hull increasingly overpowering other centres, but without the contact between the two regions there is no reason to expect either to develop beyond the types of centre they are now. Hull will assume the role of organising centre of regional activity rather than become the physical container for people and workplaces. The actual pattern of housing will vary with changing social contacts, and the region is fortunate in having available so much delightful countryside for housing and recreation. Similarly the pattern of factory development will reflect the needs of industries attracted to the area. The immediate basis of such expansion seems assured to be related to the intensification of the chemical industries and to industries using local resources. Other industries related less directly to resources and more to other industrial products and markets may follow. Traditionally such later-stage industries have been concentrated in towns, and Hull has overwhelmingly dominated this class of industry in Humberside. The emerging generation of science-based and service industries may well show a similar predilection. Towns are defined more clearly as locations than rural areas, and this may be one reason why they attract industrial investment. They are not homogeneous and this is reflected in the industrial patterns that have developed in Hull and Grimsby (Chapter 5). One interesting feature of both cities is the extension east from Hull and west from Grimsby of new industrial building; a connection across the Humber could well strengthen the development of an industrial corridor.

### Regions of Humberside

Our emphasis on the functional integration of Humberside reflects the nature of the development of a region. There cannot be a proper set of regions that exhausts a national space and fulfils all space-using purposes. A space economy develops, the pattern of settlement and workplace changes, and the structure of spatial relationships progresses to give different geographies. Within this dynamic framework a region is defined, and it has to serve a variety of purposes and have some stability so that policies can be implemented. When these policies are directed towards crystallising particular spatial relations, the region must coincide fairly closely with the area of the principal spatial inter-dependencies. The strongest feature of contemporary space economies is their polarisation about urban complexes.

Humberside is not a polarised region at present because the largest city, Hull, exerts a weak attraction on the southern side of the Humber. But it is important to remember that there is only one clearly out-standing city in the region. This is recognised by the postal frank which proclaims 'Hull capital of Humberside'. The absence of two or more fairly equally balanced cities, each contending for the dominant posi-tion, means that there is no unnecessary duplication of facilities, such as is found in Leicester and Nottingham or in Sheffield and Leeds. It could be argued that the creation of a rival city on South Humberside would be inefficient if it provided social and economic facilities that could be more readily offered by Hull.

This lack of a functional region prevents a definition of Humberside in terms of the influence exerted over the area by the principal town. However, the recognition that such organisation is likely to arise and develop the regional space efficiently is an important justification for including both banks of the Humber. Other justifications are simply related to the existence of other officially designated regions of Humberside.

### *Humberside and Planning Regions*

The Humber bridge may provide an opportunity for the functional integration of Humberside, and meanwhile its attributes continue to attract the attention of planners at a national level as a possible over-spill area for Britain's anticipated population expansion between 1981 and 2000.[8] Humberside is not one of the Economic Planning Regions established in 1964, but forms a part of the Yorkshire and Humber-side economic planning region.

The most important regional problem in advanced industrial countries is considered to be the existence of regional inequalities in indices such as unemployment or activity rates, while per capita income differences remain fairly insignificant.[9] This is reflected in the regional policy of the British government since 1945, which has usually recognised as *Development Districts* or *Development Areas* those regions of the country with above average unemployment. The solution of these inequalities has been conceived mainly in terms of adjusting the pattern of industrial distribution through a variety of controls and inducements which can be summarised as *development area policy*. This is the dominant aspect of regional economic planning, the scale of which can be judged by the current cost estimate of about £250 million a year.[10] However, the policy is almost entirely concerned with manipulating the distribution of industry in Great Britain, and is far from being regional planning in an integrated sense that embraces the whole scope of social and economic factors. The system of *regional economic planning regions*, with their respective planning councils, established in 1964, is concerned with the entire range of planning considerations—population, land use and availability, housing, transport and employment—but the powers of these councils are limited and essentially advisory. Many of the regions consist of areas grouped together for administrative convenience, so that there is an obvious lack of any functional coherence. The Yorkshire and Humberside Region is a case in point; there is no clear link between Humberside and the Pennine mill towns or the Sheffield steel area.

One aspect of this development area policy cannot be ignored, and that is the distinction between areas that qualify for substantial encouragements towards industrial expansion, and those that do not. These areas bear no close relationship to the economic planning regions. The particular inequalities which result have been examined in detail by the Hunt Committee, which investigated the problems of areas which were *intermediate* in economic status, neither declining rapidly enough to give high unemployment nor dynamic enough to give confidence in the future expansion of economic activity.[11] Yorkshire and Humberside fall into this intermediate status, which, with the increasing scale of government aid to development areas, must have inhibited the movement of new industry into the region as a whole. Following the Hunt Report, further legislative action has created a series of *intermediate areas* in which industry will receive additional inducements to expand.[12] North Humberside is one of these, and this could make a considerable difference to the projected industrial expansion of the Humberside region in the 1970s.

These development area and intermediate area policies are not directly related to regional planning in the stricter sense, but they help to explain past and projected industrial trends in specific regions. The type of planning study made for Humberside by the Central Unit for Environmental Planning represents the constructive approach to planning and uses the region as a tool of economic analysis, involving the analysis of a region and its potentialities, and the evaluation of alternative development proposals. This study recognises the meaningful position of the area in relation to national planning needs. Although Humberside's present population of about 750,000 hardly qualifies it for full regional status in equality with the economic planning regions, its particular physical advantages make it a special type of region. However, its links with the older industrialised and densely populated sections of the Yorkshire and Humberside planning region are of considerable significance. It is also interesting to observe that Humberside's main rival in southern Britain, Severnside, does not enjoy this advantage of coming within *one* economic planning region, but is divided between the South West and Wales.

The definition of Humberside used by the Regional Economic Planning Board in the Review of Yorkshire and Humberside[13] was adopted by the Feasibility Study and is a useful framework for appraising the region because it follows administrative district boundaries. This region is illustrated in figure 3 (page 26) and it can be seen that the boundary is similar, but not identical, to that of the Humberside region designated by the Department of Economic Affairs, whose definition is a collection of employment exchange areas (Fig. 8, page 66). The discrepancies in the regional boundaries occur in marginal rural parishes which contribute only a small proportion to the total populations concerned. In both schemes a distinction is made between North and South Humberside which emphasises the lack of functional unity. The administrative districts comprising North and South Humberside in the Department of Economic Affairs scheme is as follows:

*North Humberside:* the administrative districts of Hull CB; Beverley, Goole and Hedon MBs; Haltemprice, Hornsea, and Withernsea UDs; and Beverley, Holderness,

Goole and Howden RDs.
The equivalent employment exchange areas are
Hull, Hessle, Beverley and Goole.

*South Humberside:* the administrative districts of Grimsby CB;
Cleethorpes and Scunthorpe MBs; Barton-upon-
Humber and Brigg UDs; and Caistor, Glanford
Brigg, Grimsby and Isle of Axholme RDs. The
equivalent employment exchange areas are
Grimsby, Barton and Scunthorpe.

These administrative districts had a population of 770,000 in 1967
and may be considered as the core of the region, as the *Inner Humberside* which dominates the organisation of economic activity in the
region.

### Some Functional Bases of Humberside

In fixing the outer limit of the region there is no such ready coin-
cidence of administrative boundary and cessation of a predominant
orientation to the Humber. For example, the web of circulation focused
on Humberside becomes tenuous in the north along the crest of the
Yorkshire Wolds, but Bridlington RD overlaps this boundary to include a substantial area in the Vale of Pickering. The allegiance of
the areas around York, Doncaster and Lincoln is affected by the
attraction of these centres and by Inner Humberside, and cannot be
expected to coincide with traditional administrative units, so that any
region of Humberside that is confined to such areas must contradict
the real pattern of functional organisation to some extent. But the
convenience of such a framework of administrative areas is important
for data collection and for providing a stable basis for comparison
with studies at different times. In this book we have tried only to
designate an area that is approximately in sympathy with the precise
area of common economic allegiance, changing our terms of reference
to correspond with changes in data sources and types of factor considered.

The Humber Axis

'The Humber estuary is one of the few in the country offering a
combination of deep water and land suitable for industrial development.' (*Feasibility Study,* 3.17). On the assumption that the Humber
is the basis of potential development in the region, it forms an obvious
axis for regional delimitation. Its influence declines upstream and inland as stronger competing influences occur such as the coalfield of
South Yorkshire, or Leeds. An elongate Humberside region could be

identified, delimited at some distance from the estuary where its influence was subordinate to some other centre of organisation. To the north no major competing centre occurs until Teesside, but the advantage of the Humber becomes negligible as the Wolds give way to the North York moors. In the west the towns of York, Leeds and Doncaster extend their influence to varying degrees eastwards into the lowlands of Inner Humberside, and in the south Lincoln is an important city whose orientation is south and west into the East Midlands. The outer limits of Humberside can be set approximately in this way, thus emphasising the river's vital role in the past and in the potential development of the region. But this is not the only consideration in the activity of the region, as the distribution of industry in the area is related to a number of other factors.

The Distribution of Industry

A more specific basis for defining a regional boundary is the actual distribution of industries in the general area of Humberside (figure 2). Industry has gravitated to the principal towns and the waterways, and is much less dense in the rural districts. A marked area of low density extends along the Wolds from Bridlington in the north-east, passing north of Driffield into the fringe of the Vale of York to Selby in the west. From Selby it continues past Goole to Gainsborough and across south Lindsey to Mablethorpe. The nature of the industries in Selby and Gainsborough is strongly akin to that of Inner Humberside and they seem more appropriate to this region than to neighbouring ones. The pattern of industrial distribution is considered in detail in chapters 4 and 5, but it is worth recognising at this point that the size and nature of the industrial establishment increase the complexity of the industrial pattern portrayed in figure 2. Employment is an essential diagnostic criterion of industrial character and is considered thoroughly in chapter 3.

The Journey to Work

Blumenfeld[14] has described the journey to work and its characteristics as the most important index of regional interaction with the metropolis because it expresses the relationship between population distribution and the location of industrial and other employment. The pattern of work journeys defines the labour catchment area of a city or major industrial complex, and indicates the extent of the wider areas whose prosperity and future growth would be dependent upon basic employment growth in geographically more restricted locations.

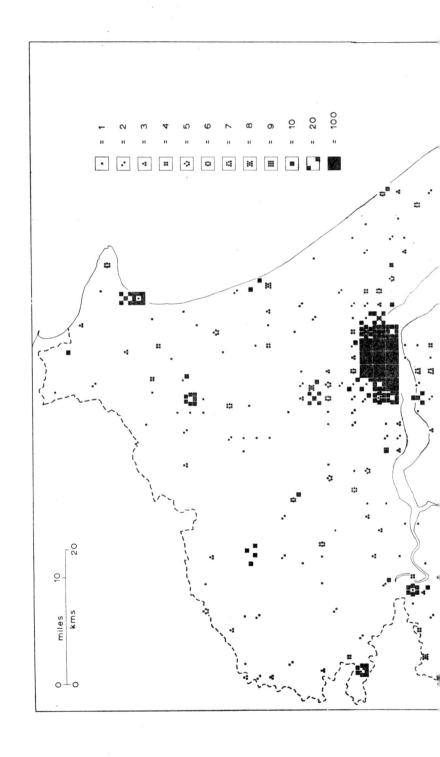

| | |
|---|---|
| ■ | = 1 |
| ∎ | = 2 |
| ▪ | = 3 |
| ▪ | = 4 |
| ▪ | = 5 |
| ▪ | = 6 |
| ▪ | = 7 |
| ▪ | = 8 |
| ▪ | = 9 |
| ▪ | = 10 |
| ◪ | = 20 |
| ■ | = 100 |

miles  0    10    20
kms    0

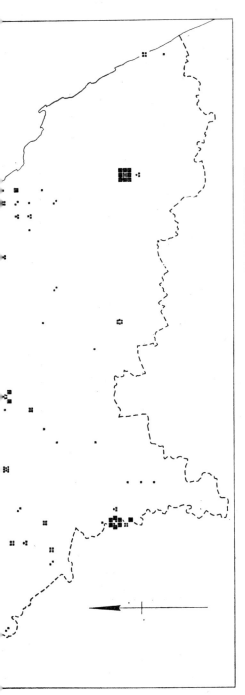

Fig 2.   THE DISTRIBUTION OF INDUSTRIAL ESTABLISHMENTS

There are over 5,000 establishments on this map, including all manufacturing industries in [sic] orders III to XVI but it also includes service industries such as laundry and dry-cleaning, cobblers, radio repair premises, bakeries with their own retail outlet and builders' establishments. The premises are undifferentiated by size; a workshop with one employee is not distinguished from a factory with 1,000s of employees. It shows the number of establishments in each kilometre square by the technique formalised by R. Bachi in his book *Graphical Rational Patterns* (Jerusalem 1968). The advantage of this technique is the precise quantitative, located information it gives, in this case from 1 to 100 establishments in each grid square, and the density of the symbol is precisely related to the quantity. It seemed to be the only map method capable of presenting the data. The method is not used subsequently because of the time used to draw the squares; the pattern is retained.

*Source*: the basic source of information was the record of HM Factory Inspectorate at Hull, Grimsby and Wakefield. The data for North Humberside were collected and mapped by P. W. and R. A. Lewis and by G. E. Skipworth, the data for South Humberside by P. W. Lewis and P. N. Jones. Substantial amendments were made on the basis of this field mapping.

Because Humberside has not yet achieved regional integration, we have to use the area designated Inner Humberside as our basic area of attraction, and examine the extent to which surrounding areas are dependent on it for employment. Calculations based on the work-

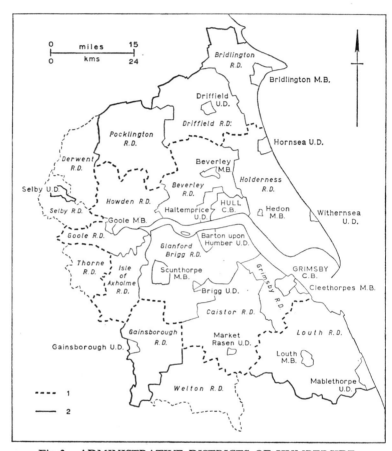

Fig 3.  ADMINISTRATIVE DISTRICTS OF HUMBERSIDE
The boundaries shown are those of 1966. (1) Boundary of Inner Humber-side; (2) Boundary of Outer Humberside where different from 1.

place statistics of the census are made difficult because of the irregular size and shape of the units for which data is collected.[15] Further difficulties are created by the sampling error implicit in the ten per cent sample taken in 1961. We attempt to show the fundamental patterns of movement and the extent of regional integration in Humberside by a straightforward method and a map (figure 4), using data from the 1961 census.

The first task was to ascertain the degree to which the three main towns, Hull, Grimsby and Scunthorpe, act as focuses for movements within Humberside. On the basis of total gross outward movement from administrative districts, those sending over half their migrants to one of the three centres have been distinctively shaded. Figure 4 indicates that most of North Humberside is strongly dominated by the city of Hull. Beverley MB appears in an anomalous role because of its strong ties with its rural district, but even so, over forty per cent of outward movement is to Hull, and the larger part of the northern section of Inner Humberside is thus closely integrated with that city. In the southern section of Inner Humberside, most of the districts are within the employment sheds of either Grimsby or Scunthorpe. Scunthorpe was dominant in 1961, although its influence was in an east-west direction and did not penetrate southwards to any great extent. Grimsby has a more restricted tributary area, comprising the adjoining residential borough of Cleethorpes MB and Grimsby RD.

Two separate areas of Inner Humberside fall outside the fields of the major centres. The larger comprises the hinge of the region's two lines of urban and industrial development, and occurs in the Selby-Goole area at the confluence of the Aire, Ouse and Wharfe. Here Goole MB, Goole RD and Howden RD form a compact area with relatively weak links with both Hull and Scunthorpe. The second is Caistor RD, which appears anomalous because it is near to both Scunthorpe and Grimsby; that it still remained essentially unintegrated in 1961 is a reflection of the slower progress of urban growth in South Humberside.

For those administrative areas lying outside Inner Humberside less rigorous indicators of association have to be selected, because distance will inevitably lead to a weakening of the direct employment linkage, and their own economic structures will be more self-contained. The measure chosen was the proportion of total gross outward movement directed to Inner Humberside districts, with a minimum of one-fifth being taken as representing a significant attachment to Humberside. Other features of journey to work are also shown where these provide further insight into the integration of the region. In North Humberside the towns of Bridlington and Driffield are closely associated with Inner Humberside and so are Pocklington and Driffield rural districts. Bridlington UD's largest single outward flow and Driffield's second-ranking outward flow are to Hull, indicating fairly important direct work-journey connections. In the peripheral districts of the map, York CB is the dominant external attraction for commuters from

Derwent RD, Selby RD and Selby UD; Doncaster RD plays the same
role for Thorne RD. The links of Welton RD are with Lincoln CB,
but Louth RD is clearly becoming a part of the Humberside orbit. The

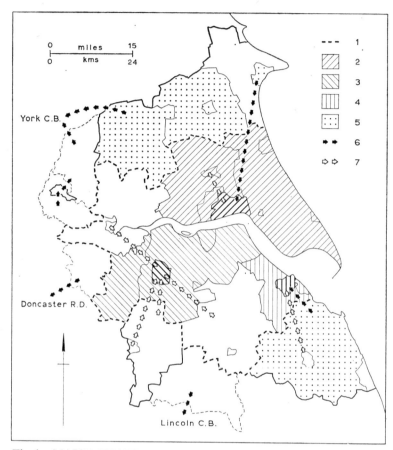

Fig 4.   MAJOR FEATURES OF THE JOURNEY TO WORK IN 1961
The map is based upon data from the 1961 Census 10 per cent sample
tables of work journeys. For district names see Figure 3. (1) Boundary
between Inner and Outer Humberside. Shaded Inner Humberside districts:
over 50 per cent of out-movement to: (2) Hull; (3) Scunthorpe; (4)
Grimsby; (5) Outer Humberside districts with over 20 per cent of out-
movement to Inner Humberside. Other selected flows: (6) First-ranking
out-movement; (7) Second-ranking out-movement

arbitrary scale of one-fifth does less than justice to its strong links,
since almost half the outward movement is directed to Inner South
Humberside, its first ranking destination being Grimsby itself. Louth
MB interacts most strongly with its rural district, but its second-
ranking outward flow is to Grimsby. The published statistics in this

case do not show whether it would qualify under the twenty per cent criterion. Gainsborough UD and RD also interact most prominently with themselves, and provide some indication of their self-contained degree of isolation. However, in both districts the second-ranking flow was to Scunthorpe, while outward movement to Inner Humberside districts was far in excess of that to the nearer centre of Lincoln CB.

The pattern of work-journey movements clarifies some aspects of the internal functional organisation of Humberside. Most of Inner Humberside is already within the intensive employment hinterland of one or other of the three major centres, while some districts in Outer Humberside have important work-journey ties with Inner Humberside. Perhaps the most difficult case is Selby UD, where industrial growth and structure are completely linked with the navigable Ouse and Humber waterways, even to the extent of a flourishing ship-building industry. Despite a lack of work-journey links with the core area of Humberside, it is most appropriately taken as part of Selby, coming in the outer sub-category. Except for the analysis of specific industrial distributions, Derwent RD and Thorne RD will be excluded. Another doubtful area is Mablethorpe and Sutton UD, which, unlike its parallels to the North, Hornsea and Withernsea, has not yet developed an important dormitory function. However, it is almost completely enclosed by Louth RD, so it can be included on the ground of future residential expansion on South Humberside.

*The Definition of Humberside used in this book*

Figure 3 presents a summary of the boundaries of the region as used in the various chapters. In chapters 4 and 5, which consider industrial distributions and sub-regions, the wider Humberside regional definition is used, including also the southern portion of Derwent RD around Barlby. But the general economic and industrial structure of the region is analysed in terms of Inner Humberside. The Humberside region is larger than both the Humberside region of the Yorkshire and Humberside Regional Economic Council and the Humberside of the Feasibility Study. But the outer parts of this larger region can only be understood in relation to Inner Humberside, and are likely to be stimulated directly by any major industrial and urban growth in the latter. The recreational and residential pressures on coast and villages in particular would increase, and rural districts such as Driffield and Bridlington in the north, and Louth in the south, are especially susceptible to such developments.

This wider Humberside framework has since been strongly emphasised by the findings and recommendations of the Maud Report on local government published in June 1969.[16] The proposed North Humberside unitary authority corresponds with the definition adopted in the book, except in so far as Pocklington RD is shared by North Humberside and York, and York incorporates Selby UD and Selby RD. As the Maud Report stresses, the regional organisation of North Humberside focuses on Hull:

> A number of places within the North Humberside unit serve as urban centres for their immediate surroundings, but the main focus is Hull. With its varied shopping and other urban services, its influence is strong and is likely to strengthen and extend with the further growth in the industrial importance of Humberside and improvements in communications.

The proposed South Humberside authority, however, corresponds closely with the southern Inner Humberside region, as used by the Feasibility Study and the Regional Economic Planning Council. It excludes Louth RD and Louth MB, and only part of Caistor RD is included.

These work-journey patterns link industry and settlement and occur in a predominantly rural environment. It now remains to describe the resources of the area and its landscape, and to note some of the recent changes that have occurred in the population of the region.

## Environment, Resources, and Population

### The Environment of Humberside

'Beyond its urban areas Humberside consists of wide areas of well farmed typical English lowland countryside largely lacking wild country.' (*Feasibility Study*, 3.19) This stresses a very significant factor about Humberside, that although in 'the North', its relief, climate, and prevailing systems of agriculture belong firmly to lowland eastern and southern England. The area is dominated by arable farming, and about half of it is contained in grades I and II of the Ministry of Agriculture's land classification system, a proportion that is approximately twice the national average.

Most of the region lies below 200 feet and forms one of the large lowland areas typical of eastern England. Only in small areas, especially in the crescent of the Yorkshire Wolds, does the relief rise above 400 feet, and the relief types are those of lowland England. Among the most significant landscape types are broad, flat, alluvial plains, now carefully drained and regulated; rolling, hummocky plains of low relief developed on the glacial boulder clays on the North Sea margins and epitomised in Holderness; and the familiar cuesta forms of vale, escarpment and gentle dip slope associated with the jurassic limestone and chalk, which add elements of landscape variety important to the future planning of settlements in the region.

The relief pattern is adjusted to the underlying geology in much of the region, and indeed can best be understood in terms of the sequence of geological formations which have their alignment in a north-south axis and dip gently to the east. The more easily eroded formations of clays and shales have been worn into vales, while the more resistant limestones and sandstones form areas of higher relief. This strong grain to the relief has been altered, very significantly from a human point of view, by Pleistocene and Holocene events which have left large areas of superficial glacial deposits and vast alluvial lowlands at or around sea level. The Humber cuts right across the prevailing north-south grain of the relief.

The main rivers of central and northern England unite to form the Humber in the *innermost* lowland vale of the sequence in our region, eroded in soft triassic rocks; it stretches from the Nottingham area in the south to Northallerton in the north. Although substantial areas are drift-covered, more significant are the flat, low-lying flood plains in the lower reaches of the Don, Aire, Ouse and Trent. These warplands, now drained and dyked, form a huge, featureless lowland of fenlike landscape and high fertility.

At the eastern edge of this vale more resistant rocks of the jurassic series, including the Northampton ironstone and Lincolnshire limestone, form an upland cuesta with a steep westward face and a gently declining dip slope to the east, so gentle, in fact, that it is liberally sprinkled with wartime airfields. In South Humberside this prominent relief feature is known as the Lincoln Cliff, but north of the Humber the harder series is only feebly represented because of an axis of uplift which greatly reduced deposition at the time of formation, so that no separate landform exists in Humberside.[17] The next lowland vale in the east-west sequence is only present to the south of the Humber, where it is often called the Lincoln Clay Vale. The most striking relief form in the region is the cuesta of the chalk, which again presents its steep face westwards; the lower easterly slopes are plastered with boulder clays, but elsewhere the relief is dominated by the rolling, typically smooth contours of chalk country. The Yorkshire Wolds are higher, rising to over 500 feet almost everywhere along the crest, but the Lincolnshire Wolds also rise to above 500 feet in certain areas, especially south of Caistor. Both wolds areas offer uniquely attractive landscapes in the Humberside region, with elevated, rolling topography, many deep valleys with considerable areas of woodland, and charming villages, usually with their own village ponds, are tucked away in the valley folds. It is hardly surprising that the villages more accessible from the large centres should be experiencing an inward movement of former city-dwellers, particularly near Hull; this, in fact, accelerated rapidly in the 1960s.

The chalk forms a buried basement to the plains which abut on to the North Sea. Boulder clays give most of the relief a very confused hummocky appearance in which drainage has long been a difficult problem, with many meres as evidence. However, the River Hull occupies a broad alluvial plain which owed its origin to a long period of inactivity in the retreat of the North Sea ice-sheets. This plain is the largest area of recent deposits in the region, and most of it is less than 10 feet above sea-level.

The relief pattern has implications for industrial and urban development. The traditional expansion of Hull has reflected the problems of drainage and sewage disposal in the low-lying plain of the River Hull. The wolds, although fairly continuous, have presented no serious obstacle to road communications, although the main road and railway routes on the North Humber bank skirt their southern margin and keep close to the estuary. More serious has been the considerable width of the Humber estuary which has so far discouraged bridge-building, and the dearth of modern bridges across the numerous wide rivers and drainage cuts of the Inner Humber lowland, which often causes serious constriction to traffic routes, as at Keadby. The outstanding characteristic is, however, the abundance of very low-lying and flat land, which is of paramount importance to the region and will be examined in detail in the next chapter.

### The Resources of Humberside

The low relief and sluggish drainage did not provide the opportunity for water-powered industry that was so evident in other parts of England, and there was no accessible coal as a basis for nineteenth-century industrial development. The enormous reserves of low-grade iron ores present in the jurassic series in the Scunthorpe area encouraged the development of the iron industry in south Humberside. This ironstone field provided about a third of

Page 33: (above) *King George V Dock, Hull, looking east towards Salt End, opened 1914. Floating grain elevators discharging overside into barges are clearly seen; (below) Immingham Dock, looking north, opened 1911. Fisons' fertiliser factory is in the foreground. The liquid storage tanks for oil and other materials are on the Humber foreshore near the western jetty*

Page 34: (above) *The Old Harbour, Hull, at the mouth of the River Hull, seen from Drypool Bridge. The Old Town is on the right, now separated from the river by warehouses; (below) River Hull looking upstream from Drypool Bridge. The old entrance basin to the Queen's Dock is in the middle foreground next to the farthest pair of barges on the left of the photograph. This basin is now used by a shipbuilding firm*

home ore production in the 1960s, and although the iron content averages as low as twenty-one per cent, conditions for quarrying and mixing are ideal, so that the ore-field is worked over a distance of about eight miles to the north of Scunthorpe.

The chalk provides the raw material for two major cement plants on the Humber estuary at North and South Ferriby, and also for numerous small whiting works in the region. Various clays are used with the chalk to manufacture cement, and clays are also used to make bricks and tiles at scattered locations, but this is not a major industry. Reserves of chalk and clay for cement production are very extensive.[18] Other local resources are sand and gravel, silica sand and anhydrite.

Much interest in Humberside has been focused on future supplies of energy. Humberside is close to the Yorkshire coalfield, the most productive in the country, and vast coal reserves have been proved at Selby and Haxey. Until recently the most easterly colliery was at Thorne, thirteen miles from Scunthorpe, but this has been closed permanently as a result of underground flooding. Even so, the collieries to the east of Doncaster, such as Hatfield Main, are only about fifteen miles from the steel town. The cheap coal of Inner Humberside, coupled with the water available for cooling purposes from the major rivers, has led to the development of Britain's largest concentration of thermal electricity generating capacity on the margins of the region. Ferrybridge, Eggborough and Drax are the major stations close to the region, and Drax will possibly be of 4,000MW capacity. In addition to this concentration of cheap base-load power generation, the CEGB has a large site reserved on the Humber bank at South Killingholme, where a power station fired either by natural gas or crude oil could be built to provide any further needs of cheap industrial power, and natural gas fields are being exploited at Sole Bank, off the Humber estuary. However, the potential of natural gas, while superficially appearing valuable, can be overrated. The main centres of concentrated heavy gas consumption are in areas such as Sheffield and the West Midlands; consequently priority has been given to serving them. A 24in diameter pipeline runs out of the region from Easington to Sheffield, where it joins the national methane grid system.[19] The gas fields are not the exclusive property of the Humber region, although the proximity of the gas fields might prove attractive to industries with a need for bulk supplies of cheap energy of the type provided by natural gas.

As in all parts of lowland Britain, water supply is a major con-

C

sideration of resource planning and projected developments. Most of Humberside's water is pumped from the chalk, and is adequate for the present demand. The water supply available in each sub-region varies considerably, but it is clear from the Feasibility Study's findings that, while the completion of the Derwent scheme in the Yorkshire moors should give North Humberside ample reserves for the 1970s, the position in South Humberside is less satisfactory, since proposed schemes will not provide sufficient surplus above the projected increase in demand of industrial and domestic consumption to allow either urban or industrial developments that make heavy demands on water.[20]

Communications

At this stage we shall be concerned solely with road and rail communications, because the Humber waterway and ports form the subject of chapter 2. The major disadvantage of Humberside has always been its inadequate road network, which was essentially local and rural in origin, and which formed the base upon which inadequate, piecemeal improvements have been made to cope with the explosive growth of road traffic since 1920, and particularly since 1950. Historically, long-distance inland communications were the province of the waterway system, and were supplemented in the nineteenth century by a fine rail network. The one important road link from the region to the rest of the country is the road from Hull to Selby and the A1, which runs along the north of the Humber estuary. There is no equivalent in South Humberside, and the external road links of the region have had to make do with a quite inadequate system of roads, designed to link market town and village. Not unnaturally, traffic saturation, congestion, slow frustrating journeys and interminable delays have resulted. Investment in the region's road network since 1945 has been quite inadequate; conditions have been described in considerable detail in a recent study made by the British Road Federation.

The seriousness of the position may be illustrated from the vital A18 between Doncaster and Thorne, which carries traffic bound for both South and North Humberside. This is a two-way single carriageway with a design capacity in parts of 6,000 passenger car units per day; it carries almost 20,000 vehicles at peak times, over a third of them heavy lorries.[21] Trunk roads out of the region to the national motorway system are constricted; the A63 from Hull to the A1 and Leeds crosses the Ouse at Selby by an eighteenth-century wooden toll bridge; the A614 from Howden on the A63 to Bawtry and the Midlands crossed the Stainforth and Keadby Canal at Thorne until recently by a single-lane swing bridge; the A18 from South Humberside has to cross the Trent by the Keadby Bridge. The region contains no motorway and only a few efficient dual-carriageway roads adequate for heavy traffic, such as the A63 between Hessle and Elloughton. Road communications between North and South Humberside are arduous, the Hull-New Holland ferry is expensive and limited in capacity, and the hovercraft service between Grimsby and Hull has not yet been operating long enough for its usefulness to be evaluated. The major planned improvements to the road system are shown on Figure 1 (page 13); it is plain that these facilities are inadequate to meet the transport needs of the region, especially the need for fast routes outwards to national markets and from the national hinterland to the Humber ports. The present industrial patterns relate to, and have to exist with, the system as it is today.

The railway system of Humberside is far more purposeful, with east-west, port to hinterland routes dominant in both North and South Humberside. These are satisfactory today, although the network as a whole has been in active retreat since the 1950s as the rural branch lines have closed. Hull is joined directly to Leeds, Manchester and Liverpool, and connects with the London-Edinburgh main line route at Selby and Doncaster, from which Sheffield and the Midlands are reached. Grimsby has three outward routes: via Scunthorpe to Doncaster, via Lincoln to Grantham, and directly south to Peterborough, although this route is unlikely to remain open long. Developments in freight-handling techniques have resulted in the construction of freight-liner terminals at Doncaster and Hull, and the rail facilities of the region are perfectly adequate for the demands being made of them. Passenger connections to the Midlands and London leave much to be desired, but improvements may come, especially if the revolutionary high-speed gas-turbine passenger trains are introduced on the east coast route. In the view of the Regional Economic Planning Council the rail network of the region is under-utilised. The cessation of coal exports through Hull, and a general decline in rail traffic from Hull, has released hundreds of acres of rail sidings and marshalling yards in west Hull and Hessle, but fortunately these redundant yards will make excellent sites for industry within the city when negotiations between British Rail and Hull Corporation are completed. Plans for a light industrial estate of twenty acres at Springhead sidings in west Hull have already been submitted to the planning authorities of Hull and the East Riding. The impact of freightliner trains could, however, redress the railway's fortunes in the region, particularly on the north bank in relation to the port traffic; and an increased reliance on imported iron ores would increase the use of the Immingham to Scunthorpe line. The railway system is undoubtedly capable of taking a considerable traffic expansion without serious modifications, which is a factor of significance in the region.

### The Population and Settlement of Humberside

In a book on industrial Humberside, treatment of such a large and important topic can only provide a broad background. Yet there is a need to understand the relationships between population and industry in the region, and two problems in particular stand out. The first is the low rate of population growth throughout the region, and the second is the basic contrast in urban development between North and South Humberside, which we shall examine first.

Settlement Structure

North Humberside has a well-integrated urban structure, with a hierarchy of urban centres culminating in the city of Hull. The city is, in fact, without rival in Humberside, having a population of almost 300,000 within its boundaries in 1968, and with a further 50,000 in the contiguous urban district of Haltemprice, making a total of 350,000. In 1961 almost half the region's total retail turnover of £112m took place in the city of Hull itself, giving a per capita turnover of £178 compared with the average for the region of £150. The remainder of North Humberside has a regular pattern of market towns and coastal resorts, whose sizes range from Pocklington, with less than 4,000 population, to Beverley, with 17,000 in 1966. Beverley has the important administrative and service functions of an English county town to supplement its considerable industrial sector, and with Goole and Bridlington acts as a sub-dominant centre, supplemented by smaller towns such as Hornsea and Driffield. Finally, below the smaller towns is a dense network of compact villages fairly evenly distributed throughout North Humberside, the only departure being the line of swollen villages along the westward communication links from Hull along the north Humber bank, including North Ferriby, Brough and Gilberdyke, which have grown in response to transport needs, industrial development and intensive horticulture. This settlement pattern is very old; Kingston-upon-Hull was a planned new town in the thirteenth century. The only additions to the settlement pattern since the Middle Ages, apart from the rapid nineteenth- and twentieth-century growth of Hull, are the towns of Goole and Bridlington. This is a startling reflection on the slowness of change in the sub-region, which is in sharp contrast to the remainder of the Yorkshire and Humberside planning region, and indeed to South Humberside.

The underlying rural settlement pattern in South Humberside is also one of an evenly-distributed network of compact villages, in origin mainly Anglo-Saxon and Danish. But both the main towns are of recent origin, Grimsby rising to real prominence only after 1850 when the railway links were built, while Scunthorpe has rapidly developed from a group of villages, such as Ashby and Frodingham, which were quite rural only a hundred years ago. Both Grimsby and Scunthorpe are far smaller than Hull, however, and less varied in their service provisions and general urban facilities. But their dominance of a hinterland which was otherwise poorly served by urban centres is complete, so that the per capita sales in Grimsby in 1961 amounted to £206, quite considerably greater than Hull, whilst Scunthorpe's figure of £178 is identical to that of Hull. The remaining towns in South Humberside are very small, only Louth and Gainsborough exceeding 10,000. Brigg, Barton, Market Rasen, Caistor and others were by-passed and lost ground completely in the nineteenth-century industrial and port growth, and consequently failed to expand both in population and service terms. As a result, post-war industrialisation in South Humberside has an inadequate base and urban infrastructure outside the two main centres. This means that post-war population growth outside Grimsby and Scunthorpe has been catered for largely by expanding rural villages, although Immingham itself is in the process of developing from a straggling and rather overgrown village into a small town. In fact, of all the market towns of South Humberside in the early nineteenth century, only Gainsborough on the navigable Trent enjoyed any substantial industrial and population growth.

The region is, in fact, strongly rural and underdeveloped; an area of traditional villages, of small by-passed market towns, with economic life focused on the three big urban centres which dwarf the others.

Internal Pattern of Population Change, 1951–66

In the intercensal period 1951–66 the population of Humberside grew relatively slowly, particularly by comparison with regions such as the south-east. The absolute increase was 62,475, or about 4,000 per annum, and this was unequally distributed, about two-thirds being on South Humberside and the remainder on North Humberside. On the other hand this population growth was well above that of the Yorkshire and Humberside economic planning region; 10·4 per cent compared with 5·4 per cent, which may indicate an increase in industrial momentum.

Two aspects of these changes are of particular relevance to the economic development of the region. First, we need to evaluate the migration movements within the region because migration, either inwards or outwards, is a sensitive index of economic change and a vital component of the labour supply position. Secondly, we need information on the distribution of population changes within the region, particularly in relation to the three main focuses of industrial development.

The first important point which needs to be stressed is that almost the entire population growth of the region has occurred in Inner Humberside, the Humberside region of the Regional Economic Planning Council and *de facto* of the Humberside Feasibility Study. This is paralleled in terms of the distribution of total population within the region, illustrated in Table 1.

**Table 1**

POPULATION DISTRIBUTION AND CHANGES IN HUMBERSIDE,
1951–66

| Subdivision | 1951 | 1961 | 1966 | Total Change 1951–66 |
|---|---|---|---|---|
| North Humberside | | | | |
| Inner | 443,389 | 458,424 | 465,390 | 22,001 |
| Outer | 76,185 | 76,998 | 78,060 | 1,875 |
| Sub-total | 519,574 | 535,422 | 543,450 | 23,876 |
| South Humberside | | | | |
| Inner | 263,489 | 288,364 | 303,140 | 39,651 |
| Outer | 67,482 | 66,761 | 66,430 | −1,052 |
| Sub-total | 330,971 | 355,125 | 369,570 | 38,599 |
| Humberside total | 850,545 | 890,547 | 913,020 | 62,475 |

*Source: Census of England and Wales,* County Reports, 1951, 1961, 1966.

Here it will be noted that the population of our larger Humberside region exceeded 900,000 in 1966. It remains heavily concentrated in Inner Humberside, however, and there has been little change in Outer Humberside. Over the entire fifteen-year period a gain of only 1,875 was recorded on North Humberside, complemented by an almost equivalent loss of 1,052 in Outer South Humberside. The outer areas are dependent to a great extent on agriculture, and agricultural employment has contracted in post-war years.

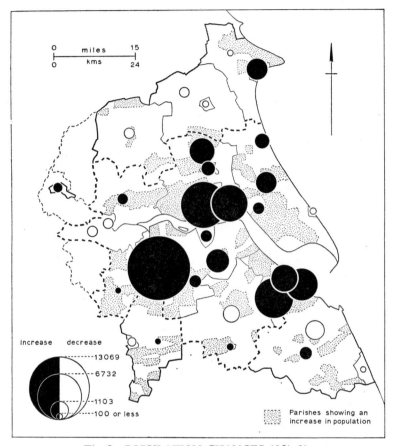

Fig 5. POPULATION CHANGES 1951–61

The map is based on data from the 1961 Census reports, and depicts the pattern of population change. The districts and boundaries are shown in Fig 3. Within rural districts only, parishes with increases in population are distinguished

Within Inner Humberside, the absolute increase in the south is almost double that in the north, a measure of the more rapid pace of industrial development associated particularly with the Scunthorpe steel industry. Figures 5 and 6 illustrate the distribution of absolute population changes in two stages, 1951–61 and 1961–66. On Figure 5 it will be seen that parishes which recorded population increases are distinctively shaded, giving a clearer indication of the spatial distribution of population change in the region. Unfortunately this cannot be done for 1961–66 as there is no parish-based data.

For the period 1951–61 there were clearly two contrasting trends in North Humberside. The three outer districts lost population, mainly through rural depopulation, with Pocklington and Driffield rural districts particularly affected. There was little change in Driffield and Bridlington. Within Inner Humberside, the basic pattern was one of a belt of high population increase surrounding Hull, which itself also recorded a slight increase. Haltemprice, Holderness and Beverley RDs recorded the greatest increases, which were supplemented by increases in the two towns of Beverley and Hornsea. Away from this major zone, there are few areas of population increase apart from the very noticeable attenuation along the principal transportation artery of North Humberside, from Haltemprice westwards to Howden. In particular the more rural areas, such as in Goole RD, have declined, but it is noticeable how all the smaller towns like Beverley and Bridlington have their own zones of population increase, minor editions of that surrounding Hull.

In South Humberside in the same period the pattern of population growth again encircles two centres, Grimsby and Scunthorpe. These centres are also almost linked by an elongated belt of growth via Caistor and Brigg, which continues beyond Scunthorpe into the Isle of Axholme. This gives a linear zone of increase within Inner South Humberside, but one which is not aligned along the Humber estuary itself, although Grimsby's ring of population increase had extended as far north as Killingholme by 1961. Elsewhere in the region the prevailing pattern was one of population losses, reflecting a largely rural-agricultural background, although small towns such as Louth and Gainsborough generated their own minor zones of increase. A major departure from North Humberside, however, is seen in the enormous population increase in Scunthorpe, which was actively expanding in the 1950s. Most of the growth of population associated with Grimsby is focused on Cleethorpes and Grimsby RD. The most rural of the districts, Louth and Caistor, not unexpectedly recorded declines.

The period 1961–66 is shorter, but even so some notable changes have occurred. The most striking change that the map reveals is the curtailment in the growth of Scunthorpe MB, as population has tended to spill out into surrounding parishes and as the employment expansion of the 1950s in the steel industry rapidly declined. Grimsby's

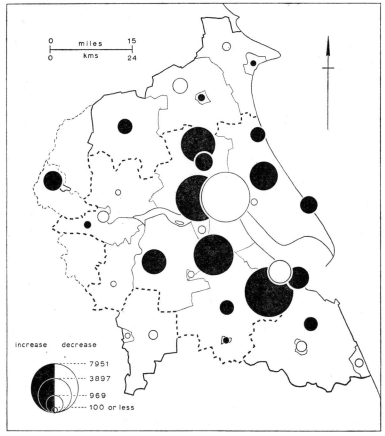

Fig 6.  POPULATION CHANGES 1961–66
The map is based on data from the 1966 and 1961 Census reports, and
shows the pattern of absolute population change. The districts and boundaries are shown in Fig 3

population has decreased and that of Cleethorpes MB has lessened
greatly. This reflects the increased rate of suburbanisation of the
population, with accompanying higher private house-building rates
and higher living standards in the region, which encourage a powerful
outward movement. Thus in Grimsby RD, surrounding Grimsby and
Cleethorpes, the absolute increase for the later five-year period is
about half as much again as for the previous ten years. In the case
of Glanford Brigg RD, tributary to Scunthorpe, the change has been
even more pronounced. The two focuses of Grimsby and Scunthorpe,
with the intervening belt, were the main growth-points of South
Humberside in the sixties. The smaller urban centres all record popula-

tion declines, and losses from the rural districts generally appear to be unchecked except in Caistor and Louth, close to the major growth points.

North Humberside in the sixties witnessed a continuation of rural population decline in Outer Humberside generally, although in Pocklington this trend was reversed. There was also a small increase in Goole RD, but Howden RD still recorded a decline in population. However, in marked contrast to South Humberside, most of the small towns of North Humberside expanded in terms of population—Beverley, Hornsea, Withernsea, Selby, Driffield and Bridlington. Only Goole was out of sympathy with this promising trend, which indicates a general quickening of economic activity throughout the sub-region. The decline of Hull, as the centre of a zone of population growth, was very marked indeed, with a loss of almost 8,000. However, much of this loss is attributable to Hull's constricted boundaries, which have forced much municipal as well as private house-building to locate outside the city boundaries.[22] But the line of population increase is very much in evidence, with ample indication of an accelerated growth of population in outer districts. Thus in five years Holderness and Beverley RDs and Haltemprice UD have grown in population as much as, or more than, in the previous ten-year period.

The most noticeable feature of recent population changes within Humberside on both banks has been accelerated deconcentration. A decline in the population of the urban centres has been accompanied by a movement outwards, helped by rising regional living standards and car-ownership rates. Population growth is becoming more diffused throughout a larger area of both North and South Humberside, transforming these districts with residential estates, shopping and other service provisions, and the influx of new populations. It is particularly breaking down the hitherto very sharp urban-rural dichotomy, and represents the emergence of a new settlement form: an embryonic 'exploding metropolis'.

Migration Trends

Table 2 summarises the estimated absolute migration gains and losses by administrative districts in North Humberside in the fifteen-year period 1951–66;[23] Table 3 is a similar table for South Humberside and Humberside as a whole.

The net migration movement from Humberside has been away from the region. From 1951–66, some 23,000 persons were lost. Admittedly this does not compare in scale with the rapid exodus from

**Table 2**

MIGRATION CHANGES IN NORTH HUMBERSIDE, 1951–66

| Subdivision | 1951–61 Total | 1951–61 Per cent | 1961–66 Total | 1961–66 Per cent | 1966 Census Population |
|---|---|---|---|---|---|
| Hull CB | −19,143 | −6·4 | −20,925 | −6·9 | 295,310 |
| Beverley MB | −177 | −1·1 | 465 | 2·9 | 17,000 |
| Goole MB | −864 | −4·5 | −894 | −4·7 | 18,470 |
| Haltemprice UD | 5,277 | 14·8 | 5,256 | 12·4 | 48,900 |
| Hedon MB | 229 | 11·5 | −138 | −5·9 | 2,230 |
| Hornsea UD | 735 | 13·8 | 688 | 11·6 | 6,610 |
| Withernsea UD | −87 | −1·7 | 750 | 15·1 | 5,790 |
| Beverley RD | 897 | 4·1 | 2,985 | 12·9 | 27,110 |
| Goole RD | −789 | −8·6 | −87 | −1·0 | 9,060 |
| Holderness RD | 557 | 2·9 | 1,674 | 8·2 | 22,880 |
| Howden RD | −232 | −2·0 | −326 | −2·7 | 12,030 |
| Bridlington MB | 2,392 | 9·7 | 598 | 2·3 | 26,110 |
| Driffield UD | −70 | −1·0 | 248 | 3·6 | 7,040 |
| Selby UD | 20 | 0·2 | 826 | 7·9 | 11,550 |
| Bridlington RD | −284 | −3·2 | −229 | −2·6 | 8,610 |
| Driffield RD | −825 | −7·4 | −1,097 | −10·1 | 10,110 |
| Pocklington RD | −756 | −5·3 | 335 | 2·4 | 14,640 |
| North Humberside | −13,120 | | −9,871 | | 543,450 |

*Source:* 1951–61: calculated from *Census of England and Wales*, 1961 County Reports; 1961–66: D. G. Symes and J. G. Thomas.[23]

larger planning regions such as Scotland, or the north-east of England, but it is clear that industrial expansion within the region has not yet reached a stage where it is able to absorb the natural increase of population, which for the same period, but in the Inner Humberside region, amounted to 10·4 per cent in North Humberside and 12·6 per cent in South Humberside, compared with a Great Britain average of 8·3 per cent.[24] The region's first task will be to hold on to its own natural increase, and only then can planners really envisage moving people *into* it.

In North Humberside the outstanding feature in both 1951–61 and 1961–66 was the high outward migration from Hull, and it will be seen that the annual average rate in the later period was about twice that for the 1950s. Much of this migration was a voluntary residential movement to the encompassing administrative districts, particularly Haltemprice and Beverley RD, but this type of movement does not account for all the loss. In the 1950s only about a third of Hull's losses can be accounted for by gains to the surrounding districts, although this ratio has since improved to about half in the 1961–66 period. This trend is encouraging, since it indicates that a higher proportion of migration losses from Hull are being retained within the region. Also, the migration losses from rural districts on North Humberside are numerically insignificant compared with Hull, although some of the percentage rates, such as in Driffield RD, are high.

In South Humberside the migration pattern for all the Outer Humberside districts (see Figures 5 and 6) has been consistently negative, but within Inner South Humberside a modest net inflow of approximately 5,000 persons occurred in the 1951–61 period. The table demonstrates that Scunthorpe played a key role in this, accounting for half the recorded migration gains in South Humberside. The trend for Grimsby CB parallels that of Hull on the north bank. During

### Table 3

MIGRATION CHANGES IN SOUTH HUMBERSIDE AND
HUMBERSIDE, 1951–66

| Subdivision | 1951–61 | | 1961–66 | | 1966 Census |
| | Total | Percentage | Total | Percentage | Population |
|---|---|---|---|---|---|
| Grimsby  CB | −5,068 | −5·4 | −5,957 | −6·2 | 95,020 |
| Barton-on-Humber  UD | 151 | 2·4 | −332 | −5·0 | 6,370 |
| Brigg  UD | 352 | 7·8 | −200 | −4·1 | 4,770 |
| Cleethorpes  MB | 1,655 | 5·6 | 160 | 0·5 | 34,140 |
| Scunthorpe  MB | 6,934 | 12·8 | −2,134 | −3·2 | 69,240 |
| Caistor  RD | −1,696 | −11·9 | 81 | 0·6 | 14,060 |
| Glanford  Brigg  RD | −341 | −1·0 | 3,261 | 9·4 | 39,940 |
| Grimsby  RD | 3,874 | 30·1 | 6,324 | 35·6 | 25,560 |
| Isle  of  Axholme  RD | −771 | −5·5 | −529 | −3·8 | 14,040 |
| Gainsborough  UD | −723 | −4·1 | −532 | −3·1 | 17,210 |
| Louth  MB | 128 | 1·2 | −527 | −4·6 | 11,170 |
| Mablethorpe  UD | −67 | −1·2 | −282 | −5·2 | 5,180 |
| Market  Rasen  UD | 113 | 5·3 | 40 | 1·8 | 2,330 |
| Gainsborough  RD | −999 | −7·9 | −837 | −6·6 | 12,420 |
| Louth  RD | −2,135 | −11·4 | −169 | −1·0 | 18,120 |
| South  Humberside | 1,407 | | −1,633 | | 369,570 |
| Humberside Total | −11,713 | | −11,504 | | 913,020 |

Source: 1951–61: calculated from Census of England and Wales, 1961 County Reports; 1961–66: D. G. Symes and J. G. Thomas.[23]

the 1960s there was a serious reversal of migration trends, the total net inflow of Inner South Humberside being reduced to under 1,000. Scunthorpe itself experienced a similar trend, recording a loss of over 2,000 people. The major gains were recorded in Glanford Brigg and Grimsby RDs.

This migration perspective is a valuable reminder of the individuality of the region, with the association of highly-capitalised, modern industries set in an area dominated by agriculture. Its demographic performance since 1951 has not been outstanding, and despite the more spectacular nature of developments on the south bank, the growth of South Humberside's population has not been fast enough to supersede, or even seriously challenge, the total population of the north bank. The weight of population distribution remains firmly entrenched in North Humberside.

In other parts the favoured play areas of childhood are now concealed by houses, by school or by factory; the annual change is slight, an erosion of memory, but the accumulation of this erosion is dramatic. A glance at the map of the London of 1800 or the Manchester of 1860 shows how the open space is absorbed by the urban need. It is still difficult to envisage the quiet fields of Humberside replaced by the noise and bustle of a large metropolitan region. The growth of Britain depends upon the closer integration of all regions into the sweep of national direction. To predict this pattern exactly is not practicable, but to assess its general form is important to investment at many levels. For some this will mean less intensive land use than at present, elsewhere a readjustment of older patterns, and in peripheral areas, such as Hull, the fuller use of local resources such as the port facilities and external trade links that have been fostered for decades and that are being thoroughly encouraged at the present time. The waterways of the region are considered in the next chapter.

The efficient use of this large area of land depends upon improving its internal communications and facilitating inter-regional exchange. At the moment the towns are 'underfit', are too small for their regional space and are incapable of extending their organisation to those parts of the area that are not oriented to other centres; a union almost by default. This weak association of parts of the region to a particular centre may be expected to change. The region is agriculturally rich and the development of this potential may be expected to accelerate under urban expansion. Already the influence of processing industries associated with fish is seen in the agricultural orientation of the region towards large-scale vegetable freezing industries.

The remainder of this study attempts to isolate those elements of recent industrial change which seem to be repetitive. In chapters 3, 4 and 5 industry is examined in terms of employment, allegiance to market or material, and its spatial specialisation. In the final chapter we return to transport networks in the region.

References to this chapter are on pages 221–3

# 2

# The Humber Estuary and its Ports

THE HUMBER ESTUARY is one of the major deepwater estuaries in Great Britain. With its confluent rivers and canals, it forms one of the most extensive waterway networks, providing cheap water transport into west and south Yorkshire and the East Midlands. The low-lying lands flanking the estuary are an important physical asset of the region, and no examination of the present industrial pattern can be complete without some knowledge of the facilities provided by the Humber and its ports.

## The Estuary and its Physical Potential

Figure 7 illustrates the major features of the deepwater estuary of the Humber. The estuary is at present completely unregulated, except where the riverside at Hull has been artificially embanked to provide quays. The Humber Estuary Model (completed at the beginning of 1969) imitates many of the dynamic features of the actual estuary, and permits a thorough investigation of various possible alterations to the channel profile, including land reclamation at Spurn Bight, deepening the channel or building quays.

The main deepwater channel swings within the overall estuary form. It provides a 36 foot channel at Hull at high tide, the depth increasing steadily downstream. It impinges on the Lincolnshire bank at Killingholme and on the Yorkshire bank at Hull itself, and this is where the main enclosed dock systems are found. Extensive use can also be made of quays and jetties which provide anchorages in deep water. The deepest water lies off Spurn Head itself, and between this point and Killingholme the deepwater channel loses depth as it crosses the middle shoal off Grimsby. This limited the size of vessel using the channel, but an artificial channel, cut in 1964, is now being regularly and inexpensively dredged to maintain easy access to Killingholme

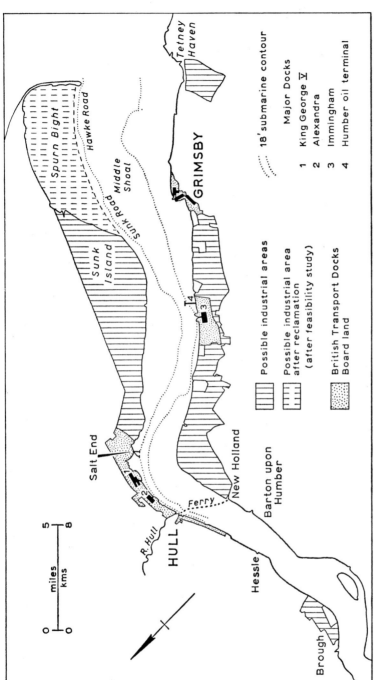

Fig 7. THE HUMBER ESTUARY

The map shows the location of the main docks and terminals in relation to the deepwater channel, and the estuarine sites with major development potential for industry. It is based on Map 11 in *Humberside—a Feasibility Study* (HMSO 1969) by permission for vessels of up to 100,000 tons.[1] The greater depth of the channel at Killingholme, 45–60ft High Water Mean Neap (HWMN), has been a major factor in causing postwar industrial development to be mainly placed on South Humberside, since the channel at Salt End, Hull, provides only 37ft. However, the ultimate development potential of the estuary will only be realised by exploiting the Hawke Road, which branches off the main channel at Spurn Point and lies close to the *north* Humber bank. Here consultants' reports for the British Transport Docks Board have indicated that the existing channel provides about 57ft of water at HWMN, which, with relatively little channel control, could be scoured to provide berths for vessels of up to 200,000 tons; these could negotiate the approaches to the Humber estuary with a minimum of dredging.[2]

The reserves of potential industrial land along the estuary can also be seen in Figure 7, and are closely related to the vital deep-water channel. The areas of possible industrial development are admittedly notional, but it is clear that there are vast areas of undeveloped land available along the estuary without recourse to land reclamation projects. Although the amount of land on the north bank appears larger, the greater part is of the highest agricultural quality, especially Sunk Island, and it is unlikely that this would be ceded without a struggle. However, the most important development on the north bank would be at Hawke Road, which is fronted at present by Spurn Bight, an expanse of sands that are exposed and dry between tides, and which could be fairly easily and cheaply reclaimed. This would provide an enormous area of flat land adjacent to one of the deepest anchorages on the east coast of Britain. Extensive land reclamation would only be necessary as part of a complete, phased plan for regional industrial development. But such a scheme is not an essential condition of Humberside development, because its existing and available land reserves are large enough. On the south bank Continental Oil (UK) have begun construction on a deepwater oil discharge terminal at Tetney Haven, to be linked with its existing south bank industrial site by pipeline; but extensive areas are also available at Tetney for industrial development, which would extend the South Humber complex far to the south of Grimsby.

The estuarine sites of the Humber are its major physical assets, for nowhere else on the east coast are deep channels and flat, cheap land in close juxtaposition. The opportunities for industries needing both imported raw materials in bulk and extensive sites are obvious, and have been recognised in the region since the construction of the first

Page 51: (above) *River Hull from Stoneferry Bridge about two-and-a-half miles up-stream on the Clough Road, looking downstream;* (below) *unloading a trawler on St Andrew's Dock, Hull. The fish is in the aluminium containers that are replacing the more traditional baskets*

Page 52: (above) *Inside a local mechanised net-making factory, Hull;* (below) *a local trawler being refitted on St Andrew's Dock*

deepwater jetty at Salt End as long ago as 1914. We shall look more closely at the nature of existing development in later chapters, but at this stage it should be borne in mind that the Humber and its waterways have stimulated a whole range of marine industries such as ship-building, barge and lighter building, marine engineering, ropemaking, and ship-repairing. The major ports have an important locational influence on industry in the region, particularly as they are being improved to meet changes in the technology of transportation.

## The Waterways

Historically, rivers such as the Ouse, Trent, Aire and Don have linked the ports of the Humber estuary with their distant hinterlands, and they continue this role today, especially for bulky goods. The relationship was strengthened in the last century with the construction of broad canals such as the Aire and Calder, and Hull in particular is a focus for inland waterway traffic. The reasons for the continued significance of water transport in the region are essentially physical (the flat topography, the broad and deep rivers, and the easy construction of canals since few locks are needed), and with the exception of the Manchester Ship Canal the network is the most important concentration of commercial inland waterways in Britain. In the words of the British Waterways Board:

> ... The Aire and Calder, the Calder and Hebble (Greenwood lock to Wakefield), the Sheffield and South Yorkshire and the Trent comprise an inter-connected group of major waterways linking the industrial areas of the West Riding and East Midlands to Goole, to Immingham and to Hull.[3]

The capacity of the waterways is the chief factor in their continued viability, strongly influencing many of the region's industries which need heavy or bulky materials; these include grain milling and seed crushing, petroleum distribution depots, building materials, timber and chemicals. The Trent Navigation accepts 200 ton craft to Nottingham, and 500 ton craft to Gainsborough; the Aire and Calder Navigation accepts specially designed craft of 500 tons, and general craft of 300 tons, while the compartment boats which dominate the coal traffic are used in formations of 700 tons. The Sheffield and South Yorkshire Navigation is also navigable for 700 ton compartment boats between Hexthorpe, near Doncaster, and the Trent at Keadby, barely three miles from Scunthorpe.

The lower reaches of the rivers are navigable by sea-going vessels

D

of up to about 2,500 tons, and include the lower Ouse to Selby and Goole, and the Trent to Flixborough Stather, Gunness and Keadby.

On the waterways the movement of bulky goods is dominant, especially coal and petroleum products. The Aire and Calder alone carries about 3 million tons of goods a year, an impressive figure especially when compared with the total tonnage of about 9 million tons handled at Hull. The internal movement of commodities such as grains is helped by the freedom from dock dues at Hull, which is the right of all lightermen on the Humber system, and this gives a competitive edge to the movement of such goods by the waterways.[4] The most impressive manifestation of this historical factor is seen in the industrial geography of Hull itself: but the size and distribution of origins of the commercial river craft of the Humber waterways, shown in Table 4, shows how widely its benefits are disseminated along the Humber waterways.

Table 4

RIVER CRAFT ON THE HUMBER WATERWAYS 1968

| District | Mechanically Propelled Vessels | Other Vessels | Total |
|---|---|---|---|
| Hull and East Riding | 281 | 145 | 426 |
| Grimsby, Barton and South Humber | 27 | 2 | 29 |
| Goole and Lower Ouse | 33 | 4 | 37 |
| York, Selby and Upper Ouse | 29 | 12 | 41 |
| Leeds and West Yorkshire | 43 | 1 | 44 |
| Gainsborough, Keadby and Lower Trent | 32 | 3 | 35 |
| Nottingham, Lincoln and Upper Trent | 2 | – | 2 |
| Sheffield and South Yorkshire | 26 | – | 26 |
| Total | 473 | 167 | 640 |

Source: British Transport Docks Board, Hull.

Although Hull itself is the main place of registration, the importance of the other ports along the waterways is particularly shown in the registration of mechanically propelled craft.

The development potential of the waterways has not been exhausted by any means. The British Waterways Board have recently placed before the Ministry of Transport a £2,500,000 scheme which would enable 500 ton barges to use the Sheffield and South Yorkshire from Keadby on the lower Trent to Rotherham. If implemented, this could undoubtedly be a further boost to the important movement of petroleum products inland from Hull and Immingham. Of more importance for regional industrial growth are the improvements taking place on the lower reaches of the rivers, which are accessible to sea-going vessels. Perhaps the most interesting are on the lower Trent, at Keadby, Gunness, Flixborough and Burton Stather, where there is already some industrial expansion. At Burton Stather a new river port, with special facilities for the direct off-loading into barges of cargoes such as timber, is under construction at a cost of £500,000. The port will be able to accommodate coastal and near-continental vessels of up to 3,000 tons.[5] A new £200,000 quay has also been recently commissioned on the lower Ouse at Howden, and has special facilities for bulk chemical handling. These developments show the degree of inland penetration of cheap water transport in the region; this is sometimes difficult for the outsider to envisage. It has allowed industry to develop in a clustered fashion well inland, and the types of industry usually present link these concentrations to Humberside as a region. Perhaps the best case is Selby, but the potential of Scunthorpe as an inland port through its location near the Trent has only recently begun to be exploited. The waterways' chief role lies in the inland distribution of imported materials, with the striking exception of coal, although this is not moved in any quantity beyond Goole. The use of water transport for exporting general goods is poorly developed, although experiments on the Leeds to Hull route were launched in 1969. The only other substantial down-movement is in dredged river gravels from the Trent valley to the Hull area, which is deficient in these vital materials for the construction industry.

## The Humber Ports

In this book we are concerned with the role of the ports in the distribution of industry, which will be reflected in their facilities for cargo handling, their pattern of trade, their development plans and their direct industrial estate facilities at the dockside. In addition, the docks have encouraged many service industries, such as the maintenance of marine navigation and radio equipment, or ships' stores, and ancillary activities such as ship repairing, and the vast fishing industry of Grimsby and Hull, with its many associated activities. The commercial and industrial functions of ports are always difficult to separate, but it is hoped that a preliminary discussion of the role of dockside industrial estates will afford some idea of the direct importance of the ports in the location of industry, a topic which will be more comprehensively treated in later chapters.

*Goole*

Goole is the furthest inland of the dock systems, being about fifty miles from the open sea. The Humber, upstream from Hessle Narrows, is a very treacherous channel and monthly revisions of the navigation charts are necessary. However, an extensive programme of engineering works accomplished between 1884 and 1935 regularised the lower Ouse, and has enabled Goole to be reached by 2,500 ton vessels, although rather larger ships have been docked.

Goole was created in the nineteenth century by the Aire and Calder Navigation Company as the terminus and transhipment port for coal traffic, and this function still dominates the port, particularly in its physical layout, which is tortuous in the extreme. With a total water area of 45 acres, there are no less than eight individual docks, many branching off at right-angles from one another and making ship movement difficult. The main entrance to the dock system, Ocean Lock, is 375 feet long and 80 feet wide. The trading connections of Goole are coastal and near-continental, with regular scheduled sailings to Belgian, Dutch, West German and Danish ports. Some of the small European ports are included, such as Delfzyl and Harlingen, and there is a weekly sailing between Goole and Brussels.

In terms of tonnage handled, Goole is essentially an exporting port, with coal accounting for about sixty per cent of its total traffic by weight. But imports are growing, and, as Table 5 shows, reached over half a million tons in 1968. The trade of the port is becoming more diverse and new general merchandise facilities are being developed around the Ouse Dock; this necessitated the filling-in of the original Harbour Basin to improve quay and storage space. The nineteenth-century planning of the dock estate prevents any major associated industrial development, since the fragmented dock layout, and a network of public roads and railways, provide little free space. The important Goole Ship Building and Repairing establishment lies outside the dock estate on the south of the Dutch River and so is separate from the system. Some regional industries use Goole for importing raw materials, such as Belgian white sand for important glass industries near Doncaster and at Knottingley, but generally Goole is a commercial rather than an industrial port. Nevertheless, large areas of flat land abut on the Ouse channel down river from Goole, and could provide sites for industries willing to rely on transhipped raw materials by lighters, or able to use small vessels for cargo-carrying. At present only a large fertiliser plant on Dutch River makes extensive use of water transport in this way. The development of general cargo services was hampered in 1968 by the loss of scheduled services to Hamburg and Antwerp; these were transferred to Hull under rationalisation schemes. This was probably inevitable, since Goole's sea connections are inferior to Hull's, but the stability of the bulk cargoes, such as coal and timber, appears assured.

## Hull

Located at the inland extremity of the deepwater channel in the Humber estuary, Hull is the major port of the system, having by far the largest docks and the most varied trade. Although recently overhauled by Immingham in tonnage handled, the value of Hull's trade is far greater, amounting to £770,000,000 in 1968. This Customs and Excise figure places Hull in third position of British seaports, measured in value of trade handled.

Hull's docks are of two contrasting types. The smaller docks of the late eighteenth century and early nineteenth century are sited to the west of the River Hull, and are generally cheek by jowl with other urban land uses, only the St. Andrew's fish dock having a small dock estate (see Figure 31, page 167). The innermost group of docks, encircling the old city and following the line of fortifications, are now too small for modern traffic, the Queen's dock having been closed and filled in before World War II. The combined water area of the Humber, Princes and Railway docks is in fact only 16 acres; they are now of negligible importance, the Princes dock having closed in 1969, but they retain an important function for ship-repairing firms. The Albert, William Wright and St. Andrew's docks are narrow, elongated docks running parallel with the Humber, which at this point provides a deepwater channel capable of direct use, as at the rebuilt Riverside Quay. The docks concentrate on near-continental traffic, handling all types of cargo, and the reconstruction of the Albert dock, with the provision of covered transit sheds, is evidence of their continued usefulness. The St. Andrew's dock is exclusively the preserve of the Hull fishing fleet, and the dock estate is densely packed with associated industrial activities, such as ice making, fish filleting and packing, fish freezing and packing, and fish meal plants. This distinctive industrial complex is repeated in Grimsby in similar circumstances, and will be commented on in more detail later.

The major docks, and those possessing the greatest site advantages for certain types of industry, lie east of the river Hull, and include the Salt End jetties. As Figure 31 illustrates, these large docks are set in a very extensive dock estate which has large areas available for industrial development, and for improvements to the docks themselves. The Alexandra Dock of 53 acres water area has been extensively reconstructed in recent years; the lock sill depth of 29ft Mean High Water Neap (MHWN) enables large ocean-going vessels to use it, and South American, African and Far Eastern sailings are handled, beside those for Europe. The King George dock, with a water area of 64 acres recently increased to 92 acres with the completion of a £7 million extension, is capable of taking ships of up to 25,000 tons and is the main dock for Hull's distant overseas trade. The diversity of modern cargo handling facilities is impressive, ranging from open storage cargoes such as timber or vehicles, to general merchandise and wool requiring extensive transit shed accommodation and special grain terminals. Furthermore, the two most important 'roll-on roll-off' berths for containerisation have been built in this dock, and further provision has been made in the new extension. Other developments, such as palletisation and mechanical handling of cargoes at the quays, are well advanced. In line with modern trends in cargo handling, seven specialised berths have been provided at Hull, and by 1968 these operated twenty five regular weekly sailings to northern Europe, handling over a million tons of general cargo in the process.

The Salt End deepwater jetties provide specialised facilities for the discharge and loading of liquid cargoes, primarily petroleum products and petrochemical feedstocks. They are used by vessels ranging from 35,000$dw$ ton oil tankers to river barges, and the eastern end of the British Transport Docks Estate is extensively developed with oil storage depots and petrochemical plants.

It is difficult to generalise about the dominant trading connections of a port as large as Hull, but northern Europe figures prominently, accounting for a third of all imports by weight; even so this is only marginally higher than imports from the Americas. However, in its export trade Hull is very clearly dominated by Northern Europe, which accounts for over three-quarters of its outward cargoes. This reflects Hull's location advantage, facing the rapidly growing industrial ports of Belgium, Holland, Germany and Sweden.

The tendency in the volume of trade through Hull in tonnage terms has been upward since 1958, but the increase in its value has risen far more sharply, as higher value shipments of general merchandise or vehicles through the specialised berths has replaced lower value cargoes such as coal exports. The imports are dominated, in weight at least, by petroleum products, followed by cereals, timber, oilseeds and nuts, and various types of foodstuffs, fruit and vegetables. (See Table 5).

**Table 5**

MAJOR CHARACTERISTICS OF THE TRADE OF THE
HUMBER PORTS IN 1968

| Commodity | Port and Cargo (in tons) | | | |
|---|---|---|---|---|
| | Hull | Goole | Immingham | Grimsby |
| Total Inward Cargo of which: | 5,785,284 | 552,703 | 6,385,552 | 1,051,494 |
| Cereals | 868,885 | 18,296 | — | 37,528 |
| Fruit and vegetables | 129,727 | — | 5,477 | — |
| Molasses and sugar | 97,726 | — | — | 55,354 |
| Dairy produce | — | 67,473 | — | 160,347 |
| Other foodstuffs | 326,882 | — | 22,635 | — |
| Oilseeds and nuts | 203,919 | — | 359 | — |
| Timber | 526,393 | 109,773 | 32,697 | 182,729 |
| Woodpulp | — | — | 41,587 | 179,963 |
| Iron ore | 4,178 | — | 625,164 | — |
| Chemicals and fertilizers | — | — | 1,155,029 | — |
| Non ferrous ores | — | — | 272,545 | |
| Fish landings | 200,427 | — | — | 185,463 |
| Petroleum | 1,910,507 | 21,945 | 3,512,074[3] | 52,500 |
| Total Outward Cargo of which: | 2,168,006 | 1,537,349 | 4,295,984 | 243,696 |
| Chemicals and fertilizers | 164,958 | 22,975 | 175,294 | 63,894 |
| Iron and steel | 203,461 | 46,365 | 459,473 | 66,895 |
| Machinery | 104,705 | 15,766 | 22,176 | 9,070 |
| Vehicles | 77,574 | 2,099 | 32,483 | 7,548 |
| Coal and coke | 323,573 | 1,371,758 | 3,102,099 | — |
| Petroleum | 464,947 | — | 457,755 | — |
| Total Inward and Outward Cargo | 7,953,290 | 2,090,052 | 10,681,536 | 1,295,190 |
| NRT of vessels arriving[1] | 6,999,348[2] | 971,860 | 5,617,157 | 534,793 |
| Number of vessels arriving[1] | 4,582[2] | 2,383 | 2,932 | 1,283 |

*Source:* British Transport Docks Board.

[1] Commercial vessels, not including fishing boats.
[2] 1967 figures.
[3] Includes 19,919 tons of Liquid petroleum gases.

The relationship between industry and the docks of Hull is of immense significance. The Salt End jetties feed a complex of petro-chemical establishments dominated by BP Chemicals, and depends at present entirely on feedstock imported through the jetties. The fish docks complex has already been mentioned, but the chief effects are indirect. Thus the Hull riverside industries, oil seed crushing, paints and chemicals and various others, are served by lighters through direct overside discharge. As Britain's second timber handling port, Hull has provided an excellent location for a large range of timber using industries. Many firms are basically dependent on the trade generated by the docks, especially engineering, metal work and transportation. These patterns are examined in detail in later chapters. With its excellent facilities and established shipping connections, its record of continuous capital investment, and an assured future judging by the interest generated by the Humber model, the port of Hull is a major asset to industry in the region.

### Grimsby

Grimsby is the smallest of the four Humber ports in terms of tonnage handled, the total traffic amounting to approximately 1·3 million tons in 1968. Its trade consists almost entirely of imports, and includes 200,000 tons of fish.

The present dock system, having begun life as an impounded creek in the early nineteenth century, has progressively grown seawards into the extensive saltmarshes and mudflats characteristic of this part of the north Lincolnshire coast. The commercial docks, the Royal and Alexandra, have a water area of 75 acres, but the sea lock is limited to a 21ft sill depth at Mean High Water Neap (MHWN). The fish docks account for a further 63 acres, split between three interconnected basins (Figure 34, page 194). The Royal dock is the main commercial dock, and has been extensively improved, particularly by the addition of a roll-on, roll-off terminal for the Danish trade in bacon, butter and other foodstuffs. However, new quays are being provided in the Alexandra dock to cope with the steady growth in trade, and accommodation for all types of cargo has been progressively improved.

Grimsby's external trade is almost exclusively with Europe, particularly Western Europe and Scandinavia. Grimsby, like Goole, has an important commercial role, acting as a collection and distribution centre for national markets. Some of the main imports of timber, all the paper pulp, and most of the fish imports are destined for Grimsby industries. Many of the exports, such as chemicals and fertilisers, although in bulk relatively unimportant, originate locally.

Grimsby docks are significant in a number of ways. The most obvious is the conglomeration of fish processing industries around the fish docks, and on the dock estate itself. This also extends to specialised ship repairing and fitting-out facilities for trawlers. The British Transport Docks Estate already contains a large number of plants, especially in the Pyewipe district. Here rail, road and direct dock access is available, and the area forms in effect an extension of the south Humber bank. Over 80 acres of industrial land is still available within the dock estate alone.[6] Fish processing plants, particularly fish meal manufacture, dominate in the Pyewipe section of the estate, with timber using industries concentrating round the Alexandra Dock.

The port facilities of Grimsby are directly responsible for the establishment of two interesting industrial concentrations. But for the general hinterland of South Humberside, its facilities are surpassed by Immingham some miles *up river*.

### Immingham

The industrial growth of Humberside is perhaps most strikingly illustrated by Immingham dock. Immingham, opened in 1911, was originally destined to export coal for the Great Central Railway, which included most of the Yorks-Notts-Derby coalfield in its hinterland. It is now one of the major ports in Britain. Although the decline of the coal trade after World War I impeded Immingham's growth, coal shipments are still high and it ranks as one of Britain's leading centres for this trade. Another feature connected with coal is the extensive rail sidings totalling over 160 miles track length, which were necessary for the storage of the long coal trains.[7]

Immingham consists of the wet dock, with a water area of 45 acres reached through a massive sea-lock 840ft long by 90ft wide, and jetties reaching out into the main Humber deepwater channel, which lies close inshore at this point. The dock facilities are being constantly improved, and the sill depth of the sea-lock will be increased from its present 32 feet HWMN by an impounding scheme. Although general merchandise traffic has been increasing rapidly with the advent of North Sea roll-on, roll-off ferries, the port's facilities are still dominated by the bulky cargoes more characteristically connected with the local industrial hinterland. Iron ore, coal, timber and potash are among the most important commodities to be moved in bulk, and quay cranage and access are adapted to these types of cargo. However, two quays have covered transit sheds for general merchandise, while the ferry terminal represents further investment to develop the all round potentialities of the port. The terminal was opened in 1966, and is used by regular overnight sailings to Amsterdam and Göteborg. Very specialised equipment, in the form of electric radial arm conveyors, can load coal at the rate of 1,350 tons an hour. The steady rise in iron ore imports for the Scunthorpe steelworks since 1960 has resulted in the establishment of a special mineral quay to handle this traffic.

Two jetties provide facilities for the direct discharge of liquid cargoes, primarily petroleum products, liquid sulphur and crude oil, to shore installations. Ocean tankers use the outer faces of the jetties for discharging cargoes, and coastal tankers and river barges use the inner faces for taking on cargoes. These jetties give a water depth of 34 feet Low Water Spring Ordinary Tide (LWSOT), and are capable of handling vessels up to 40,000 tons. However, the first stage of the new Humber oil terminal was completed in 1969 at a cost of over £3$\frac{1}{2}$ million, and this reaches farther out into deeper water. It is capable of accommodating two 100,000 ton oil tankers simultaneously, as well as coastal vessels and river barges on its inner face. Its primary function is to import crude oils for the two refineries, one partially on stream at the time of writing, the other nearing completion. A further deep water jetty was opened in 1970 for the National Coal Board up river from the oil terminal; this cost about £5 million. It will enable coal to be discharged cheaply into very large bulk carriers, and so increase the export market for British coal. Discharge rates of over 4,000 tons per hour are mentioned, and there has been recent confirmation of a sharing arrangement with the British Steel Corporation, so that the jetty can handle both coal and iron ore.[8] Immingham is the focus of much investment, closely following Hull in this respect. Some of the schemes, such as the Humber oil terminal, are expensive; others, such as the reconstruction of a large quay as an open berth specially equipped to deal with lorry traffic and smaller vessels, may be less expensive but are equally significant, indicating an appreciation of the changing demands on the port, and providing a further stage in the development of an improved regional transport infrastructure.

Immingham's trading pattern clearly reflects its largely industrial role, at least in terms of imports. In 1938 the total trade handled was only 2,700,000 tons, chiefly coal. By 1968 this figure exceeded 10 million tons for the first time. Much of the tremendous expansion in post-war years has been due to petroleum products, and this traffic has now entered its most rapid growth phase with the imminent full scale operation of two major oil refineries.

As Table 5 shows, petroleum products dominated imports in 1968, and were destined for the extensive on-shore storage installations of major oil companies such as Regent, Esso, Shell and Continental.[9]

Other bulky materials play a prominent role, especially chemicals and iron ore, and manufactured iron and steel goods are also imported in considerable quantity. Exports are naturally dominated by coal, but a high tonnage of manufactured iron and steel goods shows the increasing integration with Scunthorpe. Immingham, unlike the other Humber ports, has no dominant external trade pattern, the ferry service providing links only to Holland and Sweden.

The port of Immingham has played a major role in the industrial development of the south Humber bank since 1945. The existence of an excellent but under-used dock, isolated from major urban developments, has encouraged industries needing extensive sites and imported materials. Since the south Humber bank concentration of chemical plants (analysed in Chapter 5) is arguably the single most important industrial phenomenon in the region, the role of Immingham has obviously been of major importance in the process of industrial development.

References to this chapter are on page 223

# 3

# The Economic Structure of Humberside

THIS CHAPTER has two main aims: first to analyse the economic structure of Humberside, both as one unit and in terms of its two major sub-regions, and secondly to evaluate some of the recent changes in the region's industrial structure. In the former, it is important to keep the national context in mind, especially in identifying sectors of economic activity or individual industries as characteristic of Humberside. Any account of the industrial structure should also deal with the basic locational needs of industry. In evaluating changes in a region's industrial structure, it must be stressed that this cannot be achieved successfully with any one index; those which have often been used include population growth, employment growth, growth in per capita income, and various measures of growth in output. However, there is not necessarily a positive association between these indices, and an expansion in output, output per employee, and income per employee can be, and often is, associated with a decline in employment and a decreasing share of national employment. Perloff cites the American tobacco industry as an example,[1] while in the present period the fastest growing industries in output terms are generally highly capital intensive, with only scanty labour requirements, such as chemicals and oil refining. Many qualifications are thus needed when growth is examined. Much of the analysis is based on employment data from the Department of Employment and Productivity, and the employment exchange area boundaries are shown on Figure 8.

### The Overall Level of Economic Activity since 1953

From 1953–67 the total employed population of Humberside expanded by twenty per cent, compared with a national average of

64

only twelve per cent,[2] but this expansion has not been entirely uniform. Male unemployment in North Humberside has been consistently above the national average, and female employment relatively low. From total employment statistics the prevailing impression is one of a rapid expansion from 1953–60, followed by slower and more hesitant growth in the 1960s. Although we are interested primarily in the period since 1960, a number of important trends can only be understood with reference to the earlier period.

The degree of employment in the region is an important indicator of economic strength. In North and South Humberside the trend of male and female activity rates has been upwards, although Table 6 shows that important differences within the region remained in 1966.

**Table 6**

MALE AND FEMALE ACTIVITY RATES* 1951–66

| Year | North Humberside | | South Humberside | | Great Britain | |
|------|-------|---------|-------|---------|-------|---------|
|      | Males | Females | Males | Females | Males | Females |
| 1951 | 72 | 28 | 73 | 24 | 76 | 35 |
| 1961 | 74 | 32 | 79 | 30 | 78 | 39 |
| 1966 | 75 | 37 | 78 | 32 | 76 | 40 |

* Total employees as a percentage of home population aged 15 and over.
Source: Humberside Feasibility Study, Table 10a.

The male activity rate for North and South Humberside was below the Great Britain average in 1951, and, even after the rapid growth in employment between 1951 and 1961, still lagged behind the national level in North Humberside. A very rapid expansion of industries need-ing predominantly male labour occurred between 1951 and 1961 in South Humberside, but has not been maintained since 1961, so that a slight decline in the male activity rate is recorded for 1961–66. However the male rate has continued upwards in North Humberside, so that by 1966 internal variations in male activity rates had largely disappeared, and the region does not differ significantly from the national average.

The differential between Humberside and national activity rates for females was very wide in 1951, South Humberside recording a lag of eleven points. But whereas the national rate has only moved up slowly from 1951 to 1966, the rise in Humberside has been very steep. In North Humberside the rise from twenty-eight to thirty-seven means that the area is rapidly approaching the national average. The South Humberside rate of thirty-two in 1966 suggests waste of potential labour in the area, although the mechanism behind this continuing lag is more complex than might appear, since studies in Scunthorpe have shown that the main demand is for suitable part-time jobs for females.[3] But overall, the rise in female activity rates has been a factor

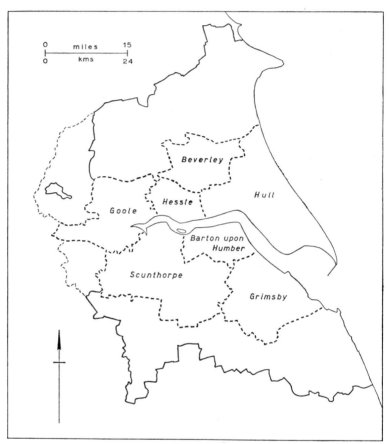

Fig 8.  EMPLOYMENT EXCHANGE AREAS OF INNER
HUMBERSIDE
The boundaries do not coincide completely with the Inner Humberside of
Figure 3; the boundary of Outer Humberside is also shown

of considerable significance for the region's income, and as an element in industrial location.

A further measure of general economic efficiency is the level of unemployment, although as an index it has been criticised on many counts.[4] In Humberside, where the docks and fishing employ large numbers, the rate of casual unemployment is always high, and was higher before the decasualisation of the dock labour force in 1966.

But unemployment in North Humberside particularly has tended to be above the national average since 1955, as Table 7 indicates.

**Table 7**

HUMBERSIDE AND GREAT BRITAIN—MALE AND FEMALE UNEMPLOYMENT RATES 1955–68

| Year | North Humberside | | South Humberside | | Great Britain | |
|------|-------|---------|-------|---------|-------|---------|
| | Males | Females | Males | Females | Males | Females |
| 1955 | 1·9 | 1·5 | 1·0 | 1·3 | 1·1 | 1·1 |
| 1956 | 1·9 | 1·2 | 1·0 | 1·9 | 1·2 | 1·2 |
| 1957 | 2·5 | 1·5 | 1·6 | 2·3 | 1·5 | 1·3 |
| 1958 | 3·8 | 2·3 | 1·8 | 2·3 | 2·3 | 1·8 |
| 1959 | 4·1 | 2·0 | 2·2 | 2·5 | 2·4 | 1·7 |
| 1960 | 2·7 | 1·4 | 1·5 | 1·8 | 1·8 | 1·3 |
| 1961 | 1·9 | 1·1 | 1·3 | 1·3 | 1·7 | 1·1 |
| 1962 | 2·6 | 1·3 | 2·3 | 1·8 | 2·3 | 1·4 |
| 1963 | 3·4 | 1·8 | 3·2 | 2·3 | 3·0 | 1·6 |
| 1964 | 2·5 | 1·2 | 1·9 | 2·1 | 1·9 | 1·1 |
| 1965 | 2·2 | 1·0 | 1·8 | 1·7 | 1·7 | 0·9 |
| 1966 | 2·3 | 0·9 | 2·1 | 1·5 | 1·9 | 0·9 |
| 1967 | 4·0 | 1·2 | 2·9 | 1·9 | 3·0 | 1·3 |
| 1968 | 4·9 | 1·2 | 3·3 | 1·7 | 3·2 | 1·0 |

*Source:* Humberside Feasibility Study, Table 10b.

Male unemployment in North Humberside has faithfully reflected national fluctuations, but with amplified rates. Thus in the period 1965–68, whilst the national male unemployment rate rose from 1·7 to 3·2 per cent, North Humberside's rate rose from 2·2 to 4·9 per cent. Female unemployment rates in both North and South Humberside have remained low in comparison with male rates, and in North Humberside since 1960 the rate has been almost identical with the national average; a favourable trend. However, the sudden rise in male unemployment in North Humberside after 1966 is disturbing, and by 1968 the rate had reached development district levels at nearly five per cent. The recent Government action in creating North Humberside an intermediate area is a recognition of the seriousness of the position. In South Humberside, although the male unemployment rate has risen since 1960, it is nevertheless similar to the national average.

Some of the major features of the region's economic expansion in the 1950s are relevant to an understanding of events since 1960. The overall growth of the employed population in the period 1953–60 was faster in South Humberside, although on a smaller initial base, but clear differences between North and South Humberside had already emerged. The most significant was that South Humberside's expansion was concentrated in manufacturing (Table 8), and North Humberside's

**Table 8**

EMPLOYMENT GROWTH BY SECTORS 1953–60
(In 1,000s)

| Sector | North Humberside 1953 | 1960 | Percentage change | South Humberside 1953 | 1960 | Percentage change |
|---|---|---|---|---|---|---|
| Primary | 10·5 | 9·2 | −12·4 | 11·5 | 10·8 | −6·1 |
| Manufacturing | 60·3 | 65·6 | +8·8 | 38·3 | 46·4 | +21·1 |
| Construction | 8·2 | 10·0 | +22·0 | 7·6 | 8·2 | +7·9 |
| Public utilities | 2·9 | 2·8 | −3·4 | 1·4 | 1·8 | +28·6 |
| Transport | 26·3 | 24·6 | −6·5 | 10·4 | 9·7 | −6·7 |
| Services | 53·1 | 63·6 | +19·8 | 28·6 | 34·3 | +19·9 |
| Total | 161·3 | 175·8 | +9·0 | 97·8 | 111·2 | +13·7 |

in services, with only a small numerical increase in manufacturing, confined mainly to the vehicle industry. But the expansion of the industrial labour force in South Humberside was also unevenly distributed, with metal manufacture and chemicals accounting for the major share.[5] This degree of over-specialisation has created a number of socio-economic problems for the 1960s, particularly as the two groups in question have lost much of their impetus to expand in terms of employment.

### The General Economic Structure and Employment Changes 1960–7

In both 1960 and 1967 the Hull employment exchange area contained approximately half the total employment of Inner Humberside (Table 9). Because some of the western suburbs of Hull lie in Hessle exchange area, the real proportion must be higher. Moreover the absolute increase in employment in North Humberside was almost entirely centred on Hull itself, and numerically this increase was equal to that in South Humberside. This corrects a prevalent impression that all economic expansion in the region is south of the Humber, and that North Humberside is stagnant. The growth of employment in manufacturing in the region since 1960 has been small in absolute terms, although the rate of increase has again been faster in South Humberside than North Humberside.

In regional planning circles employment expansion is considered desirable, yet even in former centres of rapid growth such as Scunthorpe it has been small. But caution must be exercised in interpreting employment change over a number of years, since the choice of base line can result in different patterns, depending on the phasing of

Page 69: (above) *Beverley shipyard, on the River Hull, about 10 miles upstream. The two vessels are the traditional design side-fishing trawlers;* (below) *aerial view near the site of the Humber bridge, looking south to the Lincolnshire bank, showing the main railway line to Hull, Earle's cement works and Capper Pass, the non-ferrous metal refinery*

Page 70: (above) *The Salt End factory of BP Chemicals (UK) Ltd, looking north east. This large petrochemicals complex is Europe's biggest producer of acetic acid. Hedon Creek is on the right;* (below) *the Lindsey oil refinery, Killingholme, opened in June 1968. The Humber estuary is in the background*

### Table 9

HUMBERSIDE TOTAL AND MANUFACTURING EMPLOYMENT
CHANGES 1960–67
(Employment in 1,000s)

| Employment Exchange | Total Employment | | | Manufacturing* | | |
|---|---|---|---|---|---|---|
| | 1960 | 1967 | Percentage change | 1960 | 1967 | Percentage change |
| Hull | 139·7 | 149·5 | +7·0 | 49·5 | 51·6 | +4·2 |
| Hessle | 12·1 | 13·8 | +14·0 | 7·5 | 8·4 | +12·0 |
| Beverley | 12·4 | 11·4 | −8·1 | 5·4 | 4·5 | −16·6 |
| Goole | 11·6 | 11·6 | — | 3·2 | 3·3 | +3·1 |
| North Humberside | 175·8 | 186·3 | +6·0 | 65·6 | 67·8 | +3·4 |
| Scunthorpe | 46·9 | 49·5 | +5·5 | 24·8 | 25·2 | +1·6 |
| Barton | 3·3 | 6·0 | +81·8 | 1·4 | 2·3 | +64·3 |
| Grimsby | 61·0 | 66·5 | +9·0 | 20·2 | 23·4 | +15·8 |
| South Humberside | 111·2 | 122·0 | +9·6 | 46·4 | 50·9 | +9·7 |
| Humberside | 287·0 | 308·3 | +7·4 | 112·0 | 118·7 | +6·0 |

* Standard Industrial Classification [SIC] Orders III–XIV. Employment figures rounded to the nearest hundred.

employment growth, and this is certainly true of Scunthorpe. Also cyclical fluctuations occur within the time span considered, and while it is difficult to incorporate these in a general comparison they will obviously influence the rate of change over a given period of time.

Table 10 gives an indication of the annual cyclical trends in all employment since 1960, and it shows in three areas a decline in employment since 1965. Consequently our use of the later 1967 data understates the actual maximum expansion of employment in Hull, Scunthorpe and Beverley in the intervening years. The table reinforces the pattern of total employment change shown in Table 9: Hull,

### Table 10

INDEX NUMBERS OF TOTAL EMPLOYMENT CHANGE 1960–67 BY
EXCHANGE AREA
(1960 employment = 100)

| Exchange | 1960 | 1961 | 1962 | 1963 | 1964 | 1965 | 1966 | 1967 |
|---|---|---|---|---|---|---|---|---|
| Hull | 100 | 102 | 105 | 107 | 107 | 110 | 113 | 107 |
| Beverley | 100 | 91 | 95 | 94 | 103 | 98 | 94 | 92 |
| Hessle | 100 | 107 | 109 | 113 | 112 | 110 | 111 | 113 |
| Goole | 100 | 98 | 102 | 102 | 103 | 99 | 98 | 100 |
| Scunthorpe | 100 | 107 | 106 | 106 | 108 | 114 | 109 | 105 |
| Barton | 100 | 85 | 86 | 87 | 93 | 92 | 115 | 179 |
| Grimsby | 100 | 103 | 105 | 106 | 109 | 104 | 112 | 109 |

The index numbers are rounded to the nearest integer.

E

Hessle and Grimsby have been fairly consistent in their expansion whilst Goole has been static. Scunthorpe and Barton illustrate the significance of cyclical trends, the former having an internal peak, and the latter a pronounced trough. Beverley's decline in employment was a feature of the 1960s as a whole, with the exception of a slight recovery in 1964.

In the period 1960–67, over two-thirds of the growth in manufacturing employment has been in South Humberside, and here the emphasis has switched from the Scunthorpe area to Grimsby and Barton. The expansion in the latter has occurred entirely since 1965 and is mostly connected with construction work, so that the longer term employment prospects are less promising; the Humber Oil Refinery, when operational, is expected to employ only 250. In North Humberside manufacturing employment increases have been focused on Hull and Hessle. Goole has been stagnant, and Beverley has fluctuated downwards from a peak for the series in 1960. In both areas existing industry has not provided the impetus for employment growth, and new industry has not been enough to make up the deficit.

The most important trend in national post-war employment has been the rapid expansion in services of all descriptions, such as retailing, finance, government, education and professional services, most of which are geared to local needs. Employment expansion in these services has also been more consistent than in manufacturing, and in both North and South Humberside services have accounted for most

**Table 11**

HUMBERSIDE EMPLOYMENT IN SERVICES* 1960–67
(In 1,000s)

| Employment Exchange | 1960 | 1967 | Change | Percentage change |
|---|---|---|---|---|
| Hull | 52·3 | 61·8 | 9·5 | 18·2 |
| Hessle | 2·9 | 3·8 | 0·9 | 29·3 |
| Beverley | 4·7 | 5·1 | 0·4 | 9·7 |
| Goole | 3·7 | 4·1 | 0·4 | 9·5 |
| North Humberside | 63·6 | 74·8 | 11·2 | 17·7 |
| Scunthorpe | 10·8 | 13·5 | 2·7 | 24·8 |
| Barton | 0·9 | 0·8 | −0·1 | −11·1 |
| Grimsby | 22·6 | 25·0 | 2·4 | 10·6 |
| South Humberside | 34·3 | 39·3 | 5·0 | 14·5 |
| Humberside | 97·9 | 114·1 | 16·2 | 16·6 |

* SICs XX, XXI, XXII, XXIII, XXIV. All employment figures rounded to the nearest hundred.

of the total employment growth since 1960, with growth rates high in all areas except Barton, usually far above those for manufacturing. Public utilities and transport have not been included in this definition of services, and employment in these is declining. The balance between North and South Humberside in service employment is clearly in favour of the former, and this advantage is being increased by a faster growth rate. Services are primarily concentrated in urban centres, and are unevenly distributed between urban centres of different size classes.[6] Sophisticated services are associated with large towns and cities, and, while Hull dominates within Humberside, it has not achieved the status of a major provincial city in any published scheme.[7] The regional headquarters of government departments, nationalised industries, or major commercial enterprises tend to concentrate in Leeds, and although Hull has a considerable array of non-locally oriented services associated with its international port functions such as shipping offices and marine insurance, the employment associated with these is not very large. The rapid increase in service employment is a key feature of the region's economic structure, particularly with regard to the continued dominance of Hull. Since 1960 about sixty per cent of this expansion was concentrated in Hull, and, as much of it consists of better paid white collar employment, the impact on sub-regional incomes will be most marked. A high rate of increase also occurred in Scunthorpe but this largely consisted of making up a huge leeway, the result of previously unbalanced growth. Goole, Beverley and Grimsby recorded lower growth rates, while the high rate in Hessle was related to the expansion of retail and other local services for growing new residential estates.[8]

Geographers such as Peter Hall have drawn attention to the increasing need to include service employment as well as manufacturing employment in the study of regional economic patterns.[9] Against a background of increasing technical efficiency, which reduces labour requirements in relation to output, manufacturing industry must be considered as essentially a static sector in the future. On the other hand, following American experience, a further rapid expansion of service and construction employment is anticipated by the end of the century. This will arise partly from the increased demands for a more varied range of public and private services by the general population, and also from rapid employment growth in research and development laboratories, computer complexes and so forth within manufacturing organisations. These branches are often in locations separate from the manufacturing establishments. Other service functions more closely related to the needs of industry such as automatic food vending, heating and ventilation or specialist plant design and engineering, should also expand rapidly, and many of them are urban-based. In all these growth trends, Hull should have a substantial role to play, with the aid of its elaborate range of commercial, cultural and educational facilities, which are far superior to those of any other centre within the region.

Fig 9 summarises graphically the balance between the three major

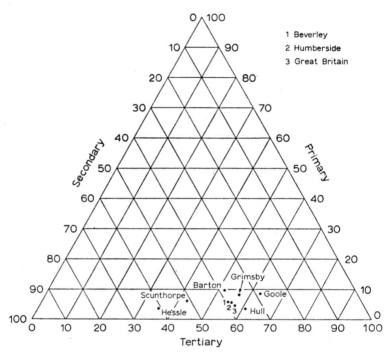

Fig 9.  EMPLOYMENT STRUCTURE OF HUMBERSIDE
EXCHANGE AREAS 1967

This triangular graph summarises the percentage of employment in the
three main economic sectors for each exchange area

sectors, primary, secondary or manufacturing, and tertiary, and this data is presented numerically in Table 12. The major feature of Humberside as a whole is the close similarity which its employment structure bears to the national average. Manufacturing, construction and public utilities do not vary significantly, and the primary sector is only slightly above the national average. The distinctiveness of the region is best reflected in a considerable excess of transport employment, accompanied by a small deficit in the services.

Of the individual exchange areas, Hull shows least variation from both the Humberside and national pattern. Despite its strong association with fishing, the primary sector employs only slightly over three per cent of the work force. A very high proportion is engaged in transport, reflecting not only the dock system but also the host of canal and road haulage firms operating out of Hull. The proportion engaged in services is virtually identical with the national average, while manufacturing is rather less significant.

**Table 12**

PERCENTAGE BREAKDOWN OF EMPLOYMENT IN HUMBERSIDE
EXCHANGE AREAS 1967

| Sector | Great Britain | Humber- side | Hull | Beverley | Hessle | Goole | Scun- thorpe | Barton | Grimsby |
|---|---|---|---|---|---|---|---|---|---|
| Primary | 4·3 | 5·2 | 3·4 | 5·8 | 3·6 | 8·2 | 6·0 | 9·4 | 8·1 |
| Manufacturing | 38·0 | 38·4 | 34·5 | 39·2 | 60·8 | 28·7 | 51·1 | 38·5 | 35·1 |
| Construction | 7·0 | 6·9 | 5·7 | 6·5 | 5·6 | 4·9 | 8·0 | 33·9 | 6·9 |
| Public utilities | 1·8 | 1·7 | 1·8 | * | 0·1 | 2·3 | 1·6 | 2·9 | 1·6 |
| Transport | 7·0 | 10·4 | 12·8 | 3·2 | 2·4 | 20·6 | 5·6 | 1·5 | 10·6 |
| Services | 41·8 | 37·3 | 41·4 | 45·3 | 27·5 | 35·3 | 27·3 | 13·8 | 37·6 |
| Miscellaneous† | | 0·1 | 0·4 | * | * | * | 0·4 | * | 0·1 |
| Total | 100·0 | 100·0 | 100·0 | 100·0 | 100·0 | 100·0 | 100·0 | 100·0 | 100·0 |
| Employment in 1,000s | 23,255·7 | 308·3 | 149·5 | 11·4 | 13·8 | 11·6 | 49·5 | 6·0 | 66·5 |

* Absent or negligible.
† Persons with employment not stated, ex-servicemen not placed etc.

Primary employment is generally well-represented outside Hull and Hessle, particularly in Barton, Goole and Grimsby. This is indicative of the prominent position of agriculture, and also fishing in the case of Grimsby. In Scunthorpe this sector includes a small and declining number engaged in ironstone mining and quarrying.

The main departures from the national average, as seen in Figure 9. are in the manufacturing or secondary sector. Hessle and Scunthorpe are clearly dominated by manufacturing, and both have low proportions in services and transport. The lowest ratio engaged in manufacturing is found in Goole, which to some extent reflects a very high transport employment and also a large agricultural hinterland. The most eccentric employment structure probably belongs to Barton. where a third was engaged in the construction sector in 1967, mainly in connection with the south bank oil refineries. Grimsby, like Hull, had a slight deficit in manufacturing which matched its high representation in transport and fishing. The best balanced structure was at Beverley, important as county town of the East Riding and for its industrial role in North Humberside; this small town is a remarkable cross section of national economic activity.

Perhaps the most distinctive features of the region's employment structure is its blend of industry and agriculture, and the dominance of transport, which emphasises the sensitivity of the region to all changes in transport technology, particularly those which may influence competitiveness of its major dock systems. It is thus understandable that communications have been allocated such a prominent position in regional affairs.

### Regional Industrial Specialisation

A discussion of regional industrial structures often involves the concept of the regional economic base. In any populated area there are some virtually ubiquitous industries, such as baking, laundering, or the manufacture of soft drinks. Other industries have a less uniform, more sporadic distribution, and in extreme cases may serve the entire national market from one or more locations. Sargant Florence has cited tinplate in South Wales and jute on Tayside as examples of industries with very uneven distribution within the national framework. Such highly localised industries will obviously not be present to any significant extent in all regions of the country, but where they are found they play important parts as generators of regional income, since a high proportion of their output will normally be sold outside the region. This creates a net inflow of capital and wealth to support other economic activities, and for this reason such industries are called 'export-base' or 'basic' industries.

The practical application of the export-base approach depends on identifying the export component of the output of every business in the region, since this is primarily responsible for initiating and controlling the pace of economic growth. The drawback is the absence of data in a readily accessible form, and the problems arising from this are discussed by Perloff.[10] The minimum requirement approach is a short cut in which it is assumed that for a given size of city or region there is a typical minimum representation of employment in various industries and activities which would satisfy regional demand. Any excess employment would be working for the export sector. Blumenfeld has stressed that the reality of contemporary economic organisation is far too complex for such a simplified approach to have any analytical value.[11] But these techniques are still useful in gauging an accurate impression of what Duncan and his co-workers have termed an industrial *profile*,[12] enabling a preliminary identification to be made of prominent regional industries.

The Location Quotient, *LQ*, measurement developed by Sargant Florence is suitable for this purpose, since it is straightforward to calculate and the data is readily available.[13] The base line for all calculations is Humberside's proportion of national employment in all manufacturing industry, which in 1967 was 1·26 per cent. Humberside's proportion of national employment in each of the 110 Minimum List Headings, *MLHs*, of manufacturing industry is then divided by 1·26 to give a series of *LQs*. An *LQ* of 1 or very close to 1, in the range 0·9–1·2, indicates that the region's share of a particular industry is roughly in harmony with its share of all manufacturing. High *LQ* values indicate that these industries are more closely identified with the region than average, while low *LQ* values indicate the reverse. The technique is static; it presents an industrial profile at a given point in time, and does not include dynamic features of growth or decline. But it does isolate effectively those industries which are positively associated with Humberside, rather than those which happen to be large employers.

Table 13 presents those industries which form the peak of Humberside's profile in terms of a combination of *LQ* and employment. A

## Table 13

### HUMBERSIDE'S INDUSTRIAL PROFILE: HIGHLY CHARACTERISTIC INDUSTRIES 1967*

| Industry | LQ | Industry | LQ |
|---|---|---|---|
| Bacon curing, meat and fish products | 8·0 | Shipbuilding | 3·4 |
| Cement | 5·8 | Timber | 3·2 |
| Cans and metal boxes | 5·7 | Fruit and vegetable products | 3·0 |
| Iron and steel | 5·1 | Grain-milling | 2·9 |
| Animal and poultry foods | 4·7 | Wooden containers | 2·9 |
| Vegetable and animal oils, fats, soaps and detergents | 4·7 | Man-made fibres | 2·6 |
| | | Paint, printing ink | 2·5 |
| Rope, twine and net | 4·5 | Contractors' plant | 2·5 |
| Leather tanning and dressing | 4·5 | Pharmaceuticals, toiletries | 2·0 |
| Coke ovens and manufactured fuel | 3·5 | Aircraft | 1·8 |
| Chemicals and dyes | 3·4 | Industrial plant and steelwork | 1·7 |
| | | Marine engineering | 1·6 |

* The table includes ONLY those *MLHs* having an *LQ* $\geqslant$ 1·5, and a total Humberside employment $\geqslant$ 500.

careful examination of this list enables us to identify the industries in terms of possible relationships with other attributes of Humberside's economic activity. The highest *LQ* belongs to bacon curing, meat and

fish products, in which the region's emphasis is firmly on fish pro-
products. Industries linked with the fishing or maritime activities of
Humberside are rope, twine and nets, shipbuilding and marine engineering, and wooden containers. Other industries shown in the table
suggest a reliance on imported raw materials through the Humber
ports, such as animal and poultry foods, vegetable and animal oils etc,
timber, leather tanning and grain-milling. Iron and steel and cement
manufacture are related to the physical resources of the region. This
type of analysis is not definitive, however, because industries such as
pharmaceuticals, cans and metal boxes or aircraft suggest that the
processes of industrial localisation and specialisation are far more
complex. It must be emphasised that these industries are not necessarily the largest employers in the region, but the list represents a stage

**Table 14**

HUMBERSIDE'S INDUSTRIAL PROFILE: POORLY REPRESENTED
OR ABSENT INDUSTRIES 1967*

| Industry | LQ | Industry | LQ |
|---|---|---|---|
| Milk products | 0·5 | Weaving of cotton, flax etc | – |
| Tobacco | 0·4 | Woollen and worsted | – |
| Synthetic resins and plastics | – | Jute | – |
| Steel tubes | 0·2 | Hosiery and knitted goods | 0·3 |
| Light metals | – | Lace | – |
| Metalworking machine tools | 0·2 | Carpets | – |
| Industrial engines | – | Textile finishing | – |
| Textile machinery | – | Other textile industries | – |
| Mechanical handling equipment | 0·4 | Leather goods | – |
| Other machinery | 0·3 | Fur | – |
| Ordnance, small arms and other mechanical engineering not else-where specified | 0·4 | Weatherproof outerwear | – |
| | | Womens' and girls' tailored outer-wear | – |
| Scientific, surgical and photographic instruments | 0·2 | Overalls, mens' shirts etc | – |
| | | Dresses, lingerie, infants' wear | 0·3 |
| Watches and clocks | – | Hats, caps, millinery | – |
| Electrical machinery | – | Dress industries not elsewhere specified | 0·3 |
| Insulated wires and cables | – | | |
| Telegraph and telephone appliances | – | Footwear | 0·3 |
| Domestic electrical appliances | 0·1 | Glass | 0·2 |
| Other electrical goods | 0·2 | Shop and office fittings | 0·3 |
| Locomotives and track equipment | – | Cardboard boxes, cartons | – |
| Hand trucks | – | Manufactures of paper and board not elsewhere specified | 0·4 |
| Cutlery | – | | |
| Bolts, nuts, screws, rivets | – | Printing and publishing of news-papers and periodicals | 0·4 |
| Wire and wire manufactures | 0·2 | | |
| Jewellery and precious metals | – | Linoleum and leather cloth | – |
| Metal industries not elsewhere specified | – | Toys and games | 0·3 |
| | | Miscellaneous stationers' goods | – |
| Spinning, doubling of cotton, flax etc | – | Plastics moulding and fabricating | 0·2 |
| | | Miscellaneous manufacturing | 0·4 |

* This table is restricted to *MLHs* with *LQs* of ≥ 0·5.

in the analysis of the region's industrial character, and for this to be meaningful we must examine the troughs of the profile as well as the peaks. Table 14 presents those industries which are either poorly represented or absent in Humberside, and they can be divided broadly into two groups. First there are industries with strong historical associations with other regions in Britain, such as the textile industries, jute, and certain branches of the clothing industry. However, most industries listed in Table 14 have reasonably wide distributions, and the virtual absence in Humberside of the whole range of electrical industries, and many branches of engineering is particularly noteworthy in view of their large employment in the country as a whole. The implications of these troughs in the profile become more apparent when the growth performance of the region is examined in a later section.

It is to be expected that the characteristic industries of Humberside's profile will form important constituents of its export-base. More consistent information on the role of industries in the region's export base has been collected by the Central Unit for Environmental Planning as part of its research for the Feasibility Study.[14] The Unit's industrial survey embraced a sample of 117 firms which accounted for three-quarters of all manufacturing employment in Humberside, but the data relating to the export-base refers to only 100 firms, of which 94 also supplied data for total sales. According to the Survey, the total annual sales of these 94 firms was over £400 million, of which 92 per cent was external to Humberside, revealing the outstanding part played

### Table 15

EMPLOYMENT ON SALES TO HUMBERSIDE MANUFACTURING
INDUSTRIES

| SIC | Manufacturing Industries | No. | Employees | Per cent | Humberside Firms Distribution of Sales | |
|---|---|---|---|---|---|---|
| | | | | | Humberside | External |
| 13 | Cement, pottery etc | 4 | 2,647 | 2·9 | 60·0 | 39·9 |
| 7 | Shipbuilding | 7 | 3,688 | 4·1 | 60·3 | 39·8 |
| 15 | Paper and printing | 7 | 2,818 | 3·1 | 25·8 | 74·2 |
| 14 | Timber | 7 | 3,101 | 3·4 | 13·8 | 86·3 |
| 3 | Food and drink | 20 | 15,063 | 16·7 | 11·7 | 88·3 |
| 8, 9 | Vehicles and other metal goods | 10 | 10,677 | 11·9 | 3·5 | 96·5 |
| 6 | Engineering and electrical | 8 | 4,986 | 5·5 | 2·8 | 97·1 |
| 4 | Chemicals | 19 | 16,920 | 18·8 | 7·6 | 92·5 |
| 10, 11 | Textiles, leather | 6 | 3,239 | 3·6 | 5·4 | 94·6 |
| 5 | Metal manufactures | 8 | 24,973 | 27·8 | 2·1 | 98·0 |
| 12, 16 | Clothing, miscellaneous | 4 | 1,858 | 2·1 | 0·9 | 99·1 |

*Source:* Central Unit for Environmental Planning, Humberside Industrial Survey, Appendix 8, Table B (1969).

by manufacturing as a generator of regional income. Almost the entire output of some important *SICs* is sold outside Humberside, either in other parts of Britain or abroad, as Table 15 indicates. In the cement, shipbuilding and repairing industries more than 60 per cent of man-hours are devoted to production for sale on Humberside, but in all other industry groups sales to Humberside represent a much smaller proportion of total activity. The most important industrial orders in terms of employment are also dominantly exporting industries, such as chemicals, food and drink, and vehicles, and this dominance of external markets for Humberside industry in general is summarised by the Industrial Survey report.

> Humberside's industries include important examples of industries serv-ing national markets and this is reflected in weaker local links on the sales side than on the side of materials and supplies.[15]

The prominent role of the local region and its waterways is thus primarily expressed in the assembly and supply of materials, and not in sales linkages. The importance of sources and flows of input, and of distribution of markets is often commented upon but less frequently examined in detail in geographical literature. Yet the interaction between materials and markets should be a matter of prime concern, since it cuts across established, often artificial groupings of industries and directs our attention to more fundamental relationships. Only in this way can a more precise evaluation of the Humber be achieved, or the dependence of industries on specific types of markets be analysed. Such an analysis would also complement our understanding of regional industrial growth.

### An Input–Output Approach to Humberside Industries

Following research into regional and metropolitan economic struc-tures in the United States,[16] we can adopt an analytical approach to Humberside's industrial structure that focuses attention on the loca-tional advantages of the region, acts as a link between the export-base and sector viewpoints of regional economic growth, and also serves as an introduction for later, more detailed investigation. This approach analyses a region's industries in terms of dominant input requirements and output destinations, and a brief outline of the major premises is given here.

The basis of the scheme is the difference in the nature of the inputs for various industries, ranging from primary, unprocessed raw materials in the early stages of production through successive stages of elaboration to the final assembly industries which embellish and assemble inputs that are already highly manufactured. Industries with a high input of raw materials will be attracted to the source of one or more of the materials, although this tendency depends on related considerations, such as the weight loss in manufacture and differential freight rates. On the basis of the relative weights of material input and product output A. Weber constructed a theory of industrial location, from which are derived terms now commonly used to express the locational tendencies of industries, such as material-oriented, market-oriented, and labour-oriented.[17] A widespread assumption is that the real costs of transport have been reduced, and that the processes of manufacture have become more complex, so that the pull of the market has increased over that of materials for most industries. In many cases the market is the general consuming public; this emphasises the importance of the major conurbations. In the scheme adopted here, this type of market is called *final demand*, and it also includes purchases by central and local government. But for many industries the market is represented by other manufacturing industries, and in these cases the market is called *non-final demand*, of which an obvious group is the component industries supplying the vehicle assembly industry. Few industries actually produce exclusively for one or the other type of market, so that an arbitrary assignment to major marketing type is necessary for the scheme to work. Moreover, the data refers to industrial categories, not to individual establishments, and the former are not homogeneous entities.[18] The categories of the scheme are as follows:

I  *Primary resource extractors* (agriculture and mining).
   This category is NOT considered in the book.
II  *Secondary Industries.*
A  First stage resource users producing for non-final market.
B  First stage resource users producing for final market. Both categories derive their inputs from the primary resource extractors in the form of agricultural, mineral, forestry and fishing raw materials. Examples include grain-milling, oil refining, iron smelting (non-final); and most direct food-processing industries, eg sugar refining.
C  Second stage resource users producing for non-final market.
D  Second stage resource users producing for final market. These industries derive their inputs mainly from the processed products of category A, but in terms of material inputs they are less weight-losing, and so are less directly related to the source of inputs.[19] Examples include chemicals, steel tubes, iron castings, bread, chocolate, clothing.

E and F. Industries for which resources are of most indirect significance. These industries either assemble a very wide range of partially manufactured articles, or use very small amounts of materials which are subjected to a high degree of skilled manufacture. Examples are the varied range of mechanical and electrical engineering industries, precision engineering industries, metal forming and metal using industries, motor vehicles, consumer durables. The ratio of material input in relation to product output is at its lowest, and a very wide range of locational forces operate. These industries are particularly influenced by external economies of agglomeration, and strong linkages between a series of plants is a characteristic phenomenon that often welds apparently unrelated industries into a close knit system.[20]

In these categories there is thus a progressive weakening of the locational attraction of resource inputs, which is paralleled by the increasing significance of other types of locational factors.

The prominent position of first stage resource using industries in Humberside is seen in Table 16, about twenty per cent of all industrial

**Table 16**

INDUSTRIAL EMPLOYMENT IN HUMBERSIDE BY INPUT–OUTPUT
CATEGORIES 1967

| Category | Humberside | | Great Britain | | LQ |
|---|---|---|---|---|---|
| | Number | Per cent | Number (000s) | Per cent | |
| I Primary Resource Extractors not considered | | | | | |
| A First Stage *NF* | 10,227 | 8·6 | 728 | 8·2 | 1·05 |
| B First Stage *F* | 13,931 | 11·8 | 456 | 5·2 | 2·28 |
| C Second Stage *NF* | 42,349 | 35·8 | 1,182 | 13·4 | 2·68 |
| D Second Stage *F* | 7,398 | 6·3 | 1,113 | 12·6 | 0·50 |
| E Resources not significant *NF* | 33,798 | 28·3 | 4,146 | 46·9 | 0·60 |
| F Resources not significant *F* | 10,931 | 9·2 | 1,213 | 13·7 | 0·67 |
| Total | 118,634 | 100·0 | 8,838 | 100·0 | |

*NF*—non-final market; *F*—final market.

employment falling in these categories. A definite specialisation in such industries is indicated by *LQs* of over one, although this is more apparent in industries producing for the final market. The rich agricultural output of the region is utilised to a considerable extent by vegetable canning and freezing plants, but the limited mineral and other physical resources indicate that most of the necessary materials are imported through the Humber. The Humberside industrial survey collected data on the geographical source of inputs of its sample firms, and the main findings are shown in Table 17, which, although based on broad *SIC* orders, nevertheless forms useful supplementary evidence. Among the *SIC* orders which can broadly be correlated with first stage resource users, food and drink derives over forty per cent of its inputs from within the region, a reflection of the rich agricul-

**Table 17**

MATERIAL INPUTS AND SOURCES BY VALUE FOR HUMBERSIDE INDUSTRIES

| Industry*<br>SIC Order | Materials as<br>per cent of Total | Percentage distribution according to material sources (by value) | | |
|---|---|---|---|---|
| | | Local<br>Humberside | Imports<br>via Humber | Other<br>sources |
| IV    Chemicals | 39·4 | 2·4 | 77·2 | 20·4 |
| V    Metal manufacture | 25·7 | 12·7 | 12·6 | 74·7 |
| III    Food and drink | 14·4 | 41·9 | 29·3 | 28·9 |
| XIV    Timber | 3·9 | 3·7 | 87·0 | 9·4 |
| X    Textiles | 3·7 | 4·5 | 37·3 | 58·2 |
| VIII    Vehicles | 2·8 | 2·4 | 0·5 | 97·1 |
| XI    Leather | 2·3 | 3·8 | 17·2 | 79·0 |
| XV    Paper, printing | 2·2 | 1·9 | 78·9 | 19·1 |
| IX    Metal goods | 1·3 | 6·5 | 3·7 | 89·8 |
| VI    Engineering, electrical | 1·2 | 12·7 | 10·2 | 77·1 |
| VII    Shipbuilding | 1·1 | 22·1 | 11·0 | 66·8 |
| XII    Clothing, footwear | 0·9 | – | – | 100·0 |
| XIII    Cement, pottery | 0·5 | 18·1 | – | 81·9 |
| XVI    Other manufactures | 0·6 | – | – | 100·0 |
| Total | 100·0 | 11·3 | 45·0 | 43·7 |

\* Ranked in terms of percentage of all material inputs.
*Source:* Based on Table 13, Humberside Industrial Survey (available 1969).

tural output. Other branches, such as grain-milling, account for the further thirty per cent imported via the Humber. Timber industries are another good example of dependence on the Humber. Cement and pottery might appear to be an anomaly until it is realised that coal, sand and gravel are waterborne from the Yorkshire coalfield and Upper Trent valley. It should be noted that oil refining had not become operative in 1967, while the employment of Scunthorpe's steel plants is grouped under category C in accordance with the original scheme; both influence to a considerable extent the representation of Category A. The most prominent single industries in the first stage, final market category are bacon, meat and fish products, and fruit and vegetable products. For all first stage industries a Humberside location appears advantageous; we shall examine later whether the distribution of establishments reflects the need for accessibility to the Humber.

Second stage resource users employ over forty per cent of Humberside's labour force, and the non-final market category has a very high $LQ$ of 2·68, the highest of any. On the other hand, the final market category has an $LQ$ of only 0·50, but this imbalance has been to Humberside's advantage, since post-war national growth has been concentrated in the non-final category. Chemicals and dyes, including explosives, and iron and steel are the most important members of the non-final category, and Table 17 shows that about three-quarters of the material inputs of chemicals are derived from imports via the Humber. The iron and steel industry gets three-quarters of its inputs from non-regional, non-Humber sources, but since inputs are measured in value this reflects to a large extent the imports of high-value coke and coal, although rail-hauled ironstone from Northamptonshire is also important. The chemicals and dyestuffs $MLH$ is a broad grouping of all divisions of organic and inorganic chemicals, dyes, fine chemicals and industrial gases, and a fairly widespread distribution might be expected. It is supplemented in Humberside by man-made fibres, paint and printing ink, vegetable and mineral oils etc, and to many of these the importance of the Humber ports for importing materials must rank high. The final market category contains no prominent Humberside representative, since the largest employer, bread and confectionery, is a residentiary-tied industry.

In Great Britain industries for which inputs are of no particular locational significance account for almost two-thirds of manufacturing employment, but in Humberside this ratio is only one-third; this shows the real intensity of specialisation on its material-oriented industries. The term 'footloose' industries entered into geographical and economic literature to describe industries with no *apparent* strong location controls, although the inertia of existing concentrations have given many older industrial regions a powerful grip on them. For industries serving national markets, needing close and frequent contacts with a tight network of specialist industrial services or suppliers, Humberside presents difficulties which stem from its relative remoteness and its low population. However, it must be stressed that these difficulties are relative and not insurmountable, being open to compensation by counter attractions such as an easier labour market and lower wage levels. Thus the $LQ$ for the final market category, 0·67, is higher than might be expected from Humberside's location away from the main axis of population concentration.

Nationally, the non-final market category consists of many industries in *SIC VI*, engineering and electrical, which lie at the heart of modern industrial technology. However, as already seen, these industries are poorly represented in Humberside, and this gives rise to much concern. The generally low representation of basic engineering and metal industries is a further drawback compared with established regions such as Greater London or the West Midlands conurbation. It is difficult to amend in the normal run of events, as the Feasibility Study has pointed out,[21] particularly because of the resulting limited supply of skilled labour. At the same time Humberside contains many firms with international reputations engaged in a variety of complex engineering industries, which suggests that the deficit is relative and not irreversible. The most important non-final industry is probably shipbuilding and marine engineering, which is largely a market oriented industry, trawlers and small but very specialised craft being characteristic outputs. Other prominent representatives are cans and metal boxes, contractors' plant and equipment, pharmaceuticals and toiletries, printing and publishing, rubber, copper and base metals.

Over ninety per cent of Humberside's employment in the final market category is in vehicles, *SIC VIII*, represented by motor vehicles, aircraft and bicycles. These employed almost as many workers as chemicals, *SIC III*, in 1967, and more than shipbuilding, an indication of their importance to the regional economy. Although dominated by large concerns, a particular Humberside speciality is caravan manufacture by small and medium size firms. All other industries are poorly developed.

The broad analysis has revealed the high degree to which Humberside industry is geared to large material inputs, and within this analytical framework the deficiencies in Humberside's industrial structure begin to fall into a coherent pattern governed by factors of material and market accessibility. The concept of the market inevitably brings in the sector approach to regional analysis. Growth prospects for a region's industries are related to market trends rather more than to material inputs, and any scheme which bears this in mind has considerable merit. However, any detailed assessment of the growth performance and prospects of Humberside's industries meets the difficulty of treating Humberside as one unit when discussing the expansion or contraction of employment, because the implied diversion of labour is in fact taking place within two quite separate sub-units. Consequently North and South Humberside are mainly considered separately. But before examining this aspect, it is essential that the loss of detail incurred by using rather broad sub-units is understood.

### The Individual Exchange Areas

Despite the greater degree of local mobility of labour in the post-war period, many of the fundamental problems of regional development are concerned with small units. Consequently Scunthorpe has its own particular problems deriving from an excessive local specialisation in an industry whose labour force is largely male. But this is a very localised problem, and not even characteristic of South Humberside as a whole. Moreover its solution can only be accomplished within a local framework. It is therefore instructive to examine the degree of industrial diversification or otherwise of the seven exchange areas constituting Inner Humberside.

Figure 10 presents a graphical representation of the industrial struc-

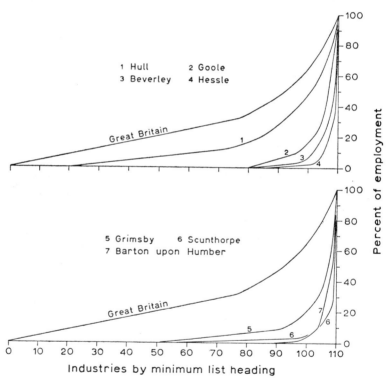

Fig 10.  INDUSTRIAL SPECIALISATION IN HUMBERSIDE
EXCHANGE AREAS 1967

The graphs illustrate how employment in manufacturing industry is distributed among the *MLH* categories represented. The *MLHs* for each area have been ranked in decreasing order of importance from right to left, and the curves should be read as a cumulative frequency graph. Only Great Britain has all 110 *MLHs* represented

Page 87: (above) *The industrial townscape of central Hull, a zone of peak manufacturing employment density;* (below) *a factory in outer Hull in a suburban location with spacious plant layout, uncongested site and good road access*

Page 88: (above) *Part of central Hull, with Queens gardens and the colleges of technology and commerce;* (below) *artist's impression of the Humber bridge, designed to have a main span of 4,580 feet, which would be one of the largest in Europe*

ture of Great Britain, and the local exchange areas. The degree of
curvature of the graphs is an indication of the degree of specialisation
in the industrial structure, as measured in terms of 110 *MLHs*. No
unit has a perfectly diversified industrial structure, since an economy
needs more of the output of some industries than others, and industries also differ in their export participation. But the curve for Great
Britain shows a well diversified industrial structure.

From the graphs it appears that total size of employment is an
important factor; Hull and Grimsby in particular have noticeably
smoother curves, while Scunthorpe runs counter to this generalisation.
The degree of diversification in Hull is quite remarkable since only
twenty out of a possible 110 *MLHs* are not represented, and some of
these are present in the adjoining built-up area which forms part of
the Hessle employment area. The small employment areas are all
obviously specialised, whilst Grimsby occupies an intermediate position. Table 18 is largely self explanatory; it shows the important

**Table 18**

HUMBERSIDE EXCHANGE AREAS: A BROAD MEASURE OF
INDUSTRIAL SPECIALISATION 1967

| *Area* | *Number of MLHs which account for:* | | |
| --- | --- | --- | --- |
| | *⅓ Employment* | *⅔ Employment* | *All Employment* |
| Great Britain | 10 | 33 | 110 |
| Hull | 6 | 18 | 90 |
| Goole | 4 | 6 | 30 |
| Grimsby | 3 | 6 | 59 |
| Beverley | 1 | 4 | 30 |
| Barton | 1 | 4 | 21 |
| Hessle | 1 | 2 | 22 |
| Scunthorpe | 1 | 1 | 54 |

internal distinctions which must constantly be made between Hull and
Grimsby on the one hand, and all other areas. Largely because of Hull,
North Humberside is more diversified than South Humberside. Over
half the region's industrial workforce is employed in the major industrial zone of Hull, including Hessle employment area, in a well
diversified complex in which ninety-three *MLHs* are represented in
some form. South Humberside is less fortunate, and contains the
highly specialised Scunthorpe. Specialisation is not necessarily a disadvantage; much of South Humberside's has been in industries with
a good expansion record. But attendant social problems, such as lack
of outlets for female employment, and the difficulties of introducing
a balance of industries in the shadow of one or more overpowerful ones,

F

are disadvantages. As the Maud Commission has recently found, South Humberside is not yet an integrated areal unit, though North Humberside is.[22] The impulses of industrial expansion in North Humberside are felt to some extent throughout the sub-unit, whereas changes in South Humberside are more local in impact; a basic dichotomy which must be borne in mind.

Table 19 presents the broad pattern of industrial specialisation in each employment area, as a preliminary to more detailed investiga-

**Table 19**

HUMBERSIDE EXCHANGE AREAS: STRUCTURE OF MANUFACTURING INDUSTRY EMPLOYMENT BY *SIC* ORDER 1967 AS PERCENTAGES

| SIC Order | | | | Employment Area | | | |
| --- | --- | --- | --- | --- | --- | --- | --- |
| | Hull | Beverley | Hessle | Goole | Scun-thorpe | Grimsby | Barton |
| Food, drink | 16·6 | 5·6 | 1·3 | 16·2 | 3·6 | 44·6 | 4·3 |
| Chemicals | 21·8 | 11·0 | * | 16·8 | 6·0 | 16·0 | 10·3 |
| Metal manufacture | 6·7 | * | 8·5 | 0·5 | 73·4 | 0·5 | 1·5 |
| Engineering, and electrical | 12·7 | 2·3 | 2·8 | * | 7·3 | 3·6 | 50·3 |
| Shipbuilding | 7·9 | 3·2 | 4·0 | 18·2 | * | 11·0 | 1·4 |
| Vehicles | 2·3 | 45·6 | 70·3 | 0·6 | 0·2 | 0·4 | 8·1 |
| Other metal goods | 7·4 | 11·2 | * | 0·5 | * | 0·7 | * |
| Textiles | 1·4 | * | * | * | 1·2 | 8·1 | 8·6 |
| Leather | 1·8 | 14·2 | * | * | * | 0·2 | * |
| Clothing | 1·2 | 0·4 | * | 19·5 | 2·1 | 0·6 | * |
| Cement etc | 2·8 | 3·6 | 4·8 | 15·2 | 4·6 | 0·6 | 15·3 |
| Timber | 10·2 | 1·0 | 1·0 | 4·1 | 0·5 | 4·0 | * |
| Paper, printing | 4·8 | 1·2 | 7·2 | 3·3 | 0·6 | 6·6 | * |
| Miscellaneous | 2·4 | 0·7 | * | 5·0 | 0·4 | 3·1 | * |
| Total | 100·0 | 100·0 | 100·0 | 100·0 | 100·0 | 100·0 | 100·0 |

* Absent or less than 0·1 per cent.

tion. Hull, with over 50,000 workers in manufacturing in 1967, is notable for its chemicals and food and drink industries, which employed over a third of the total. It has already been shown that both *SIC* orders contain a very wide range of individual industries, ranging in Hull from pharmaceuticals and paints to petrochemicals, or from chocolates and grain-milling to fish products. A feature of both chemicals and the food industries is the variety in size of firms and plants which adds a degree of diversification not adequately conveyed by a percentage breakdown. Other high ranking Hull industries are *SIC VI*, engineering and electrical, and *SIC XIV*, timber, which also contain a large number of individual enterprises. Although Hull is not now of major importance as a shipbuilding centre, both shipbuilding and marine engineering, with their associated repair services, are important to the local economy, employing about eight per cent of the labour force. The most prominent branch of *SIC IX*, other metal goods, is the manufacture of metal canisters and boxes, for which the local paint and chemical industries in particular form a locational attraction. The metal manufacturing industries, *SIC V*, are mainly concerned with ferrous and non-ferrous castings, the latter being linked to the needs of marine engineering. Other industries are relatively minor in total employment, although, as we have seen, some are highly characteristic industries, such as leather.

Hessle and Beverley are dominated by the vehicle industry, so that Hull is surrounded by specialised exchange areas. The most important branch of the vehicle industry in Hessle is aircraft, based on the former Blackburn factory at Brough, but caravans and road trailers are also made. In Beverley a firm manufactures a wide range of components for the motor industry, but again the making of caravans is represented in the order. The Hessle employment area also contains other important industries peripheral to Hull, including non-ferrous metals, cement works and the Hessle Haven shipbuilding yards. In Beverley, some employment balance is provided by chemical, leather and metal goods.

In Goole a large number of industries are unrepresented, but employment is remarkably well distributed amongst a variety of industries so that the specialisation associated with Hessle or Beverley is absent. Five *SIC* orders are of approximately equal importance, with food and drink, chemicals and shipbuilding emphasising the significance of the waterway system. Cement and clothing complete the range, the latter being a postwar introduction to use female labour in a town dominated by male-employing industries.

In South Humberside the areas are much less diversified than in North Humberside. Scunthorpe's employment breakdown needs little in the way of commentary, since industries not closely connected with iron and steel are of quite minor importance in employment terms. In 1967 the industrial structure of Barton was dominated by the large labour force employed by industrial plant and steelwork within *SIC VI*. This work force was mainly engaged on oil refineries contracts. Chemicals and vehicles, and clothing, were the only other important industries and employment in vehicles had sharply contracted since the early post-war years. Grimsby's employment structure is also highly specialised in the same *SIC* orders as Hull, although it certainly is not a one-industry town like Scunthorpe. In the Grimsby employment area, which includes both the town and the most developed section of the south Humber bank, the chemical and food orders employ sixty per cent of the work force; Grimsby's textile industry is the essentially chemical industry of man-made fibres. Shipbuilding and repairing activities are also prominent, specialising in fishing vessels. Thus three *SIC* orders employ about seventy per cent of Grimsby's industrial labour force, although the varied constitution of industries within the orders ensures a degree of stability not found in areas where just a few dominant enterprises exist. The paper industry in Grimsby completes the range of industries oriented to their material supplies.

This outline of the major internal variations within Humberside's industrial structure shows the distribution of its industries, and also conveys something of the intricate place-to-place differences in the region.

### Industrial Growth: The Sector Approach

In its widest application, the sector approach to national or regional economic development traces the sequence of internal changes in an economy, beginning in a primitive stage and dominated by primary activities such as agriculture, forestry or mineral exploitation. Economies pass through successively more elaborate stages until an advanced economy is developed in which the largest sector is services, followed by manufacturing, and with only a small proportion engaged in primary production.[23] In a narrower context the sector approach emphasises the need for a balanced representation of nationally expanding industries, or sectors, within the particular region. These are classed as growth industries, a term which has been increasingly used in geographic writings.[24]

Thus the sector approach to a regional economic development programme aims at ensuring that the region possessed at least its *pro rata* share of all expanding industries and activities in the economy as a whole, so that a balance would be preserved between growth and decline. Although not denying the importance of growth industries, Perloff and his fellow researchers have shown that this is too formal a view of regional economic growth,[25] and that rapid rates of regional economic growth have been attained in the United States with non-growth industries:

> . . . a given region may contain, at one extreme, an increasing share of a growing sub-category of a nationally-increasing industry, or at the opposite extreme a declining share of a declining sub-category of a nationally-declining industry, with many combinations in between. (Perloff and others, 1960)

The identification of national growth industries is thus only a partial solution to the more difficult task of isolating and accounting for regional industrial growth. Moreover, the presence of these growth industries within a region will not in itself ensure equality with the national growth rate, although it does constitute an advantage on *a priori* grounds. Much regional growth in fact stems from industries shifting between regions in relation to differential investments of capital and other inputs, generally in response to the real or assumed advantages of one location as opposed to another. Consequently, regardless of whether an industry is a growth industry or not, a region may be gaining employment in that industry if, as often occurs, there is a differential pattern of inputs investment. This aspect complements and modifies the sector theory of growth, and has been summarised by Perloff as a contrast between the differential or shifting effect, and the proportionality or sector effect:

> Sources of change in the regional structure of the economy are divided into two classes . . . the *differential* effect arises out of the fact that some regions gain, over time, a differential advantage in their access to important markets and inputs for each of one or more specific activities. The *proportionality* effect arises out of the fact that the various regions start with a different industry mix or composition—that some regions claim a larger (or smaller) proportion of the nation's rapid growth (or slow-growth) industries. (Perloff and others, 1960)

Problems connected with data mean that an analysis along these lines on a long time scale can only be conducted in terms of the grosser *SIC* orders, rather than specific industries. However, this does enable us to map the main areas of industrial growth.

During the ten years 1958–67 the overall increase in total industrial employment was over eight thousand, or about seven per cent. But, as Table 20 shows, an employment decrease was expected on the basis of the regional structure of 3,223, so that a massive positive differential shift in favour of Humberside had occurred, accounting for almost the entire growth of manufacturing employment. This is one indication of the underlying strength of the region and the attraction which it has exerted on industrial growth. Within the individual orders the major differential shifts have occurred in chemicals, metal manufacture and vehicles, with smaller but still significant gains in engineering and electrical, shipbuilding and textiles. Humberside has clearly no major declining industry to burden its economic development, as in the North-East or North-West. However, the amalgam of industries was not as beneficially weighted towards fast growing industries such as

Table 20

CHANGES IN INDUSTRIAL EMPLOYMENT IN HUMBERSIDE
1958–67 BY *SIC* ORDER

| SIC Order | | Total Employment | | Net Total employment shift | Expected Increase or Decrease* | Net Differential shift + = upward − = downward |
|---|---|---|---|---|---|---|
| | | 1958 | 1967 | | | |
| III | Food | 21,863 | 20,893 | −970 | −831 | −139 |
| IV | Chemicals | 16,088 | 17,775 | 1,687 | −531 | +2,218 |
| V | Metals | 21,508 | 22,872 | 1,364 | −817 | +2,181 |
| VI | Engin. elect. | 7,816 | 10,756 | 2,940 | 1,430 | +1,510 |
| VII | Shipbuilding | 9,401 | 7,749 | −1,652 | −2,896 | +1,244 |
| VIII | Vehicles | 7,489 | 9,472 | 1,983 | −757 | +2,740 |
| IX | Other metal goods | 4,711 | 4,523 | −188 | +806 | −994 |
| X | Textiles | 2,376 | 3,116 | 740 | −459 | +1,199 |
| XI | Leather | 1,300 | 1,611 | 311 | −140 | +451 |
| XII | Clothing | 2,375 | 1,959 | −416 | −420 | +4 |
| XIII | Cement | 3,426 | 4,170 | 744 | +257 | +487 |
| XIV | Timber | 5,734 | 6,532 | 798 | +373 | +425 |
| XV | Paper | 4,224 | 4,952 | 728 | +431 | +297 |
| XVI | Miscell. | 1,896 | 2,254 | 358 | +331 | +27 |
| TOTAL | | 110,207 | 118,634 | 8,427 | −3,223 | +11,650 |

Totals are algebraic sums of individual industry categories.

* Obtained by multiplying the 1958 employment figure by the percentage increase or decrease of the particular industries in the U.K.

*Source:* Regional employment exchange statistics; Annual Abstracts of Statistics.

other metal goods, or engineering and electrical, so that some of the impact of the differential trend has been lost. We must therefore look more closely at the role of growth industries, which can only be studied with reference to the more detailed *MLH* categories. This analysis covers the period 1960–66.

Following Perloff, we class growth industries as those which have expanded in employment terms on a national basis. Although other possibly more refined measures are possible, none has quite the same significance for regional development as employment creation or contraction, particularly as the direct impact of any change is magnified by multiplier effects within the region.[26] The upper third of national growth industries, defined in terms of percentage rate of growth, employ about a quarter of Great Britain's industrial labour force. This subset of industries record employment increases greater than ten per cent in the period under review, and as Table 21 illustrates, both North and South Humberside are relatively deficient in them, since the percentages of total employment were 18·6 and 15·6 respectively. Among the industries in this group, plastics, radio and electronic apparatus, small tools and gauges, miscellaneous metal industries have already been noted as deficient in Humberside (Table 14); these are industries in which strong associations with advanced technological skills have developed, so the position cannot be viewed with equanimity. North Humberside fares much better in this respect than South Humberside, whose employment in this group is largely concentrated in one industry only, bacon-curing, meat and fish products.

**Table 21**

PERCENTAGE OF TOTAL MANUFACTURING EMPLOYMENT IN
GROWTH INDUSTRIES 1960–66

| Area | All Growth Industries | Upper Third of Growth Industries |
|---|---|---|
| Great Britain | 67·4 | 25·9 |
| North Humberside | 58·9 | 18·6 |
| South Humberside | 80·6 | 15·6 |

*Source:* Annual Abstracts of Statistics.
ERIIs, Humberside exchange areas.

Taking the entire range of growth industries, North Humberside again lags behind the Great Britain average, although in view of the relatively small sample population in the sub-region, its performance is reasonably satisfactory. In fact, the limitations of this formalised scheme for small sub-regions are quickly realised, because a principal North Humberside industry, aircraft, is omitted. The aircraft industry is in many respects the epitome of the modern, highly technical industry and stimulates a supply of skilled personnel in North Humberside, but is classed as a declining industry on the basis of its employment history in the 1960s. South Humberside at first appears to be in an exceptionally favoured position until it is realised that over half the employment in growth industries is in iron and steel, which has now entered into a phase of labour contraction.[27] However there is a strong representation of chemicals and man-made fibres. Other more detailed aspects of growth industries are examined in the following chapter.

In 1940 D. S. Creamer published an approach to industrial growth analysis geared to the concept of the *relative* performance of regions and industries and not solely concerned with growth and decline industries.[28] Through a comparison of the rate of change of regional and national employment in different industries over a given period of time, various classes of shifts, to use Creamer's terminology, can be identified. But if the region's share of the national total of any industry is greater at the end of the period than at the beginning, a *shift towards* the region has occurred; if the proportion is less, there has been a *shift away* from it. These movements are quite independent of the growth performance of the industry in the national context, as the following list of classes of movement suggest (all measurements are comparisons of percentage rates of change):

1. Shifting towards a region
   This occurs in industries in which:
   (i) expansion in the region is greater than national expansion.
   (ii) expansion in the region is paralleled by a decline nationally.
   (iii) decline in the region is less rapid than national decline.
2. Shifting away from a region.
   This occurs in industries in which:
   (iv) decline in the region is faster than national decline.
   (v) decline in the region is paralleled by national expansion.
   (vi) expansion in the region is less rapid than national expansion.

Humberside's industries were allocated to these categories of shift on the evidence of their record in 1960–66 (See Tables 22, 23). An analysis of the changes in the region's labour force in terms of these categories provides further insight into the composition of industrial growth. In particular, the most favourable category is (i), in which the region is attracting a larger proportion of nationally expanding industries, while the category giving cause for greatest concern might well be (v). In North Humberside there was a net positive balance of about 5,000, and most of the employment gains in the industries shifting towards the sub-region were concentrated in national growth indus-

**Table 22**

HUMBERSIDE: SUMMARY OF INDUSTRIAL SHIFTS 1960–66

| Category | North Humberside Industries* | Total Employ-ment change | South Humberside Industries* | Total Employ-ment change |
|---|---|---|---|---|
| 1 *Shifting Towards* | | | | |
| i expanding>national | 28 | +8,098 | 25 | +4,204 |
| ii expanding—national decline | 18 | +1,873 | 13 | +2,113 |
| iii declining<national | 3 | −238 | 1 | −106 |
| Sub-total | 49 | +9,733 | 39 | +6,211 |
| 2 *Shifting Away* | | | | |
| iv declining>national | 16 | −1,924 | 17 | −2,091 |
| v declining—national expansion | 13 | −3,482 | 11 | −455 |
| vi expanding<national | 4 | +346 | 4 | +154 |
| Sub-total | 33 | −5,060 | 32 | −2,392 |

* Only industries employing>10 workers.

tries (Table 23). Only a small proportion of employment growth was the result of expansions in nationally declining industries, although in some cases, such as aircraft, mentioned above, a measurement based on employment does not provide a full or a very accurate picture. Among the growth industries expanding faster in North Humberside are bacon curing, meat and fish products. This industry has a very rapidly expanding frozen food branch which is no longer confined to

**Table 23**

REPRESENTATIVE INDUSTRIES IN VARIOUS CLASSES OF SHIFTS
IN HUMBERSIDE (ALL INDUSTRIES EMPLOYING>1000) 1966

| | *North Humberside Employment Per cent of sub-regional total* | | *South Humberside Employment Per cent of sub-regional total* |
|---|---|---|---|
| **1 Shift Towards** | | | |
| (i) *Expanding>National* | | | |
| 214 Bacon curing | 3·7 | 271–3 Chemicals, dyes | 9·5 |
| 271–3 Chemicals, dyes | 9·4 | 311 Iron and steel | 38·4 |
| 322 Copper, brass, base metals | 2·1 | 341 Industrial plant and steel work, 411 Man-made fibres | 6·3 |
| 338 Office machinery  342, 349 Ordnance, other mechanical engineering | 3·4 | | |
| 381 Vehicles | 4·7 | | |
| 471 Timber | 5·5 | | |
| 489 Other printing, publishing etc | 3·3 | | |
| (ii) *Expanding, National decline* | | | |
| 313 Iron castings | 3·7 | 218 Fruit and vegetable products | 4·8 |
| 370 Shipbuilding | 6·8 | 370 Shipbuilding | 4·6 |
| 383 Aircraft  431 Leather tanning | 10·3 | | |
| (iii) *Declining>National* | | | |
| 275 Vegetable and animal fats | 2·9 | | |
| **2 Shift Away** | | | |
| (iv) *Declining>National* | | | |
| 211 Grain-milling | 2·2 | | |
| 217 Cocoa, chocolate etc | 1·5 | | |
| 274 Paint and printing ink | 2·3 | | |
| (v) *Declining, National expansion* | | | |
| 212 Bread and flour confectionery | 2·0 | | |
| 339 Other machinery | 1·6 | | |
| 395 Cans and metal boxes | 3·9 | | |
| (vi) *Expanding<National* | | | |
| 272 Pharmaceuticals | 2·9 | 214 Bacon curing, meat and fish | 12·3 |
| 336 Contractors' plant  399 Miscellaneous metal industries | 4·1 | | |

the simple freezing of fresh fish, but has developed a complete range of convenience foods in response to a high demand elasticity for such goods in a generally rather static food sector. Similarly the high rate of increase in the consumption of the products of the chemical industry has benefited North Humberside, with its large petrochemical sector. Motor vehicles, mainly components and caravans in North Humberside, timber and joinery, copper, brass and base metals, letterpress printing, rubber, animal and poultry foods, and other mechanical engineering and industrial plant and steelwork are prominent in this category.

Three *declining* national industries are growth industries in North Humberside: shipbuilding, aircraft and iron castings. It is perhaps significant for North Humberside that all three are associated with a high level of managerial and technical skill, producing a fortunate specialisation in products which have resilient or expanding markets such as domestic central heating systems or powerful marine tugs. Moreover the industries create considerable demands for skilled and semi-skilled labour which can only benefit the region's development. Similar, on a more localised scale, are industries such as Hornsea Pottery, which in the post-war years has built up a national reputation and quality market for its products.

Of the shifting-away industries the majority are also declining nationally (Table 23). But it must be stressed that industries classed as declining in employment terms might be very buoyant in output, because advanced mechanisation and nationalisation have effected many closures in representative industries such as grain-milling, brewing, or paint manufacture. Causing greater concern are national growth industries which failed to keep pace with national rates of expansion. Cement, cans and metal boxes, contractors' plant and quarrying machinery, and pharmaceuticals and toiletries are the most important of these, but on the evidence of a relatively limited time span it would be quite erroneous to read much into this, especially as most are well established regional industries.

In South Humberside the net employment gain in the time period was just under 4,000 (Table 23). By far the most important group of industries shifting towards the region were national growth ones. Chemicals and dyes, and man-made fibres were the major post-war investments in chemical and related industries along the estuary. Another important representative is industrial plant and steelwork, reflecting the continued high level of capital investment in the sub-region. The only doubts surround the future of the iron and steel industry, strongly localised in Scunthorpe. Although the British Steel Corporation has selected Scunthorpe as a major complex for steel production, this will certainly be accompanied by a sharp reduction in the present large work force.[29] Further rapid employment expansion can be anticipated in the fruit and vegetable products industry, which is related to the growth in the market for frozen foods of all descriptions, even though this is nationally a declining industry. Also, one would expect sections of the declining clothing industries to expand in South Humberside as efforts are made to correct Scunthorpe's employment imbalance.

In industries shifting away from South Humberside the loss of employment was concentrated in nationally declining industries, but most of them are of very minor importance to the sub-region's total industrial employment anyway, so there is no burden of a major but declining industry. Nevertheless the local effects of decline can be quite severe, as with the once flourishing cycle industry at Barton-on-Humber.[30] Similarly, growth industries which failed to keep pace with national expansion were mostly small, except for bacon curing, meat and fish products. But the short term fluctuations in employment associated with the latter are so considerable that no particular significance can be attached to its appearance in the shifting away category.

Thus there is positive evidence of an underlying current of industrial attraction towards Humberside in recent years, even if it is less than desired. In addition, the region has very few important declining industries and many important expanding ones. Its short term future thus appears reasonably propitious, particularly in view of the designation of North Humberside as an Intermediate Area in 1969. Humberside has also seen a very rapid expansion in service sector employment, which has tended to act selectively in favour of the larger centres such as Hull and Grimsby.

References to this chapter are on pages 223–5

# 4

# Industrial Distribution in Humberside

THERE ARE over 2,250 industrial establishments in this region, providing employment for nearly 120,000 people. This employment is not distributed uniformly among the factories; over half of them (57·4 per cent) employ less than ten people and contribute only 4·5 per cent of the total. Half the employment is provided by forty establishments, each with 450 or more workers, and of these fifteen factories together employ two-thirds of the labour force. Such concentration is typical of manufacturing industry and it is found to varying degrees in each industrial classification. For most of these the proportion of total employment in each industry group offered by firms of less than ten employees is slight, yet the relatively small firm is of considerable importance in the employment structure of the smaller towns and villages.

Very little insight into the general pattern of industry in the region would be gained by confining our study to the iron and steel industry, whose few plants dominate the total employment so thoroughly; the greater maturity of industrial linkage, the development of auxiliary services and a wealth of local colour would be lost. In many respects, it is the firms whose size of employment lies between the very small factory of less than ten employees and the five or so giants with a quarter of the total employment, that provide the fabric of industrial structure that must be the basis for subsequent development. These are firms that may be encouraged to expand or that will provide the nucleus of skills for the growth of newer industries. In this chapter attention will be directed to firms employing more than nine people, and specific attention is directed more towards the firms of median size or larger than the smaller firms because of this concentration.

## Size of Establishments

For practical purposes of cartography the 1300 establishments employing less than ten people had to be omitted from all maps except Figure 2 (page 24–5). This map gives an immediate visual impression of the density of industry in the region, and the number of units can be counted for each square kilometre as indicated in the caption. It includes establishments primarily engaged in service industries, such as the repair of domestic electrical equipment, the small bakery with its own retail facilities, the repair of boots and shoes, laundries, dry cleaning premises and builders' yards. These last categories are not included in subsequent maps because attention is directed to manufacturing industry, as it is from such industry that the prospects of substantial growth in employment arise. As such growth occurs, it is to be expected that this service sector of employment will also expand and it is plain from this map, which contains over 1200 such establishments, that service industry is important in this region as in others. In general, service is very much smaller in terms of employment than manufacturing industry. In this region, for example, over 1000 of the establishments employ less than ten people and only five employ over 100.

Figure 2 presents the basic industrial location pattern in the area, which must now be examined in more detail. To do this, it is necessary to discard the service industries from consideration in subsequent maps and to discard the small establishments from most of the discussion. Once size of plant is introduced, some basis is needed for distinguishing large factories from smaller ones. In subsequent maps and the discussions they prompt, the whole range of plants with more than nine employees is divided into three size classes, each containing approximately the same number of factories. The divisions are not exact because in some cases an exact division would mean allocating factories employing the same number of people to different size classes and this seems unwarranted. The division into equal parts is simple, and the term 'large' then means one of the largest third of factories in a particular industry grouping, while 'small' means one of the smallest third of factories with ten or more employees. The actual sizes at which the divisions are made varies substantially from the timber industry, whose largest third of factories begins at greater than twenty-eight employees, to the metal manufacturing industry where the largest third begins at 120. When all manufacturing industries are grouped together the distinction of small, medium and large plants is made at less than twenty-one but over nine employees for small factories, at less than eighty-six but over twenty for medium size plants, so that large establishments are those with eighty-six or more employees. The distribution of small, medium and large factories by these definitions is shown in Figures 11, 12, and 13.

It is reasonably plain from all three maps that industry has accumulated at Hull and at Grimsby. It is also relatively easy to pick out

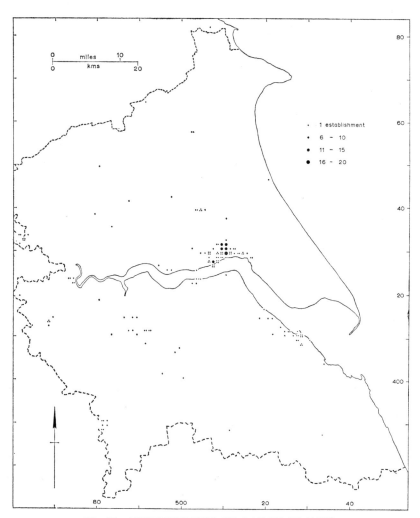

Fig 11.   DISTRIBUTION OF LARGE PLANTS

A large factory is one employing more than 85 people. This range is defined as the upper third of establishments employing ten or more people. For five or less establishments in any grid square the number is shown precisely in a standard pattern. For more than five establishments, larger graded symbols are used. The key gives the range of values

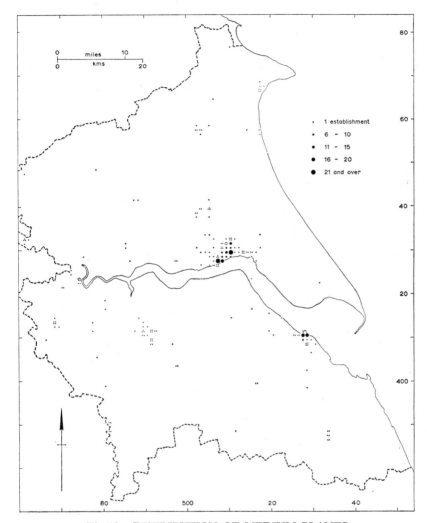

Fig 12. DISTRIBUTION OF MEDIUM PLANTS

A medium factory is one employing from 21 to 85 people. This range is defined as the central third of establishments employing ten or more people. For five or less establishments in any grid square the number is shown precisely in a standard pattern. For more than five establishments, larger graded symbols are used. The key gives the range of values

Bridlington, Beverley and Driffield in North Humberside; Selby and Gainsborough are on the boundary and the factories do not stand out quite as readily from the body of the map. In the rest of South Humberside, Scunthorpe and Louth, Barton-on-Humber and Thorne can also be recognised. There is a scatter of points elsewhere in the region, but in general industry is concentrated and in fact the extent of the

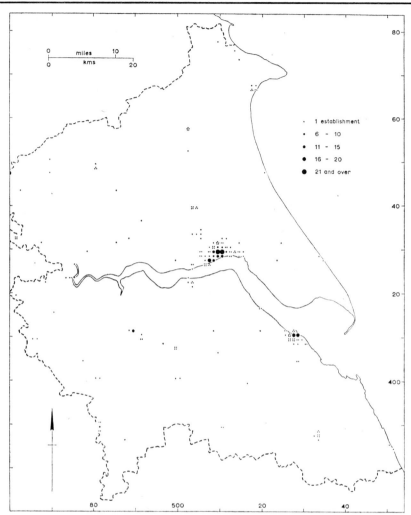

Fig 13.  DISTRIBUTION OF SMALL PLANTS

A small factory is one employing from 10 to 20 people. This range is defined
as the lower third of establishments employing ten or more people. For five
or less establishments in any grid square the number is shown precisely in a
standard pattern. For more than five establishments, larger graded symbols
are used. The key gives the range of values

clustering is similar in each map: the three maps do not reveal any
different tendencies to cluster. That factories are clustered implies
some deliberate location preference is exercised and an examination
of the frequency with which plants of each size are located in the
areas of Hull, Grimsby, Scunthorpe and Gainsborough reveals a discrepancy of preference.[1] There are significantly more large plants in
the Hull area and fewer in the Grimsby area than would be expected

from the distribution of all establishments regardless of size, Scunthorpe has more medium-sized plants and Grimsby more small plants than expected. The precise borough boundaries were not used for this examination, which include the eastward extension of Hull to Salt End and the north-westward extension of Grimsby to the area beyond

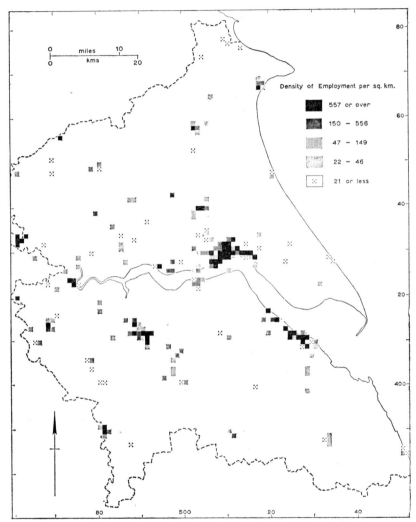

Fig 14.  DENSITY OF EMPLOYMENT IN MANUFACTURING

For this map the employment of each factory shown in figs 11, 12, 13 was summed by grid square so that the pattern of employment density refers to establishments employing more than nine people. This map shows just over 95 per cent of the total employment in the region, and the range of values is divided into five approximately equal groups. The mean size of the remaining establishments is four employees; together these very small premises contribute less than 5 per cent of the total employment

G

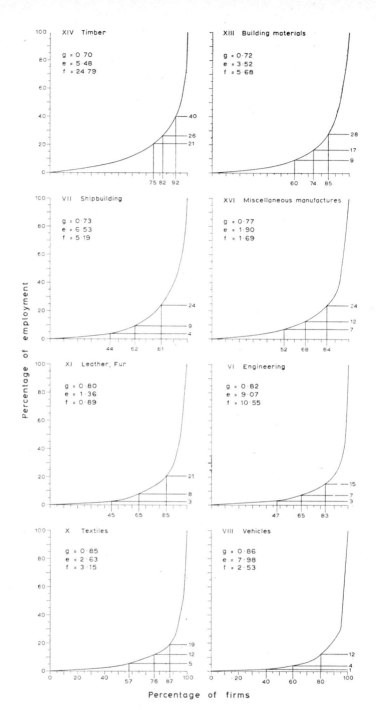

Fig 15.

## LORENZ CURVES OF MANUFACTURING INDUSTRIES I, II

This series of sixteen graphs was divided for cartographic convenience. Each graph shows what proportion of employment is offered by a particular proportion of establishments. If employment were divided equally the graph would be a major diagonal from the origin. The more concave the curve, the greater the concentration of employment in a few firms. A measure of

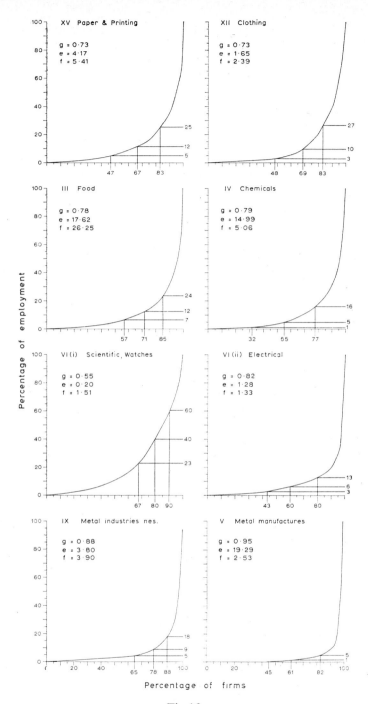

Fig 16.

this concentration is given by the *Gini coefficient g*, which is the ratio of the area between the curve and the major diagonal. The proportion of the total employment represented by each *SIC* is given as *e*, and the proportion of the total number of firms is given by *f*. The values for VI(i) and VI(ii) are not to be included in a sum of percentages as they are included in *SIC VI*

Immingham to take in the recent development of the chemical industry (this scatter of large plants is evident from Figure 11).

Thus even in these gross terms, some differences are revealed in locational preference with respect to size of plant. In the remainder of this chapter different and more detailed aspects of location preferences are examined, with size, type of industry and place of industrial location considered in finer units. But before considering the relevance of size of plant more systematically it is worth while to examine Figure 14, showing the density of employment provided by all the plants included in Figures 11, 12, and 13, together. The same impressions emerge, but their intensity has changed. Scunthorpe and Gainsborough are seen as rather more important than was apparent from the maps showing the number of establishments, because of the very large size of a few iron and steel firms in the former and of some very large engineering firms in Gainsborough. Brough, (west of Hull) with a large aircraft factory, and Beverley (north of Hull) with large tanning and motor vehicle component factories, are also more strongly demarcated. The large plants extending along the Humber bank from Hull and from Grimsby are also clearly visible, while the rural areas are perhaps less readily noticed. But what is revealed is a complex pattern, and some strands of this complexity must now be separated.

As an indication of the extent of the dominance of manufacturing capacity by a few large firms in each industry, the proportion of total employment can be referred to the proportion of firms and shown as *Lorenz curves* for each *SIC* group (Figures 15, 16). The use of the total number of firms in each group seems particularly appropriate to this region where each *SIC* has some importance as an employer and where almost every *MLH* category is involved. The curves are useful in that they present visually the proportion of total business activity, when measured by employment levels, which is operated by a given proportion of the firms. In each case the proportions are shown for those firms that employ less than ten people; this proportion is highest in the timber industry *(SIC XIV)* in which some twenty-one per cent of the employment is confined to such small businesses, and lowest in the iron and steel industry *(SIC V)* where firms with less than ten employees have a share of only 0·44 per cent of the total employment. These two curves differ considerably in the degree of their departure from the major diagonal from the origin, or the line which represents the condition of an industry with all firms of equal size.

In general, firms are not of equal size and the few large establishments will control more than a proportionate share of the market or the employment. A measure of this departure is found by expressing the area between the actual curve and the straight line as a ratio of the area of the complete triangle. These ratios are known as *Gini coefficients*, and estimates for the particular curves are shown on Figures 15, 16. This coefficient provides a measure of dominance, and the *SIC* groups are arranged in ascending order of concentration. In the building materials industry *(SIC XIII)* the smaller firms contribute a relatively important share of the work, which may have been anticipated from its general orientation to the supply of local needs, although later in this chapter we shall examine particular *MLH* categories of this industry and observe its lack of homogeneity. In some ways *SIC III*, the food industry, may be surprising by its median rank of concentration because this, too, contains a great many small businesses widely dispersed in the region. However, its degree of concentration reflects the importance of a number of *MLH* categories that serve a nationally important role, especially fish and vegetable processing, grain-milling and animal foods. Shipbuilding *(SIC VII)* is commonly associated with the few massive yards of the Clyde or Tyne rivers and the large labour forces involved, but in this area the tendency is towards rather more small and medium-sized concerns making relatively small vessels, and the industry has only equal fourth rank in terms of concentration. To illustrate the extent to which *SIC* orders can obscure features of smaller numbers of *MLHs*, the engineering industry *(SIC VI)* is subdivided by *MLHs 351–9*, referring to scientific instruments and watches and clocks, and *MLHs 361–9* relating to electrical engineering. In the first case the coefficient is 0·55 and in the latter 0·82. In general the coefficients for *SICs* vary from about 0·70–0·95; the industries with the highest coefficients have the greatest dispersion of size, and the overwhelming impression is one of substantial concentration in each major industrial group.

This is a factor of considerable importance in any consideration of the ways in which industrial developments are likely to occur, because it provides the basis of an assertion of considerable standing in industrial literature, namely that the chance of a given *relative* increase in size over a specified time period is the same for all firms regardless of their size. Thus a large firm may increase or decrease by a larger *absolute* amount than a small firm, but the proportionate change tends to be the same. This is implied by the idea that firms in the same industry tend to have the same minimum costs and below a certain critical cost the profitability of unit production falls rapidly, but at the minimum costs various levels of output are possible. In general the firms that increase their output with reference to other firms will be able to grow in size, whereas other firms may remain at a particular size class or decline in importance. In a particular region it is usually possible to discover from company histories that certain factors have seemed to be associated with expansion. These factors may be fiscal, involving high levels of investment or amalgamation with other firms, they may refer to a market preference for a particular product, and this underlies the importance of the market research that is extensively pursued in a number of the large local firms, they may relate to pre-ferential access to certain factors of production in the sense of some geographic advantage, or the industry may be an element of a class of industry that is growing rapidly relatively to the general level of growth.

An example of business amalgamation at a greater than regional level is evident in some of the flour-milling firms in Hull, and there, too, market preference operates with respect to the products of the pharmaceutical industry that is strongly represented in Hull. The Humber ports are renowned for their dominance of domestic fish supply, and the region seems to possess some particular advantage to industries associated with fish processing, as they have a rank import-ance of employment level that is significantly higher than the equiva-lent national level. Many regional administrators and representatives of Chambers of Commerce recognise the importance to a region of the development of a branch of an industry that is growing more rapidly than the mean rate of growth. This region is particularly for-tunate in already having a number of these industrial categories and is apparently able to offer special advantage to the chemical industry.

A basis of firms able to expand is valuable. Few firms are initially large. Of course, firms that are can be instanced such as the oil refineries sited on south Humberside by Continental and involving a £30m investment, the largest initial investment in an oil refinery in this country. Equally, other examples can be cited where large firms have grown from small origins. In this region, a particularly good example of this is seen in the Beverley firm of Armstrong Patents Ltd., making motor vehicle components. It expanded from a very small general engineering factory to become the dominant employer in Beverley within fifty years, benefiting from the business skill of its founder and from the production of essential components for a most rapidly grow-ing national industry. The expansion of employment in a region is a result of new firms being initiated or by the expansion of existing firms. About ten per cent of the growth of assets in the UK is due to the formation of new firms, and new firms are generally small. They are not necessarily the smallest firms in the industry because the smallest size class contains firms that are residual and, in the case of industries that require a substantial level of capital investment, the tendency may be for such new firms to be in a median size class. This may well apply to firms in order *SIC IV*. In respect to the growth of local firms to provide large increments in employment, we may expect the idea of proportionate growth to apply to size classes, and on the *Lorenz curves* the firms of more than ten employees are split into three size classes, and the per cent employment up to the class boundary is shown. For each class we may anticipate growth roughly proportionate to the size of the class and to the general level of growth in that industry. But the change in size is unlikely to apply to each firm in a particular size class because expansion is related to recent changes, but the importance of momentum is not constant; it tends to diminish. However we can expect firms that have experienced recent growth to be likely to grow more rapidly than firms of the same size whose growth occurred earlier, and we shall expect large firms to grow proportionately more rapidly than small firms. These modifications to the rigid idea of proportionate growth are consistent with the important qualitative assessments of industrial change; unfortunately we have been unable to acquire comparable employment data for the region's firms, over a time period of ten years or so, that could have provided some estimate of changes in the size structure of firms.[2] Final level of size is not independent of early stages but the degree of dependency may not be great. The development of the present or near present pattern of industry possibly depended more strongly on the prior state of industry than will anticipated expansions based upon contemporary types of initially large industry introduced into the area. In some ways this is a doubtful proposition, and the present structure of industry may be more important as the basis for the bulk of any expansion that occurs.

In this context it seems essential to examine, first, the pattern of industry orders in some aspect of their size, and secondly, the detailed characteristics of particular *MLH* categories, to ascertain whether the region reveals preferential selection by industries that show common features. This will establish a basis for examining less general aspects of industry in Chapter 5, and for a conclusion dealing with regional prospects.

### Selected Industrial Distributions

*Bases of Selection*

A summary of the importance of each *SIC* order in terms of the employment it offers is provided by the Figure showing the *Lorenz curves*. With the coefficient of concentration, this Figure indicates the importance of the industry in the region and implies its distribution in terms of whether the industry has a large number of small and medium sized plants or a few very large ones. However, these data do not indicate whether large plants are dissociated from the smaller plants, whether there is any tendency to concentrate in particular locations, nor whether the industry as a whole is equally shared between the areas north and south of the Humber.

A series of maps has been prepared to show something of the particular distributions. Eight of the fourteen *SIC* orders are considered, and their selection was made on a number of criteria. The principal division was made on the basis of their overall allegiance to raw materials and the compactness of the production sequence. SIC orders *III*, *IV*, *V* and *XIV* all use raw materials in their first and second stages of conversion. For example, logs are used directly in the local sawmills and farm produce in the vegetable canning industry, but in the latter the freezing or packaging is the final stage in a very compact, one stage, industrial sequence. In the case of the chemical industry the production of pharmaceuticals is much further removed from the basic chemical raw materials, although for chemicals as an order ninety per cent of the processing is concerned either with first or second stage resource use. As a contrast *SIC* orders *VI*, *VII*, *VIII* and *IX* use the products that have already been processed by other industries, and their links are most closely associated with these or with the final market. In this group are the manufacture of metal canisters which may be sent for food packaging or to the chemical industry, and the production of aeroplanes.

Some impression of the general, national characteristics of these orders of industry, in terms of such resource relations, can be gained from Table 24. This shows the mean percentage of total costs of raw materials plus fuel, of wages and transport, together with the mean value added by manufacture in the industry. This last figure provides a useful index of profitability and these measures are frequently referred to in the remainder of this chapter. A more detailed breakdown by *MLH* is used for Figures 25 to 30, but at this stage it is useful to make the following statements about the data in Table 24. In the first place there is an almost perfect rank correlation between value added in the manufacturing process and transport costs and a very strong inverse rank correlation between the expenditure on raw materials and on wages. This latter is to be expected; it is surprising that they are not more strongly associated. Secondly the *Gini coefficient* that measures the degree of concentration in those industry groups locally is inversely associated with the proportionate expenditure on raw materials: a high expenditure on raw materials is related to a substantial dispersal of size class in the industry.

A second criterion for industrial selection was the significance of these eight orders in local employment. Together they comprise 85 per cent of the region's employment, 57 per cent from the first group and 28 from the second: a significant reflection of the bias to a resource base of local industry rather than to a non-resource or market base. The nature of the employment varies from the diverse and often

**Table 24**

COST CHARACTERISTICS OF INDUSTRY ORDERS, 1963

| SIC ORDER | Value added per caput £s | | Purchases Per cent | | Wages Per cent | | Transport Costs Per cent | | Gini coefficients |
|---|---|---|---|---|---|---|---|---|---|
| | 1 | | 2 | | 3 | | 4 | | 5 |
| 3 | 1876 | 2 | 75·11 | 4 | 18·50 | 13 | 6·39 | 2 | 7 |
| 4 | 2212 | 1 | 81·99 | 1 | 15·30 | 14 | 2·71 | 6 | 8 |
| 5 | 1399 | 4 | 75·61 | 2 | 21·85 | 12 | 2·53 | 7 | 14 |
| 6 | 1285 | 6 | 56·08 | 12 | 42·00 | 2 | 1·92 | 9 | 10 |
| 7 | 1060 | 11 | 50·40 | 13 | 48·82 | 1 | 0·78 | 13·5 | 4 |
| 8 | 1054 | 12 | 73·15 | 6 | 26·07 | 8 | 0·78 | 13·5 | 12 |
| 9 | 1094 | 10 | 73·68 | 5 | 24·16 | 10 | 2·16 | 8 | 13 |
| 10 | 1162 | 9 | 72·86 | 7 | 25·60 | 9 | 1·53 | 11 | 11 |
| 11 | 1021 | 13 | 75·21 | 3 | 23·19 | 11 | 1·60 | 10 | 9 |
| 12 | 771 | 14 | 63·46 | 9 | 35·20 | 5 | 1·35 | 12 | 4 |
| 13 | 1629 | 3 | 50·04 | 14 | 39·03 | 3 | 10·93 | 1 | 2 |
| 14 | 1170 | 8 | 62·80 | 10 | 32·41 | 7 | 4·79 | 3 | 1 |
| 15 | 1381 | 5 | 59·09 | 11 | 36·94 | 4 | 3·98 | 4 | 4 |
| 16 | 1223 | 7 | 63·83 | 8 | 33·38 | 6 | 2·79 | 5 | 6 |

Ranks are shown in italics.

rho $(1,4) = p0·01$ positive

rho $(2,3) = p0·01$ inverse

rho $(2,5) = p0·05$ inverse: for column 5 a rank of 1 was given to the industry with the least concentration

*Source:* Derived from information in the Census of Production for 1963, published from 1966–69. In July 1969 some *MLHs* were not available and data were taken from the earlier census of 1958. As only five *MLHs* were involved the overall result is unlikely to be affected significantly

rho is a measure of correlation for ranked variates

$p$ is a statement of the likelihood that such a value would arise in a sample from a population in which the variables were unrelated.

small-scale nature of the establishments, as in timber and shipyards, to the considerable concentration found in orders *V* and *VIII*. These groups also contain most of the categories of industry which show a significantly high preference for the region in terms of their national employment levels. Indeed much of the essential character of the region is contained in these orders and the different qualities of location patterns are represented. Some of the other industries are also important; in particular, leather tanning and cement manufacture are of considerable local significance; the relative lack of a paper-making industry is surprising and is one possibility for future growth. Its share of the regional employment is the highest of the non-selected group, but the bulk of this figure is made up of a large number of relatively small printing, not papermaking firms.

There is an interesting regularity shown in these maps (Figures 17–24) between the number of establishments and the size of employment opportunity. The eight *SIC* orders constitute 85 per cent of the local labour force and involve 85 per cent of the establishments. 63 per cent of these are in north Humberside and employ 63 per cent of the labour force, Hull has 40 per cent of the region's establishments and employs 40 per cent of the labour force. This relationship between number and size of establishments does not hold for smaller subdivisions; there is a substantial departure in Scunthorpe whose labour force is about as great as that for the Grimsby area but has 3 per cent of the region's establishments compared to 15 per cent in Grimsby. This very simple arithmetical comparison illustrates a fundamental feature of the area's industrial structure. A decrease in the size of the centre implies an increase in the dominance of one type of manufacture, and this feature is admirably illustrated by Figures 17 to 24.

These maps show the establishments employing more than nine people, the largest third of the establishments being shown in black. The factories in this range dominate employment and in all cases represent at least 60 per cent of the labour force, in most cases over 80 per cent. The size of factory qualifying as a large factory varies with each industry and is 120 employees in *SIC V* and 30 in *SIC XIV*. Some of these large factories have grown rapidly in recent years, and this may be expected to continue in any future period of accelerated growth; the expansion of other large plants may have happened some time ago and these may be expected to grow less quickly. The remaining medium size plants which are represented as open symbols may be expected to provide some new focuses of accelerated growth; this pattern of growth opportunity varies within each industry.

**Table 25**

SHARE OF EMPLOYMENT BETWEEN NORTH AND SOUTH
HUMBERSIDE IN SELECTED *SIC* ORDERS

| | Percentage of Employment | |
|---|---|---|
| *SIC* Order | North | South |
| III | 50 | 50 |
| IV | 70 | 30 |
| V | 10 | 90 |
| VI | 50 | 50 |
| VII | 50 | 50 |
| VIII | 97 | 3 |
| IX | 93 | 7 |
| XIV | 80 | 20 |

*Source:* Calculated from data in the records of HMFI.

In the case of orders *III*, *VI* and *VII* the employment is divided equally between North and South Humberside. Of these, the engineering and shipbuilding industries refer least to resources and most to industrial links, whereas all the food industries are closely tied to the resources of the region or to those made accessible by imports. Table 25 shows that in the other five orders the industries are considerably concentrated; in South Humberside in the case of iron and steel, and in North Humberside in the remaining four cases. To a large degree the existence of intrinsic resources, imports and inter-industrial connections explain these patterns.

## Industries with a Resource Base

### Local Resource Base

More establishments are involved in food processing than in any other industrial order, and just under half the 600 factories are shown on the map (Fig. 17). The 334 *small* establishments have a mean size of four employees and provide less than seven per cent of the employment in this order. They are concentrated in the large centres and smaller market towns, a few being dispersed throughout the villages of North and South Humberside. The plants with more than ten employees are in Hull and in Grimsby, each with approximately a third of the employment in this industry. The large factories shown in black on this map have at least 45 employees, most of them clustered in Hull and, of the 10 largest, 5 are in Grimsby, offering nearly a quarter of the employment in the order; Hull has only 2 of these first 10 ranking factories but most of the smaller plants employing from 100 to

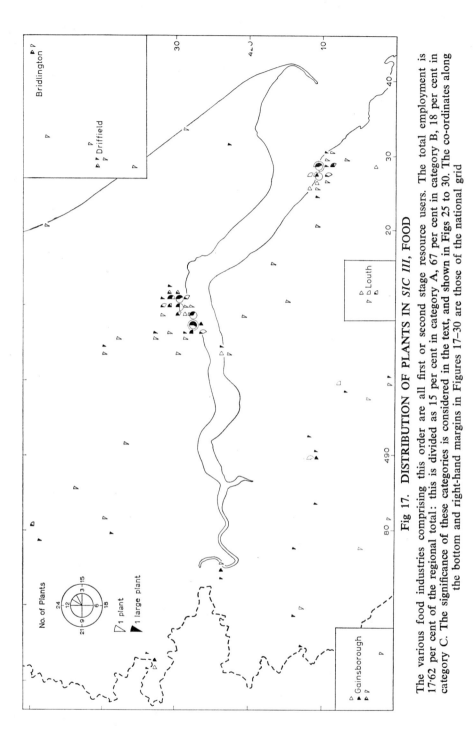

Fig 17. DISTRIBUTION OF PLANTS IN *SIC III*, FOOD

The various food industries comprising this order are all first or second stage resource users. The total employment is 17·62 per cent of the regional total: this is divided as 15 per cent in category A, 67 per cent in category B, 18 per cent in category C. The significance of these categories is considered in the text, and shown in Figs 25 to 30. The co-ordinates along the bottom and right-hand margins in Figures 17–30 are those of the national grid under 300 employees. This difference largely reflects the type of food industry located in each centre. The older industries of grain milling and animal feedstuffs are dominated by Hull. A series of large mills with a mean size of 65 employees is strung along the river Hull, which is overhung by elevators and carries barge traffic, indicating the dependence of these industries on imported resources. Similar collections of flour milling and provender manufacture are found at the older market towns of Beverley, Selby and Gainsborough, which share a number of common features of industrial structure. Sugar processing is in this same category of industry and there is a large factory, opened in 1927, processing sugar beet at Selby, another at Scawby, south of Scunthorpe, and a smaller sugar grinding plant at Driffield.

The most important industries in this order are those that compress the processing into one stage, using basic resources and converting them so that no further manufacture precedes consumption. This sector involves 67 per cent of the labour force shown in Figure 17, and is very much more important in South Humberside. This importance is revealed by the line of large establishments bisecting the area and ranging from poultry processing in two plants near Caistor to food canning at Goole, all based on local produce. Even more typical is a fascinating collection of factories engaged in sprout-trimming, culling the fields around Keadby, Scunthorpe and Barton-upon-Humber; they belong to frozen food firms with national marketing reputations. These establishments are closely related to the fish processing industries centred in Hull and in Grimsby. There has been no comparable rural employment in North Humberside, apart from two milk-processing plants at Holme-on-Spalding-Moor and Driffield, and even in South Humberside the largest factories and the greatest concentration are in Grimsby, where the mean plant size is over 120, well over double the mean size in Hull. Thus Hull and Grimsby have different biases in their partition of food processing, with Hull, as the older manufacturing centre, attracting the grist mills with a typically high value added and a high proportion of their expenditure on raw materials, and Grimsby and South Humberside being preferred by the newer and more rapidly growing food industries with median value added and lower transport costs. Again a division by type of product rather than a proportionate division across the range of industries found in this group occurs in the remaining factories, Hull having the cocoa mills and confectioners and Grimsby the only biscuit firm in the region.

There is a higher degree of concentration in order $V$ than in any other industry. Of the 57 establishments, only 25 employ less than ten

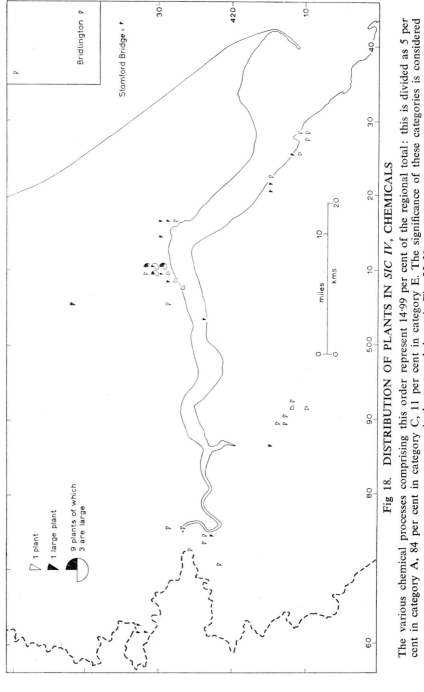

Fig 18. DISTRIBUTION OF PLANTS IN *SIC IV*, CHEMICALS

The various chemical processes comprising this order represent 14·99 per cent of the regional total: this is divided as 5 per cent in category A, 84 per cent in category C, 11 per cent in category E. The significance of these categories is considered in the text, and shown in Figs 25–30

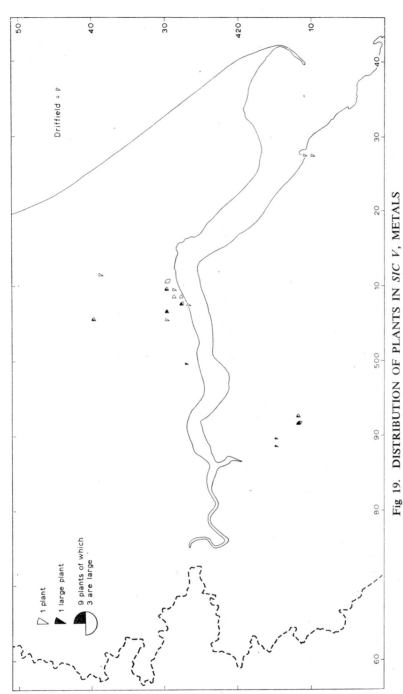

Fig 19. DISTRIBUTION OF PLANTS IN *SIC V*, METALS

The various metal trades comprising this order represent 19·29 per cent of the regional total: this is divided as 94 per cent in category C, 6 per cent in category E. The significance of these categories is considered in the text, and shown in Figs 25–30 people and these constitute less than $\frac{1}{2}$ per cent of the total employment. All the major firms are based in Scunthorpe and are related to local low grade iron ore, the four largest employing over 80 per cent of the people in this category. It is little wonder that the location pattern is as concentrated as the employment. The other component of this order is non-ferrous metals and this is confined to North Humberside and largely to Hull. The establishments are much smaller but still have a mean employment of over 90. Two firms dominate the industry and specialise in copper and brass founding and casting; the industry has close relations with the building and repair of ships, but has not developed in Grimsby. A lead smelting factory at Melton, west of Hull, and a firm in Beverley manufacturing light alloys complete this rudimentary pattern: rudimentary because iron and steel making tend to be linked more strongly backwards to coal mining than forwards to metal using industries. The best developed of these forward links are with engineering categories; Hull has the most strongly developed engineering industry in the region and Scunthorpe is second in importance after Gainsborough in South Humberside. It seems clear that the serial movement of processed resources must continue but that a locational sequence is not necessary. Raw material and fuel costs are the second highest at 75·61 per cent and the local iron industry is associated closely with its resources. In engineering the raw material and fuel costs are 56·08 per cent and the bases of attraction are more diverse, hence the locational hiatus in this area.

Imported Resource Base

Still related to a resource advantage of the area are those industries that have developed from and remain largely dependent on imported raw materials arriving at the Humber ports and especially the Hull and Grimsby dock areas. North Humberside dominates both, with seventy per cent of the chemical industry's employment and eighty per cent of the employment in the timber industry. One person in twenty in Humberside is employed in timber and the small firms with less than ten employees have a more important part to play than in any other industry, with just over a fifth of the work. The importance of small firms seems implicit in the diversity of ways that timber can be used and the extent of its demand in most forms of construction. Something like half the labour is in fact found in sawmilling factories and the 422 smallest establishments are not shown on this map; their mean size is four employees and, as in the food industry, they are found in most of the smaller towns and villages throughout the

Page 121: (above) *Hull freightliner terminal, opened 1968, from which Freightliners Ltd operate liner trains to London, Southampton, Liverpool and Manchester and linking services to places as far apart as Harwich, Cardiff and Glasgow;* (below) *manufacturing caravans at the Hull factory of Astral Caravan Co, one of many large firms concentrated in Hull and Beverley which together make up a significant proportion of national manufacturing capacity*

Page 122: (above) *Assembly of Buccaneer low-level strike reconnaissance aircraft at the former Blackburn Aircraft factory at Brough, near Hull, now part of Hawker Siddeley Aviation (HSA);* (below) *assembly of Harrier 'jump-jet' wings at Brough; although an advanced technological industry, aircraft production is prone to cyclical fluctuations, but as part of HSA Brough now plays an important role in sub-assembly production for aircraft such as the Harrier and Trident finally assembled elsewhere*

region. A further twenty per cent of the employment is provided by 92 firms with from 10 to 26 employees, leaving 60 per cent of the employment in the 46 firms employing from 28 to over 700. These large factories are shown in black and it is plain that most of them are located in Hull. The eight largest firms, with a quarter of the labour force, are in Hull, and indeed two-thirds of the largest firms employing half the people in this industry are in this port, while most of the remainder are in Grimsby. In both centres the industry is closely related to the food industry, providing boxes for fish and packing cases for vegetables, and to the shipbuilding industry. There is an interesting extension of the industry to furniture and upholstery in Grimsby and cabinet-making in Hull. A number of firms in Hull have recently specialised in the manufacture of portable buildings and doors; they are all large concerns and provide a most important source of employment on the northern edge of the city. In strong contrast with the food industry, few large plants are located outside Hull and Grimsby, away from the Humber in the rural areas, a distinction reflecting the difference between a widespread local resource and an imported resource with some primitive development of inter-industry dependence.

In this region the chemical industry depends on imported raw materials. The association is plain to see on the map, with lines of establishments along both sides of the river Hull, on the Ouse at Selby, at Rawcliffe and Goole and particularly along the Humber east of Hull and west of Grimsby. As an *SIC* group this industry has the highest expenditure on raw materials, eighty-two per cent of the total costs, but it also has the highest value added per employee with a mean value of £2,212. This association with raw materials is emphasised by the cluster of ten establishments in Scunthorpe which are generally associated with the iron and steel industry, using by-products such as slag and involved in the distillation of tar. This industry provides fifteen per cent of the regional employment and is third in importance after the food and iron and steel industries, but it may be seen by some as the epitome of prospective industrial growth for this area. At present it is concentrated in north Humberside, which has seventy per cent of the industry's employment to which Hull contributes slightly more than forty per cent, and the eastward extension of the industry along the Humber a further twenty-five per cent. There is no comparable industry in Grimsby, which lacks the provender mills with their oil by-products that are of considerable importance in Hull. In particular, bordering the river Hull, is a series of mills engaged in

H

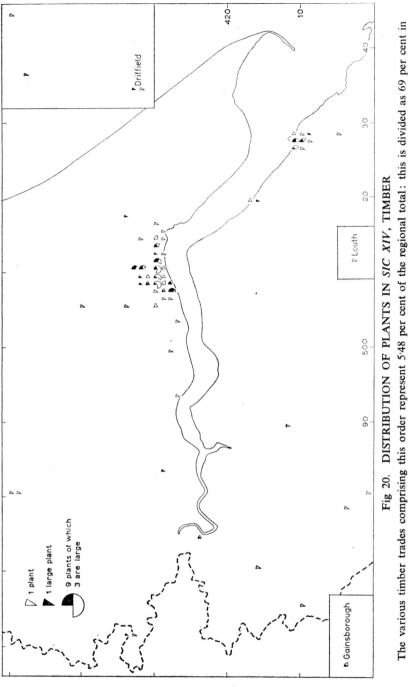

Fig 20. DISTRIBUTION OF PLANTS IN *SIC XIV*, TIMBER

The various timber trades comprising this order represent 5·48 per cent of the regional total: this is divided as 69 per cent in category A, 17 per cent in category C, 14 per cent in category D. The significance of these categories is considered in the text, and shown in Figs 25–30 extracting oil, making oil-cake and grinding paints. North-west of Grimsby, near Immingham, the new, large chemical factories employ an average of over 450, a figure almost identical to the large but more established firms at Salt End on the north Humber bank. Both these values are substantially greater than the mean size of eighty employees for the more traditional factories in Hull making paints, oils and soaps. Some of these have hundreds of employees but there are small firms too, and this reflects the differences of structure within the chemical industry.

The dominant aspect of chemical manufacture in the area is in the second stage of resource conversion, composed of vegetable and animal oils and soaps, paints and inks, basic chemicals and dyes, lubricating oils and greases which together constitute eighty-four per cent of the employment in this order. Such factories are located in Selby, where a Leeds soap manufacturer began to produce oil after a disagreement with Hull millers over irregularity of supply and fluctuating prices.[3] The Ouse is navigable for barges and the Selby canal provided a link with the Leeds soap works. A large dyeworks and the production of fine chemicals established in 1946 as an extension of a Midlands firm complete this industry's activities in Selby. The production of fertilisers is not surprising in view of the presence of a strong chemical industry in an area of major agricultural importance; three large firms cling to the Humber from Goole, Barton on Humber to Flixborough, and a fourth makes nitrogen fertiliser in Scunthorpe. The chemical industry is unimportant in Grimsby; its vigorous development past Immingham represents its concentration in South Humberside.

In every other case the share of South Humberside's industrial strength is allocated to one or other of the main centres, but in the chemical industry a new centre is nascent reflecting the needs of this industry dependent on imported resources. It is hoped that this will develop in a similar way to the iron and steel industry in Scunthorpe, using local resources. One characteristic of mature industrial structures seems to be a considerable degree of interdependence, and though this has not been stimulated to any great extent in Scunthorpe the opportunity in the chemical industry for the development of such associations may be greater than in other industries. These related industries are newer and have not therefore already reached the same established locational pattern as the engineering industries. There is a lower proportion of such related industries as plastics. The chemical industry is also closely associated with engineering, and as industrial

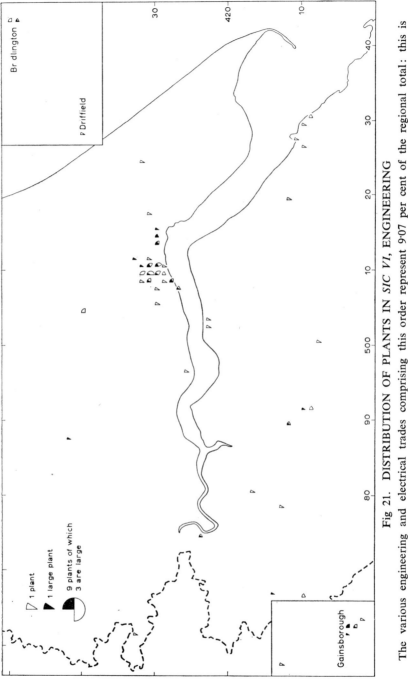

Fig 21. DISTRIBUTION OF PLANTS IN *SIC VI*, ENGINEERING

The various engineering and electrical trades comprising this order represent 9·07 per cent of the regional total: this is divided as 99 per cent in category E, 1 per cent in category F. The significance of these categories is considered in the text, and shown in Figs 25–30 production reaches the stage in the sequence where basic resources have least direct significance and other industries and final markets have most relevance, we see how it is the most mature centre in the area that has attracted such establishments.

### Industries Dependent on Linkages and Markets

Engineering incorporates a greater number of separate trades than any other industrial order and illustrates the best developed inter-industry connections. These are most strongly associated with the larger firms, but the more numerous smaller firms also show a strong connection with at least one other local industry. There are approximately 250 establishments, of which three-quarters are in mechanical engineering trades and twelve per cent are associated with electrical engineering. The large plants distinguished on the map (Figure 21) employ over 40 people and constitute over 84 per cent of the jobs in this order, but the largest seventeen plants offer three-quarters of all the employment.

The industry is concentrated into a few factories, confined to three centres. In Scunthorpe the industry is dominated by constructional steel work with a mean employment of over 150, and is associated with United Steel in one large plant. This sort of development is encouraging. Currently, constructional steelwork composes only seven per cent of the employment in engineering in the region; this is ten times more than in Grimsby where the mean size is fifteen employees, but far below Gainsborough, which is the most important engineering centre in South Humberside and has almost as large an employment figure in engineering as Hull, so that in terms of total employment it is much more dominant. The mean size of establishment is over 400; much larger than in any other centre, and these firms provide practically a third of the region's engineering employment. Particular mention can be made of the firm of Marshall Sons and Company Ltd, which specialises in the production of steam-and-oil-engine automatic boilers. Founded in 1848, the firm has helped to change Gainsborough from a market town of food industries to the broader industrial structure of today. This change has been closely linked to the growth of Rose Forgrove Limited, an engineering firm making wrapping and packaging machines. This firm is now a member of Baker Perkins Holdings Limited of Peterborough, and is tied to other packaging machinery firms in Leeds. A gear cutting factory, also an important source of employment, was started as a subsidiary company and this underlines the way some industries stimulate the location of others and such industries can assume real importance in a town's development.

In North Humberside the influence of rural activities has been condensed into a series of establishments in the older market towns making agricultural machinery. The largest of these is R. B. Massey of Market Weighton, but smaller factories are found in Driffield, Beverley and Bridlington, where there is also an interesting development of a firm specialising in the manufacture of amusement machinery. Practically forty per cent of the engineering industry's employment is in Hull and practically half the establishments. The small firms have a mean employment of four people and together offer two per cent of the jobs; some, such as scale-making, are related to the fishing industry; others repair lifting tackle or are more generally described as jobbing engineers prepared to deal with a whole range of tasks and flexibility is the basis of their survival. There is a nostalgic sprinkling of farriers and blacksmiths throughout the East Riding of Yorkshire, many turning to the repair of agricultural machinery or decorative wrought-iron work as the horse is replaced.

The larger establishments show more specialisation, a substantial proportion making machine tools and jigs. Others make machines for Hull's more basic activities; one factory making fish processing machinery, another making oil-cake machinery. Some are auxiliary establishments developed by a parent company, for example Reckitts, the Hull chemical firm, and another makes pulleys and speed reducers as an auxiliary to Fenners' belt-drive systems. Many are maritime, making boilers and renovating them; these are usually found near the docks and some of them are among the region's largest firms in this industry. Along the Humber, east of Hull, Priestmans make excavators, and Imperial Typewriters is on a neighbouring site: both are very large firms and important sources of employment. The electrical engineering industry is weakly developed in the area, one Hull firm making electric lamps is in the largest class, but the major factory is the AEI works at Thorne, a very large employer and important in that town now that the coal-mine has closed permanently because of flooding.

There are a number of links between the engineering industry, brass and copper founding and the shipbuilding industry, which in turn is associated with fish imports and the timber trades in a number of stages. Shipbuilding is not a large industry, employing just under 7 per cent of the regional labour force, with 95 firms employing less than 10 people and confined, like the larger establishments, to a few

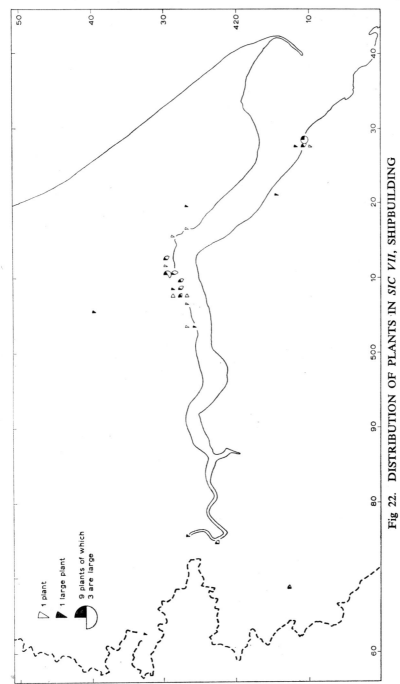

Fig 22. DISTRIBUTION OF PLANTS IN *SIC VII*, SHIPBUILDING

This order represents 6·53 per cent of the regional total: it is contained in category E. The significance of these categories is considered in the text, and shown in Figs 25–30

1 plant
1 large plant
9 plants of which 3 are large

locations on navigable waterways. North and South Humberside share the employment equally, dominated by Hull in the north with forty per cent of the employment and by Grimsby in the south with twenty per cent. In employment terms it is Grimsby's most important industry after food processing, and it is the last industry we shall consider in which South Humberside makes any important contribution in these terms.

In Grimsby the industry is dominated by its fish trawling connections, and most yards are operated by the Ross Group, and the descriptions of particular units vary from marine engineering to boiler making and shipbuilding. The largest unit in the region, at Immingham, employs rather under 1000 men and carries out general repair work. In Hull there is less dependence on one particular fish trawling group, but there is a close link with the fish industry and with engineering. For example, a firm on St Andrew's dock is concerned with brass finishing and boat-making, another on the same dock with ship repairs, electrical engineering, nets and sailmaking. Others make ships' engines and repair them, deal with welding and fashioning non-ferrous metals. Relatively few are concerned with boat and barge building, which is found in four places away from Hull; at Beverley on the river Hull, and at Goole, Thorne and Selby, whose boat-building firm moved from Beverley in 1898, apparently because there were fears that the river Hull was too small, and therefore incompatible with the trend to increasingly large vessels. The continuation of these enterprises illustrates to some extent the persisting use of the region's waterways for the transshipment inland of imported raw materials delivered to Hull and Grimsby. These are long-established links. Furleys of Gainsborough have operated vessels on the Trent since 1770; today they have over twenty diesel-powered barges plying between Hull and Gainsborough, and many people believe that these routeways should be even more fully used than at present.

In contrast, modern transport and packaging developments in terms of container shipments from ports and on railways are well in evidence at the Humber ports and this seems appropriate in an area whose employment in canister and aircraft manufacture is higher than the national level. These industries are subsumed under orders *IX* and *VIII*. The appropriate maps (Figs 23, 24) show how North Humberside monopolises the employment in these categories of industry, with 93 per cent producing various metal goods and 97 per cent in vehicles. Both industries have high coefficients of concentration and are confined to three parts of North Humberside. Holloware production is

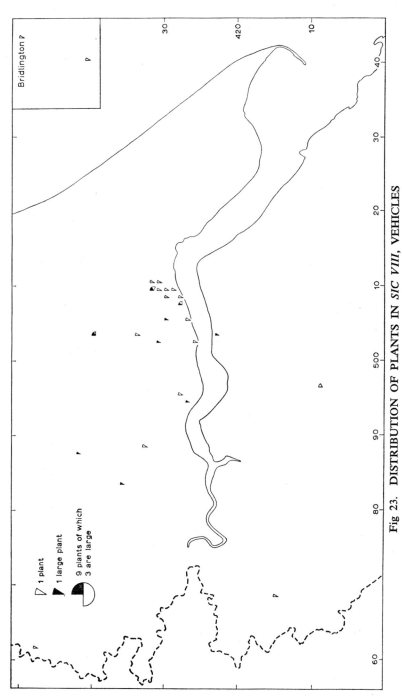

Fig 23. DISTRIBUTION OF PLANTS IN *SIC VIII*, VEHICLES

The various industries comprising this order represent 7·98 per cent of the regional total: this is divided as 3 per cent in category E, 97 per cent in category F. The significance of these categories is considered in the text, and shown in Figs 25–30

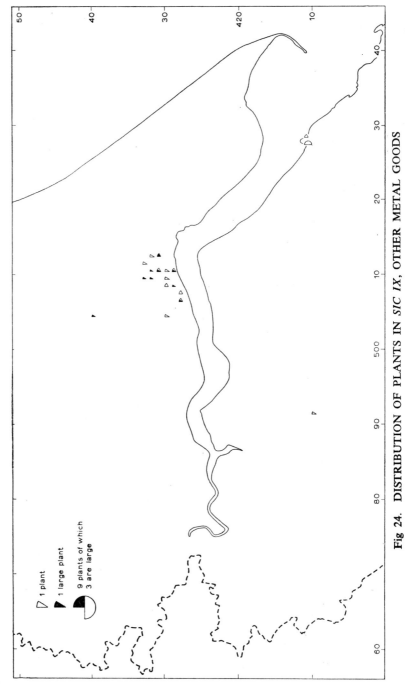

**Fig 24.** DISTRIBUTION OF PLANTS IN *SIC IX*, OTHER METAL GOODS

The various trades comprising this order represent 3·8 per cent of the regional total: this is contained in category E. The significance of these categories is considered in the text, and shown in Figs 25–30 in Hull, with the Metal Box Company providing a large part of the employment; other firms of substantial size are on the northern edge of the city and make metal canisters and containers for local industrial use as well as for the national market. This industry is vertically integrated with iron and steel foundries and with mechanical engineering, and its market is the food and chemical industries. Its concentration in Hull and its absence elsewhere is not surprising. The particular association with chemicals is seen in a firm adjacent to the river Hull which makes kegs and drums, while Reckitts, the largest manufacturer of basic chemicals in Hull, has its own subsidiary firm making canisters for such things as polishes, and aerosol containers. The lack of a complementary development in cardboard and paper packaging industries has been noted earlier.

Vehicles, too, are basically connected with mechanical engineering. Two firms dominate employment. Beverley imitates the towns of southern Humberside in this category by its specialised importance in one industry entailed by the large firm of Armstrong Patents Ltd produces shock absorbers for the motor industry, while the recently accelerated growth in employment at the Brough aircraft works contrasts with the lack of a basic vehicle industry in Hull. Two establishments on the Yorkshire Wolds make components for the aircraft factory at Brough, a firm at Market Weighton makes motor bodies, and a number of firms in Hull also make motor bodies, radiators and car components. South of the Humber, in Barton, is a large firm making cycles and there are two related coachbuilding establishments at Broughton. In and around Hull there is a strongly developed and specialised manufacture of caravans, with eleven such establishments shown on the map.

*Summarising the Patterns*

The location patterns implicit in these maps have been described in terms of the use of resources, in the link between industries, and in relationships between the size structure of the industry and the pattern of concentration between North and South Humberside and within them. In South Humberside, each centre is specialised, Gainsborough for engineering, Scunthorpe for iron and steel, Grimsby for food, shipbuilding and timber, but in North Humberside these specialisations are not found because Hull absorbs them. A useful distinction between basic resources found locally and those imported seemed consistent with the map patterns, and this distinction helps to explain the different distributions of food from timber or chemicals from iron and steel. In food as in chemicals the emerging pattern of new, large establishments was similarly distinguished. The usefulness of industrial connections was present in each pattern, but the influence becomes clearer as the direct dependence upon resources diminishes and the separate nature of North and South Humberside in maturity of industrial structure emerges. Hull itself is not in this respect of comparable maturity with many other centres, and it may be expected that the contemporary pattern of maturity is the one towards which a developing region moves. This may not be so if a significantly different variant of the established pattern is implied by the locational and cost characteristics of the industries of accelerating importance in the country today. For this reason constant reference will continue to be made to the proportionate expenditure on raw materials and transport of particular industrial categories as well as to their profitability characteristics as indicated by value added per employee.

In terms of mean size of establishment, of newer compared to traditional industry types, and of restricted as opposed to highly connected industry, there is strong evidence that Hull and its immediate neighbourhood, as the major centre of population and with the most diverse industrial structure, has been the preferred location for all industries except iron and steel. If the future strength in industrial structure is to be contained within a framework of industrial connections consistent with the pattern that has evolved over a century, then we must envisage a variety of industries in this region that are interlocking and overlap in the production sequence extending from basic resources to final markets. And for this growth we must see the present size structure being retained for a substantial period, so that growth will be essentially proportional to size-class, with an emphasis biased to large units that have grown in recent years. The pattern of growth by industry order and the cost characteristics are not uniform for each component trade. Industry will now be regrouped by separate categories on a resource basis irrespective of industry order.

## Stages of the Production Sequence

### Bases of Allocation

Some of the data on structural details of an industry which are needed to answer questions of locational cost advantages are not available at even a regional level and are not disclosed in the case of individual firms. In national terms the Census of Production contains very important and valuable information by *MLH* category for firms employing more than twenty-five people about the value added per employee, purchase costs of raw materials, the cost of wages and the expenditure on transport. An appraisal of these three costs, taken to be the total expenditure of an establishment, provides a useful background in national terms to the maps in this chapter. The date of the 1963 Census of Production coincides with the beginning of the period for which the data used in this chapter was collected.

When the data is arranged by *SIC* in Table 24, we note that the highest proportion of total costs constituted by raw materials and fuel is in chemicals, and it is this industry that enjoys the highest added value by manufacture. The lowest value added is for clothing, but this is only just less than halfway down the scale of raw material charges, and there is no evidence of a relationship between value added per employee and the proportion of total costs constituted by raw materials and fuel. It may well have been anticipated that as labour costs increase so the costs of raw materials diminish. There is no evidence of any association between a large usage of raw materials and high transport charges; in fact, there is almost no relation whatsoever in terms of these figures for *SICs*. This shows the very substantial importance that must be attached to transport charges. Raw materials, fuel and labour are determined by factors other than location, transport charges are variable. The fact that there is comparatively little variation in charges for transport may be taken to indicate that industry adjusts to reduce it: ideally transport cost should tend to zero. Of course the figure given by the Census of Production is not a true reflection of movement costs; freight costs are included in many cases in the cost of imported raw materials, and only movement from the port to the factory is allocated to transport. There is a very close relationship between a high transport charge and a high value added.

Materials are often converted to their final form in a number of processes, and some industries such as cement-making depend directly on basic raw materials, while others, such as newspaper publishing, are producing for the final market. Some, such as dairying, combine both features. In this section, each *MLH* category is allocated to one of six classes on the basis of its being typically a first stage user of resources, a second stage user or in that class of industry for which resources have least direct significance: each major resource group is then subdivided according as the industry produces for the final market or for some other, and therefore non-final market. The proportion of total costs associated with the supply of materials and with transport was noted for each *MLH*. An analysis of these values reveals that there is a pronounced tendency for the proportion spent on both materials and transport to diminish as basic resources become of less importance and as the industry produces for final market. This trend is very markedly linear. The two facets of the classification must be considered jointly because there is clear evidence that there is no real difference between the group $A + C + E$ and $B + D + F$, that is of resource stage, distinguished on the basis of final and non-final market. But there is evidence that industries which depend least on resources do differ from classes $A$ and $C$ with respect to raw material costs, and when such class $F$ industries, such as printing of newspapers, produce for the final market, they have different transport costs from Classes $B$ and $D$, which are more closely related to resources.[4]

*First Stage Resource Using Industries*

Producing For Non-Final Demand

Figures 25 to 30 show the distribution of industry in the region according to the degree of dependence upon resources and upon final market, and this division accords with the details of the same industry types for the country as a whole. Locations are confined to the standard kilometre square of the Ordnance Survey map in which they occur, so that any location can be in error by about 700 metres, but at the scale of representation these maps are extremely accurate and any pretence of greater accuracy is precluded by the scale of reduction. If the number of establishments is less than six in one square then the precise number is shown by a standardised pattern. This sort of representation was not considered feasible for greater densities and for larger values one symbol is used, the size is graded and explained in the caption. This standardisation aids comparison of the various maps and serves to avoid any disclosure that may be unwelcome to a particular firm, although in many cases it would doubtless be seen as laudable advertisement. To avoid a confusingly large number of symbols the maps refer to establishments employing ten or more people and in this way the workplaces of the bulk of the region's labour force is considered.

The first map in this series shows those industries which process basic resources and whose products are absorbed by other industries before reaching their final form. Such industries have to spend a much larger proportion of their total expenditure on these raw materials and fuel than on labour which are always the dominant variables in industrial costs. In fact the mean expenditure of this class on raw materials is 74 per cent of their total outlay and labour constitutes a further 21 per cent. Over 150 establishments are shown in this category with a size range from 10 to over 340 employees and a density of employment ranging from 10 per square kilometre with just one factory to over 1000 in a similar area in parts of central Hull. Indeed

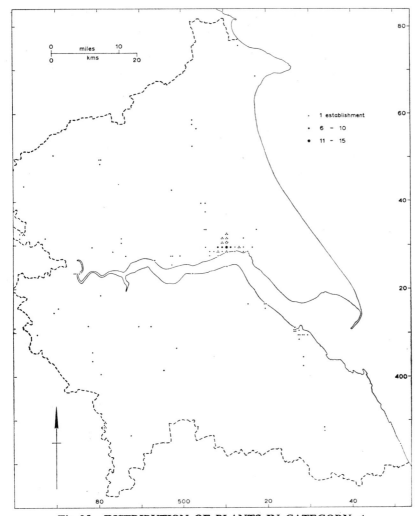

Fig 25.  DISTRIBUTION OF PLANTS IN CATEGORY *A*

This category of industries constitutes 8·62 per cent of the regional total. The mean proportion of total costs comprised by raw materials plus fuel is 74·17 per cent and by transport 4·54 per cent

there is a very plain concentration of employment in this category of industry in Hull, which contains over half the total jobs available.

Although the proportion of total employment contributed by these industries is the same locally as nationally, the allocation of importance within the various *MLH* categories involved is very different, and these differences are most instructive to an understanding of the nature of the area and indicative of the sort of development that can be expected or usefully encouraged. It is in the three classes of non-final demand—classes *A*, *C*, *E*—that the region differs most from the national pattern of employment, and the difference is most marked in this class of *first stage resource* industry. In terms of employment within this class the most important is the timber industry *MLH 471* which offers forty-five per cent of the jobs; the large firms are located near the docks at Hull and Grimsby, with smaller mobile sawmills peripatetic in the dock area. The collective buzz of saws and the shifting pattern of log stacks and cut wood is a particularly fascinating part of the dockside; the small-scale timber-using industries from packing cases for kippers to the one-man firewood vendor add to the interest. In fact timber *MLH 471* is the sixth ranking employer locally and the seventeenth nationally, an important difference, but a number of industries show much more telling discrepancies in their rank importance of employment. Animal and poultry feedstuffs *MLH 219*, coke ovens and manufactured fuel *MLH 261* and cement *MLH 464* are the most extreme differences, and there is also a substantial concentration of grain milling *MLH 211* and sugar refining *MLH 216* as compared to the national picture. Except for cement, these industry types are peculiar in that over 87 per cent of their expenditure is on raw materials and fuel and they have similar expenditures on labour and transport. Together they provide a third of the employment in this class and are concentrated in Hull. We may infer that they reflect the port advantages offered by Hull, together with the various inter-industry linkages that are most thoroughly available in this best-developed city in the area.

Cement, like timber, has a slighter expenditure on raw materials— 66 and 71 per cent respectively and both below the class mean—and a higher expenditure on transport than the four industries selected previously. It gives employment significantly higher than the national figure and on an important site, where the chalk abuts the Humber, some 500 people are employed making cement, cement slurry and whiting. This is on the north bank; there is a factory of comparable size on the south bank. The considerable expansion of construction

Page 139: (above) *Part of the production area for the manufacture of telescopic shock absorbers at* Armstrong Patents Ltd's Hull *factory which opened in 1969. This has released space at the original Beverley factory for the production of other motor components;* (below) *the finishing and painting shop at the Hull factory of* Priestman Bros Ltd, *which has a long tradition of specialisation in excavating machinery*

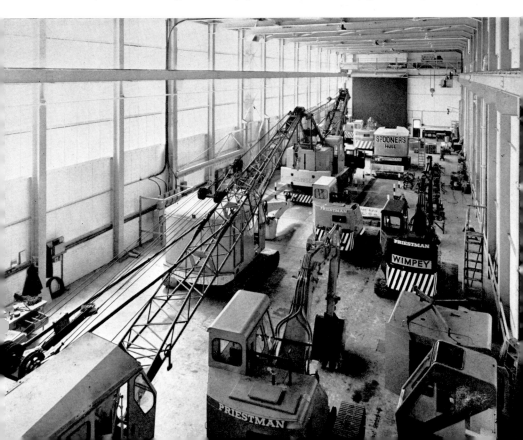

Page 140: (above) *Aerial view of Victoria Street industrial estate, Grimsby, successfully developed by the Corporation as part of its inner urban redevelopment programme: older dockside industrial premises can be seen in the foreground, and Grimsby fish docks and associated small industrial plants in the background; (below) Ladysmith Road industrial area in Grimsby, lying outside the compact pre-1914 zone of development. It contains many large plants, some connected with the fish processing and sub-zero storage for which Grimsby has been noted since the war*

for the Bransholme Housing Estate north-east of Hull and other building developments have given a notable impetus to ready-mixed concrete industries in the area, with a particularly interesting collection
lining the lower River Hull and using barge facilities for gravel and
sand deliveries from the large working in the glacial overlay of the
region. There is no shortage of such industry and materials for any
major construction work on roads or bridge.

Use of local prime resources is seen in the scatter of industries in
this class over the region. Bricks and tiles *MLH 461* are made near
Crowle on the riverside with two factories close together, each giving
over the median employment for the class. A factory near Driffield
specialises in drying and grinding grass, and there are a number of
small provender mills in the same area, one qualifying, by employing
well over ten people, for display on the map; the same firm has a flour
mill there as well. One surprising feature of these pastoral industries
is the substantial number of small enterprises, seed cleaning, provender
and grist mills, employing from one to five men; a charming relic of
a pattern of livelihood that recedes as the large establishments gravi-
tate to Hull and Grimsby.

National firms of millers and suppliers of provender, such as Ranks
and Spillers, have large plants in Hull. A similar sprinkling of these
industries is found in South Humberside, and a large tile works in
Glanford Brigg RD, a number of smaller plants not shown on the
map making bricks and tiles, a large cement works at Hibaldstow and
a stone products factory near Scawby, large provender mills in Gainsborough, and smaller ones in the countryside beyond its boundary;
these retain local labour and await new competition.

The area is distinctly unusual in its attraction to these five industry
types; within this group of industries, the principal exceptions are
textiles *MLH 412, 413, 414, 423* and mineral oil refining *MLH 262*,
but of course the recent considerable developments on the south
Humber bank will remedy this. Indeed the advantage of this particular
form of classifying industries and of providing an index of type is
that it shows there is good reason for encouraging the mineral oil
industry, as other industries of essentially the same cost structure have
been attracted to this area more than to the rest of the country. Mineral
oil refining is capital intensive, and over 95 per cent of its total expenditure is on materials, so that very little is spent on labour or transport
within the country.

One other notable feature conveniently introduced by this industry
is that these industries of exceptional local importance in this class

I

include four of the industries with the highest value added per employee and exclude three of the lowest: the textile industries. In terms of this index it seems consistent with the pattern that has emerged during the development of the area to encourage links between mineral oils, the second highest ranking industry by value added and manmade fibres and resins, value added ranks of three and fourteen respectively. The mean value added for this class as a whole is £1770 per employee, which is second of the classes behind category B at £1907, and the lowest is category C at £1104. When the data are considered in respect of each MLH within each of the six classes, there is a tendency for a significant linear diminution in value added from first stage resource industries producing for other industries to the industries in category F with consistently low values added. It is interesting to see how this region has a preference for industries in the classes with generally high values added, and that in this first class the highest ranking industries in terms of this index are very much more strongly represented regionally than nationally. This index provides a useful common basis for the two types of industry seen on this map: the typically port industries and the local resource industries.

Producing for Final Demand

This class of industries consists entirely of products for personal consumption, food, drink and tobacco, and although the last is of no importance locally, employment in these industries is twelve per cent of the regional total and more than twice the national proportion. The establishments are less widely dispersed than in the previous map and this emphasises the dominance of Hull and Grimsby in these essentially one-stage food industries. Grimsby has an importance in these industries that was lacking from the previous class, and thus reflects the basis of its growth on regional primary resources and contrasts to some extent with the far more diversified structure of Hull. These industries occupy over 170 basic unit areas with employment densities ranging from 10 to well over 3000 per square kilometre; the highest value being in Grimsby, not in Hull. In both cities there is strong clustering of these industries and adjacent areas have very high densities with over twenty establishments in the focal squares. They employ from ten people to thousands, the median number being forty.

Fish dominates this distribution, and these areas of dense employment and factory sites in Hull and Grimsby are adjacent to their fish docks. They are areas of tightly-packed streets with coastal names— from Eastbourne Street and Scarborough Street in a medley of fish-

filleting and box-making, to the more generally named Neptune Street
and its ice making—all bustling with early morning activity and
redolent of fish in various stages of preparation, in factories varying
from the very large freezing establishments of national renown to the
many small factories smoking haddock or curing cod. The largest
factory employs well over 2500 people and half of them employ more
than 40, but the common size class is less than this and there is an
interesting conjunction of the large and the new with the older and

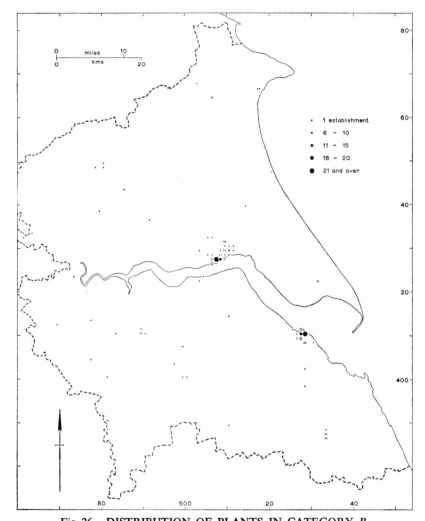

Fig 26.  DISTRIBUTION OF PLANTS IN CATEGORY *B*

This category of industries constitutes 11·72 per cent of the regional total.
The mean proportion of total costs comprised by raw materials plus fuel is
73·46 per cent and by transport 7·08 per cent

very small; one factory depending on its neighbour for ice, on another for packing cases or for fish waste to convert into animal food; small sheds for smoking and drying fish, with their flues and slatted shutters. Part of a complex of inter-industry linkage of an intimate sort, but even in 1966, when some of the original mapping was completed, the larger factories were expanding and the small blocks housing cheek-by-jowl industry were being demolished. But the activity retains its local and national importance, constituting something like sixty-five per cent of the employment in this class and exemplifying a satisfactory degree of industrial linkage. Fish provides a significant employment in the coastal resort towns, too, with the more specialised production of, for example, crab meat at a Bridlington factory.

Pastoral industries of brewing and malting are of longer standing than fish processing and traditionally they were more dispersed, culling the local barley and supplying the market towns with beer. The brewing industry like most other older industries in this country has contracted in the number of establishments and is now concentrated in the major centres, although in these, too, some breweries have recently closed, as at Grimsby. A number of malting industries of various employment sizes are still found in Gainsborough and in other market towns, but the brewing industry has contracted substantially. The industries concerned with making soft drinks or bottling wines and spirits are most vigorous in the main centre of Hull, and a number of associated service industries such as bottle washing, cork manufacture and packing cases are found close by in small premises in the older sections of the city.

The conjunction of some of the most intensely farmed lands of England with the principal centre of fish freezing almost inevitably entailed the development of an industry packaging and freezing vegetables, particularly the peas and beans for which the region is widely known. Not all these factories are in the cities; some have recently moved large packing plants into the older market centres of Lincolnshire, but the bulk remains near the Humber estuary. And as convenience dominates food purchasing and the seasonal supply of crops becomes unacceptable, we may expect this sector of local industry to expand even more rapidly in relation to national industrial growth. Over seventy-three per cent of the outlay of these industries is absorbed by raw materials and over seven per cent by transport. This reflects the relatively large areas involved in supplying industries like vegetable processing and dairying, and this has important implications for the total organisation of this region as it develops its industrial structure.

Any lessening efficiency in supplying these industries will adversely affect a set of industries that supply a much larger proportion of the labour force with work than is true for this country as a whole. The bulk of this employment is, of course, due to the fishing industry, which has relatively low transport costs, more akin to class *A* industries: this is not surprising, as the principal movement of fish is from fishing ground to port and is reflected in fish prices, not in transport. In this sense fish is similar to grain, sugar and timber.

Dairying is no more important in this region than in the nation as a whole, but any sustained increase in population could be easily accommodated by its expansion. It is a form of intensive rural land use with typically small units of production associated with metropolitan markets, and the processing of milk has a high value added. In general the dominant industries in this region are those which add considerably to the value of the material by manufacture, or which enjoy some local advantage of resource: both criteria are combined in dairying, and the stimulus of general economic growth and population increase in the region may be a catalyst. The present trend is to absorb the general surplus of liquid milk production in this country into processed forms, and the most rapid change seems to be towards dried milks. Already a number of factories with substantial employment in the rural districts are processing milk and making dried milk powders.

*Second Stage Resource Using Industries*

Producing For Non-Final Demand

Over a third of the regional labour force works in these industries, a proportion that is more than two-and-a-half times the national figure. These industries convert materials that have already been processed, and in this region, as in the country, the chemicals *MLHs 271, 273* and the iron and steel *MLH 321* categories dominate the employment, providing respectively 26 and 44 per cent of the employment represented in this stage of industry. Both have large plants, but the iron and steel industry includes what were formerly three of the largest firms in the country, United Steel, GKN and Richard Thomas and Baldwin, so that there are relatively few establishments involved in this classification, and rather more in related categories. Indeed the inclusion of these large plants is anomalous in this particular instance because the iron industry at Scunthorpe exploits a local resource of iron ore directly and so is not typical of this classification in general, which properly is a second stage resource user. The iron and steel industry does, however, spend over 76 per cent of its total costs on raw materials, a rather higher figure than the mean expenditure for all *MLHs* and 7 per cent higher than for this class of industry as a whole. This resource has encouraged a stronger cluster of industry around Scunthorpe than is seen in either of the two earlier class maps. There is a variety of foundries, from those employing less than 40 to over 250 within a short distance of each other; there are rolling and cutting

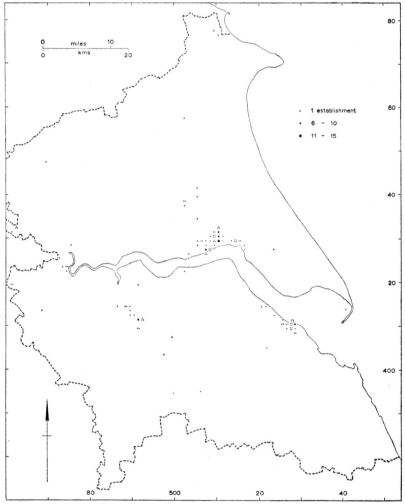

Fig 27.   DISTRIBUTION OF PLANTS IN CATEGORY *C*

This category of industries constitutes 35·70 per cent of the regional total. The mean proportion of total costs comprised by raw materials plus fuel is 69·92 per cent and by transport 4·39 per cent

shops related to the three large works, and other plants recover steel from slag, crush slag for tarmacadam, make slag cement for shot blasting, distil benzol and tar. Together these industries extend across Scunthorpe and provide a contrast with the bare areas around. In fact ten basic chemical firms have been attracted to Scunthorpe, but they are generally smaller than those along the Humber with a median size of forty employees and ranging from fifteen to eighty.

*MLH 271*, chemicals and dyes, has no establishments of the same order of size as the large iron and steel plants, but nevertheless there are a number of plants that rank within the largest twenty in the whole region and give some high employment densities of up to 2000 per square kilometre. A number of chemical firms are close to the iron factories of Scunthorpe, but the majority of them are concentrated on the Humber and especially in Hull. The mean employment density on this map is 190, and 77 squares are involved with a median density of 100. Nine firms in this group employ more than 100 people and they range from the largest firm, east of Hull, with nearly 2000 employees, to smaller firms in Goole and Selby making fertilisers and dyes. All the firms are adjacent to waterways and there are four large establishments on the south Humber bank between Immingham and Barton, three of them making fertilisers. In fact fourteen of the twenty-three firms in this category are in South Humberside and those in North Humberside are restricted to Hull or its dock extension, to Goole and Selby, and are generally smaller with the exception of the one large plant mentioned above. This class of chemicals, *MLHs 271, 273*, has a mean expenditure of 66·75 per cent on raw materials, which is rather lower than the class mean, and an expenditure of 5·5 per cent on transport which is rather higher. It is then indicative that the largest firms in the region are on Humberside and the smaller firms seem to show some spatial association with raw materials supplied conveniently and locally at Scunthorpe from coke ovens and slag.

This class of industries shows the second strongest discrepancy with the national pattern, and particular attention is due to lubricating oils *MLH 263*, paint and printing ink *MLH 274*, vegetable and animal oils and soaps *MLH 275* and synthetic resins and plastics *MLH 276*. All except this last category are very much larger employers than in the nation, and categories *274* and *275* are particularly important, ranking 17 and 13 respectively in terms of employment in this region. They differ from the chemical industry previously discussed in showing an almost complete preference for location in Hull; doubtless an historical basis can be suggested for this and particularly for category *275* with its high expenditure on raw materials of 80 per cent. There are 20 firms shown on the map as category *275* with a size range from 15 employees to just under 1000; 3 relatively small plants are in South Humberside at Grimsby, the remaining 17 are in North Humberside, with the largest near Selby, one in Beverley and the remainder in Hull. There are two principal locations. The fish oil extracting industries are on the docks or close to them, part of the complex of industries mentioned above and to be shown in a more detailed map in the next chapter. Oils derived from seed crushing are associated with the grist mills and are concentrated in a sinuous line of industries marking the course of the River Hull from its mouth to Stoneferry some three miles upstream. Some of these factories consist of multiple units concerned with separate aspects of oil refining and the making of oil cake and fertiliser, soaps and tallow extraction. They vary in size from fifteen to many hundreds of employees. In close physical association with them are firms making paints and varnishes *MLH 274*. All the plants shown are in Hull, most of them near the River Hull and the dock system. This pattern is clearly picked out by the heavier symbols and clusters of dots. Most of the plants blend oils, grind paints, extract tallow and make varnishes and lacquers, and some have extended their interests to specialist lacquers, adhesives and glass fibre moulding. Two firms are shown that specialise in the manufacture of printers' inks and one of these is located on the western outskirts of Hull in quite different surroundings from the majority.

It was announced early in 1969 that one firm of national standing in paint manufacture was to close down its Hull plant. In some ways this is contrary to the pattern of industry type in the area. The industries in this class considered so far, *MLH 263, 271, 274, 275*, all of which are of considerably more importance to employment locally than nationally, are also industries with very high value added ranks, 1, 12, 17, 8 in order, and they have the highest proportions of total costs of raw materials. The consistent association of these two variables, and their concentration in this region and especially in Hull and along Humberside, may indicate that a high value added reflects the supply of the raw materials. They generally use imported raw materials for which the transport costs beyond the port would involve an unnecessary expense of bulky materials, an idea reinforced to some extent by the general relationship between high value added and expressed transport charges.

Two other industries, rope, twine and net *MLH 416* and wood containers and baskets *MLH 475*, that are much more prevalent in the area than might be anticipated from their general importance, have a low value added and mixed proportions of raw material costs. These industries are associated with others of great importance in classes *A* and *B*, timber *MLH 471* and bacon, meat and fish *MLH 214*. All but one are in either Hull or Grimsby in close association with dockside industries making ropes and braiding nets, fixing nets, making camouflage netting or rigging. The largest plant is at Barton, on South Humberside; it spins hemp and makes ropes. Hull and Grimsby share the box and case making industry, the median size is forty employees, well under half the size for the class as a whole, and indeed the biggest firm, which is in Hull, is little larger than the class median. Clearly these are not growth industries and cannot be expected to provide expanded employment, but they are interesting examples of links between strong primary resource industry and subsequent stages in the production sequence. This feature of industry is less strongly developed than in the larger industrial complexes of, say, Manchester and Birmingham. The association between the various elements of the chemical industry could perhaps be an important development. At present the link is with paints, oils and fats and there is no strong development to plastics or to man-made fibres, both of which are included in this class of second stage resource users. Plastics provide negligible employment and this contrasts with the national employment opportunity, where it is of median and increasing importance. The largest establishment near this region is at Stamford Bridge, another makes plastics for thermal insulation, and two are concerned with fibreglass. Man-made fibres *MLH 411* are a greater source of employment than in the country, concentrated into one firm on South Humberside, just outside Grimsby. Recent developments in the fibre market indicate that Courtaulds intend to strengthen their already considerable contribution to their production, and this is the sort of industrial development that has been attracted to this area, an industry with high value added, the third highest nationally, and a relatively high proportion of expenditure on materials, some seventy-two per cent.

A further example from this section of an industry with high value added and material costs greater than the mean is paper and board *MLH 481* which provides only the level of local employment expected from the national value. In national terms this industry shows a strong tendency to locate adjacent to sources of raw material, and for the majority of papers this implies a location that is on an estuary or navigable river. Two paper mills are shown on Figure 27, one at

Grimsby and the other at Selby. The association and development of industry on south Thames-side has many features of similarity with Humberside, especially in chemicals and cement works, but on the Thames there is the largest collection of papermills in the country and it is this industry that is most weakly developed on the Humber. The projected expansion of population in Humberside would provide an enlarged local market and increase the supply of waste paper, a raw material that is becoming of considerable importance and that is basic to the papermaking firm at Selby. Local timber from the extensive afforestation in the Yorkshire Moors could be a useful incentive, as recent reports from mills that are using domestic or imported pulp wood at Fort William and at Ellesmere Port are encouraging.

Producing for Final Demand

This class of industries contrasts sharply with the preceding class. In particular there is only half the employment provided by the same industries in the nation, 6·25 per cent compared with 12·59. This slighter importance is reflected in a lower incidence of areas with such industries, 49 rather than 77, less than 100 establishments with a median employment density of 120 per square kilometre and a maximum density below 850. Again there is a concentration in Hull, with over a third of the establishments and the highest densities, although there is a large plant near Grimsby. Raw materials are the lowest item of their expenditure, nearly forty per cent being spent on labour. They are also uniformly low ranking in terms of the value added by manufacture, with only three categories greater than the median for all *MLHs*, namely carpets *MLH 419*, other textiles *MLH 429* and shop and office fittings *MLH 474*. The first two are of negligible importance to the employment structure of the area and are significantly below the national employment level, while *MLH 474* provides practically the same level.

In fact there is a closer relationship of the rank importance to the area and their rank importance nationally among this class of industries than is found in any other class and one interesting departure is found in the clothing and millinery industry *MLHs 441–9* whose importance does not compare with its national importance as an employer. The industry's establishments are equally divided between North and South Humberside, but in terms of employment South Humberside dominates with over seventy-five per cent of the total. Two important plants making children's clothing and lightwear are at Thorne, there are five establishments in the Scunthorpe area and one very substantial firm with a number of factories in the region makes up hosiery. There is an important tailoring factory at Goole and equally important factories located at Gainsborough and Immingham. In North Humberside most establishments are in Hull, but they are relatively small and the largest factories are in Driffield, Bridlington and Selby. Many of the emigré European Jews who established such important clothing workshops in Leeds in the nineteenth century stopped only briefly in Hull, a principal port of entry, and today there

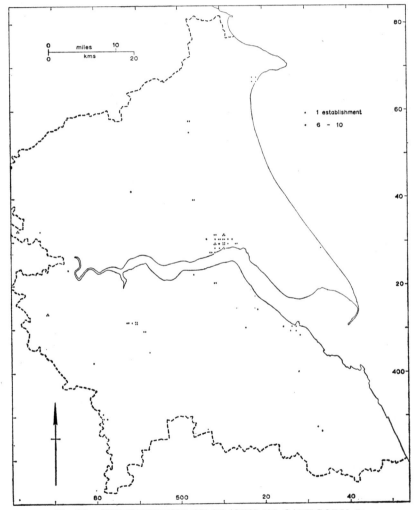

Fig 28.  DISTRIBUTION OF PLANTS IN CATEGORY *D*

This category of industries constitutes 6·24 per cent of the regional total. The mean proportion of total costs comprised by raw materials plus fuel is 58·12 per cent and by transport 4·44 per cent

is slight reminder of their settlement there. Typical of the fabric industries, clothing has practically the lowest value added by manufacture, and in this sense its absence from the area is consistent. The rest of the fabric industries in this class provide a rather slighter proportion of work in this region than in the nation as a whole, but in some of the smaller market towns these factories have considerable importance. At Market Weighton there is Allard Exclusive Knitwear which provides substantial employment, bedspreads are made at Bridlington, a large factory well above median size for the class makes textile small wares, knitwear is made at Louth and a large factory at Brigg makes stockings. Seven establishments, employing from sixteen to forty, are grouped in Hull, and the largest firms in this set of fabric categories makes belting and related narrow fabrics.

All these industries are directed to the final market and in general may well be associated with the larger towns and with metropolitan areas. These industries are lacking in most of the region but are found in such traditional market centres as Market Weighton and Louth. In particular we can note the gravitation of this class of industries to Hull, indicative of the urban, market-directed nature of what are essentially labour intensive industries in terms of costs. A third of the employment in this class is in the bread and flour confectionery category *MLH 212*; this sort of manufacture, with less than ten employees is very common and is found in practically all the centres, and there are also many large establishments supplying the surrounding rural areas. For example, one moderately large bakery in Beverley supplies bread over most of the Beverley Rural District, the western suburbs of Hull and parts of other RDs. Transport, at 12 per cent, constitutes a relatively very high proportion of total costs, and yet we must assume that these overall proportions are deliberately depressed towards a practical minimum by manufacturers, and this relatively high value indicates the difficulty of reducing the cost of transport in common with brick making and brewing. Such industries are ubiquitous and for this area as a whole the industry shows no significant difference in employment from the rest of the country. Nor indeed do *MLH* categories *213* biscuits or *214* cocoa, chocolate and sugar confectionery, but they do differ markedly from *MLH 212* in their transport costs of 5·77 and 4·30 per cent respectively, and in their distribution which is far more concentrated. The three largest employers in category *MLH 214* are in Hull, with establishments also at Driffield and in Grimsby. Only one firm, a very large one, shown on this map on South Humberside, near Grimsby, makes biscuits.

*Resources of Least Direct Importance*

Producing for Non-Final Demand

Almost thirty per cent of the region's labour force is employed in these industries, but this is only two-thirds of its importance nationally. It is under-represented in this area and shows the third highest discrepancy with the national figure in rank importance of employ-

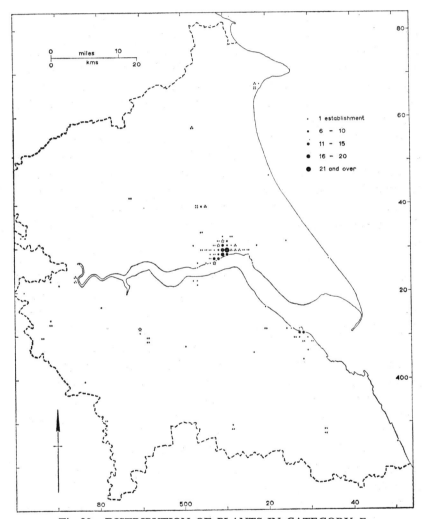

Fig 29.  DISTRIBUTION OF PLANTS IN CATEGORY *E*

This category of industries constitutes 28·50 per cent of the regional total. The mean proportion of total costs comprised by raw materials plus fuel is 59·98 per cent and by transport 3·23 per cent

ment. In many ways these industries are typical of large urban complexes such as the areas around Birmingham and Manchester, because in such complexes industries benefit from close links with other stages of the same production sequence, with other industries that provide services, packaging materials or component parts. These tend to be labour intensive, typically with forty per cent of their costs paid in wages, and transport costs that are substantially below those of any preceding class of industry. These factors are intimately associated with their location in large industrial cities and with the pattern on this map. There are well over 300 establishments occupying 97 areas with a median employment density of 100 and a range from ten to 2500 people per square kilometre; the greatest number of establishments is found in Hull and the general dominance of this city in terms of the employment is considerable. But Beverley is more marked than in earlier maps, Grimsby is of clear importance, and Scunthorpe is also readily recognisable.

Some of the industries on this map are major sources of employment regionally and in the wider national picture. The whole gamut of the engineering industry *SIC VI* is included; it represents the third ranking source of local employment and occupies prime place nationally, providing a third of the employment in this sector. In some ways this is an unfair comparison, because a number of *MLHs*, the basic unit used in this analysis, have been grouped together to reduce the detail of what is in many ways a usefully homogeneous industry. The conjunction of electronic engineering in the communications industry with the non-ferrous foundry will be an unhappy marriage to some, but in the local context their location pattern is comparable. *MLH* category *370*, shipbuilding and repair, constitutes an *SIC* class, too, and these two sectors of industry have a lot of common features and show a considerable degree of interdependence. The specialist use of brass in shipbuilding and the development of navigational aids exemplify the conjunction indicated above. Shipbuilding is the fifth ranking employment category and is rather more important than its national position at ninth.

Engineering is concentrated in North Humberside with over two-thirds of the total number of plants, and more than three-quarters of these are in Hull. The industry is more widely spread south of the Humber with Grimsby, Scunthorpe and Gainsborough having similar numbers of establishments and Goole, Barton and Brigg each with at least one plant. South of the Humber the median size of the engineering industry is forty employees. The large establishments are in Gainsborough, with factories making packing machinery, steam and oil engine boilers, and in Thorne where AEI has a large factory making light power electric motors. Four factories in these two towns offer forty per cent of the employment in this *SIC* group and over ten per cent of the employment in this class. Elsewhere in South Humberside the plants are generally of less than the median size. In North Humberside the median size is twenty employees and nearly two-thirds of this is concentrated in the ten establishments employing more than 100 people, the largest being in Hull. The association with the needs of other local industries is seen in one firm that makes oil-cake hydraulic pressing machinery and located near to the line of oil-cake factories on the River Hull, another making pulleys and speed reducers, others making scales, boilers and fish processing machinery. There are scores of plants employing from 30 to 3 or 4 people concentrated in the area near the River Hull and behind the docks and engaged in making and repairing equipment for class *A*, *B* and *C* industries; small plants but often specialised. The traditional market towns such as Market Weighton, Driffield and Beverley have a preponderance of agricultural machinery factories ranging from below the median size to some seventy or more employees, while at Bridlington a firm makes amusement machines.

Although shipbuilding *MLH 370* is important in the area, it is not of course, comparable in type with the large yards on Tyneside or on the Scottish estuaries. It is related to fishing boat repair, building trawlers, tugs and barges, small coastal vessels, especially tankers and also smaller pleasure craft. Two-thirds of the establishments are in North Humberside and with only four exceptions, less than one-tenth of the total, the industry is shown in Hull on the map. Half of these establishments employ forty people or more, they cling to the waterside, often in older docks that are not used for the basic commerce of the port of Hull and are owned or associated closely with the large fish trawling enterprises and the shipping lines based in Hull. The shipyard at Beverley has provided an important source of employment for the borough and has had to combat the problems of its lack of a deep water access to the Humber as the demand for larger ships has increased. In South Humberside there are fewer boat yards; the majority of them are in Grimsby, their median size is thirty employees and the largest are at Immingham and Goole, with another large establishment at Grimsby associated with the fishing industry's trawlers.

Three industries have an unusually large proportion of the labour force when compared with the pattern in the country: cans and metal boxes *MLH 395*, pharmaceuticals and toilet preparations *MLH 272* and leather tanning *MLH 431*. Together they employ eighteen per cent of the labour force in this class. The branch of the chemicals industry appropriate to each class will probably emerge as an unusually large employer in the region and will have one of the highest value added scores; in this instance it is the highest, ranking tenth over all *MLHs* followed by rubber *MLH 491* ranking twenty-sixth, and only four others in this class are of higher than median rank. The largest employers are Smith & Nephew and J. Reckitts, firms of national reputation and large by standards greater than that operative in this region. In this category there are other large and important firms at Hull, Rawcliffe and near Grimsby.

In contrast the two other industries have low value added scores ranking 66 for *MLH 395* and 73 for *MLH 431*. Essentially the leather tanning industry is confined to North Humberside and is concentrated in Beverley and in Hull, where one tannery in the north of the city employs rather more than the median for the class and has an associated manufactory of leather goods. The other tannery is on the River Hull and specialises in heavy leathers: a more expected location for an industry with 79·51 per cent of its expenditure on raw materials, the second highest in the class after *MLHs 321, 322*, and very much higher than the class mean of 60 per cent. Further up the River Hull at Beverley is the largest tannery in the area, employing many hundreds of people and traditionally one of the most important sources of work in that charming borough since the mid-nineteenth century. The development of extracts such as glue and gelatine was incorporated into the firm's structure during the early twentieth century as a natural by-product which was not exploited by any other local firm.

Metal canisters provide well below median employment nationally, but rank eleventh regionally. In fact the three establishments shown are all in Hull; two are just below median size and the largest, the Metal Box Company, is nearly ten times larger than these. In contrast to the metal canister industry is the lack of any substantial employment in paper packaging manufacture *MLH 482*, which is of negligible importance compared with its national labour force. The sort of developments in papermaking indicated earlier, typical of the Thames estuary, may well encourage associated paper-using industries of the same order of importance as in south-eastern England. Other industries that are severely under-represented are glass *MLH 463* and plastic

Page 157: (above) *Keadby Bridge across the Trent near Scunthorpe, showing the flat warplands of the Isle of Axholme. The riverside wharves and storage facilities form a Trentside industrial 'foyer' for Scunthorpe, along with similar facilities downriver at Flixborough and Burton Stather;* (below) *Lysaght's Normanby Park iron and steel works, sited well away from the built-up area of Scunthorpe*

Page 158: (above) *Production of industrial fastenings at the Grovehill estate factory at Beverley of Armstrong Patents, a relatively recent diversification away from dependence on motor components; (below) manufacturing gear unit components at the Hull factory of J. H. Fenner & Co, which produces power transmission equipment. The firm is representative of a varied range of engineering industries in Hull, many of whom have their origins in the nineteenth century*

mouldings and fabricating *MLH 496*. The former may well remain absent, but the development of a plastics industry in association with similar, adjacent industries in the production sequence is a likely change. At present it ranks forty-seventh in the area compared with twenty-third in the country, and its share of employment has accelerated in recent years.

Hull's dominance of this class of industry is considerable. It is the only centre providing the variety of industry and services on which such development depends, and emphasises the inferences made above in terms of the cost structure of the industry. Grimsby also shows some interrelation between industries, but the association is less mature than in Hull, being more closely dependent on fishing and ship repair. Beverley is seen most clearly on this map, a reflection of its established shipyard and leather industry, as well as its large lead smelting works. A feature of large cities and their industrial structure is that a complex of industry has properties that are emergent, that are greater than the simple composition of the individual enterprises, and in this sense, too, Hull is unique in this region. In contrast, some of the largest establishments are not in Hull, but exist almost in isolation at smaller centres such as Thorne and Goole. Large plants do not necessarily entail the close network of interdependent manufactures that is the epitome of the metropolis. It is interesting to note the greater sense of maturity in the older centres such as Gainsborough, and in Beverley where the problem may well be one of sustaining growth, but this may well be easier than initiating it.

Producing for Final Demand

Industries more closely linked to markets than to identifiable sources of raw material are shown on this map. The region has rather less employment in this sector than is nationally the case, providing 9 per cent compared to 14 per cent of the employment. The number of jobs offered is similar to the number in class *A*, but their distributions contrast markedly. This industry class is confined to 50 establishments and 35 squares, a third the number of firms and nearly a third of the areas. The median employment of forty is very similar, but the range is from 10 to some 5,000 or so and is very much greater than the range in class *A*. The general pattern is for most areas to contain only one establishment; only eight have more, and half of these are in Hull.

A reasonably close association of employment importance exists between the rank of these industries regionally and nationally. In both, the highest ranks are to motor vehicles *MLH 381*, ranking seventh in

K

the region and second nationally and to aircraft *MLH 383*, ranking sixth and eighth. The aircraft industry at Brough, west of Hull, has received a considerable fillip from recent orders. Employment has increased substantially since 1965 and is drawn from a wide area of the East Riding. It has had a history of fluctuating employment levels since its inception by a Leeds firm in the early twentieth century.[5] Amalgamation and war have resulted in both expansion and subsequent contraction, together with an increasing tendency to depend

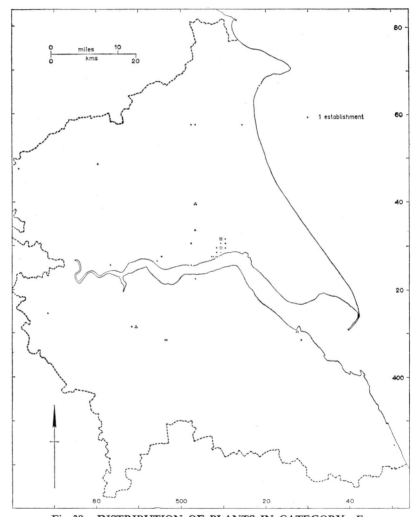

Fig 30.  DISTRIBUTION OF PLANTS IN CATEGORY  *F*

This category of industries constitutes 9·22 per cent of the regional total. The mean proportion of total costs comprised by raw materials plus fuel is 61·44 per cent and by transport 2·24 per cent

on one aspect of aircraft production. It is an industry notoriously dependent on national decisions and international competition, but, while some measure of stability is assured, it provides employment of very considerable importance. Similarly the assembly of motor vehicles has a history of substantial fluctuation, but in this region employment in *MLH* category *381* is confined to motor vehicle components and caravan manufacture. Coachbuilding provides employment for six per cent of the labour force in this category; the largest firm is at Market Weighton, and smaller firms have factories at Broughton in South Humberside and at Beverley.

Other works employing less than ten people are involved in the repairs and small-scale engineering related to garages that are, of course, of importance in most cities. From one such small workshop in Beverley the production of shock absorbers grew into the firm of Armstrong Patents, which employs rather less than 2000 people and is the largest single source of employment in the town. The firm's expansion, as part of the general expansion of the motor vehicle industry, has been considerable. Indeed making components for this industry constitutes 69 per cent of the employment in this category. A further 25 per cent is provided by the manufacture of caravans, a sector which has recently begun to expand rapidly. This industry is focused on Hull and most of the factories are in the newer industrial developments in north-east Hull or in the generally residential area of Haltemprice. One firm is recorded on the map at Bridlington. Timber provides a large proportion of the raw material for caravans, and this association may partly explain its considerable concentration in this region; certainly the pattern seems to be one of local diffusion in a favourable environment.

Of the industries that are much more poorly represented than anticipated, two seem worthy of note. They are the manufacture of domestic electric goods *MLH 365*, which ranks thirty-seventh nationally and fifty-eighth locally with a relatively high value added rank of twenty-seventh, and the printing and publishing of newspapers and periodicals *MLH 486*, which ranks twelfth nationally, thirtieth regionally, and sixteenth in order of value added, the highest figure in this class. Both categories may well be expected to expand through the substantial increase in population that is assumed in planning proposals for this area.

As a whole, this class of industry tends to have high labour costs, the mean expenditure for *MLH* category *365* being about 36 per cent, and that for *MLH 486* fifty-three per cent, and this class has the lowest mean expenditure on transport. Many of these industries appear to be labour intensive and dependent on the complex of industries in urban areas for their materials and on concentration of population for labour and a market. Apart from jewellery *MLH 396*, with over 95 per cent of its expediture on materials, the motor vehicles category has the unusually high value of 78 per cent, 18 per cent higher than the mean for the group.

### *Summarising the Location Tendencies*

There is a general level of agreement between the relative importance of the various industrial categories to employment levels in this region when compared with their national importance. In this sense the region shows a small scale reflection of the national industrial structure. But there are differences; in this chapter we have examined both the discrepancies and the similarities, and where there are similarities we have put particular emphasis on the industries that offer substantial employment such as chemicals *MLH 271*, iron and steel *MLH 311* and engineering *SIC VI*. Other general aspects of industry were discussed, and in particular, industrial expenditure was allocated to raw materials plus fuel, wages and transport, because if any hypotheses concerning this region's industry and the national industrial structure are to be made they will include such factors as orientation to materials, a preference for large urban markets, or minimised transport costs. The available figures do not permit any definitive statement of such allegiance for any particular *MLH* nor for a given establishment in local or more general terms. But certain general regularities were noted earlier and these patterns of relationship have been carefully presented in terms of the regional industries employing ten or more people. To enable such preferences for materials or markets to be recognised and accepted, the whole range of industries was partitioned to give six classes, graded according to their use of resources and their directness of marketing. One further aspect of industry was used systematically as a reasonable indication of its profitability: the value added per employee by manufacture.

In each class some of the industries showed a much higher level of employment locally than nationally. An analysis of the frequency of such discrepancies encourages the statement that there is a tendency for this region to be most attractive to industries in classes *A*, *B* and *C* (is first stage resource using industries producing for non-final demand and final demand and second stage resource using industries producing for non-final demand) and that no real difference in preference seems evident within that subset of classes or within the remaining subset *DEF*. There is some reason, too, to suppose that class *D* is ambivalent in its allegiance. A division of the six classes into two subsets based on material orientation, that is classes *ACE* as opposed to *BDF*, the final demand set, is unwarranted on this evidence. There is also some reasonable evidence for supposing that a linear trend relates the progressive preference from class *A* to class *F*. The situation is, of course, not simple; the region is itself heterogeneous, and its comparison with the nation in terms of these classes is complicated by industrial links within *SICs* when *MLH* categories within a particular *SIC* fall into different classes. In this way an *SIC* group particularly strong in an *MLH* category in class *A* can engender strong links in later classes to a degree that may be contrary to the general pattern; chemicals are a case in point. In a converse sense a very weakly represented *SIC* can obscure the more common occurrence and this seems the case in *SIC X*, textiles, with respect to class *A*.

Industries with discrepantly high regional employment levels show a very strong tendency to spend more on raw materials and fuel than the mean for their class, and less on transport costs, which, in our view, is consistent with general concepts of port based industries.

The region also seems particularly attractive to industries with a high value added by manufacture, and the strongest partition of the industries in this respect is into classes *ABC* which dominate this preference. This dominance is reflected by a linear tendency for value added to diminish from *A* to *F* significantly more sharply than is generally the case for all industry. Regularities such as these encouraged the emphasis given in the discussion of the maps to particular sequences of industry that seem worth noting as possible sources of future development. Not that there is any real reason for going counter to the prevailing pattern in an effort to diversify the economy of the region and avoid what to some may seem to be weaknesses; this is an unresolvable argument at this stage of understanding.

Hull dominates the present industrial pattern; most industry has gravitated to Hull or has been stimulated to develop there. In many ways this progressive dominance is regenerative. Any flow of the economic bases of this attractiveness would be encouraged by improved communications. In this respect most readers will have noted how often the largest plants in a particular category are on the south bank of the Humber as a part of the line of newer industry extending west from Grimsby and complementing a similar and older development

east of Hull. Contact between these could well prove extremely bene-
ficial. The existing patterns of industrial relationship and of diverse
employment opportunity have established themselves gradually and
future developments can ignore these patterns only wastefully. Industrial development is relatively slow, very expensive and makes stringent
auxiliary demands on an area; new centres are not typically spon-
taneous in their establishment, and their gradual development distinct
from established centres may prove unnecessarily expensive. Industry
in the past has spread, and we have only to note the changes in
density around the nodes in this region to see that it is a continuing
feature of industrial change. The clearer recognition of the current
directions of diffusion is the important task.

References to this chapter are on pages 225–6

# 5

# Industrial Patterns within the Region

INDUSTRIAL DEVELOPMENT is principally contained by the region's towns; this has emerged as the dominant feature of the maps presented in the previous chapters. The association of town and factory is common to the rest of the country, but in many industrial areas neighbouring towns have fused to give a complex amalgam of industries which needs subdividing for a proper understanding. The isolation of industrial centres is convincingly expressed by the density of manufacturing employment within Humberside (Fig. 14). It is a large region of approximately 5,350 square kilometres, but of these only 228 contain significant industrial activity, with a combined employment of some 105,000. This intensity of industrial employment stands in sharp contrast to the West Midlands conurbation with 429 square kilometres containing manufacturing establishments that together employ 529,000 workers in a far smaller region of 700 square kilometres.[1] Thus about twice the number of grid squares employ five times as many workers. This emphasises the difference between one of Britain's most intensive and well-established industrial regions and an emergent manufacturing region with lower employment densities. In the West Midlands Johnson simplified the industrial pattern by isolating ten sub-regions in the conurbation, of which the Central Birmingham sub-region employed nearly 140,000 workers with a mean density of 5,770 workers per square kilometre.

The situation in Humberside is simpler, the pattern more readily distinguished, the towns stand by themselves in a firm rural setting, so that any subdivision of industrial character coincides with particular towns. Some rudimentary mixing of neighbouring settlements is occurring along South Humber bank as industries develop between Immingham and Grimsby, linking the factories in Greatcoates with

the newer establishments at Killingholme. But this riparian development is newly fashioned and cannot warrant sub-regional status
although the novelty and character of its industries are considered in
detail. This south Humber bank zone is taken to extend northwards
to include Barton and a great deal of land which as yet has not been
affected by post-war industrialisation, but where future growth is a
strong possibility; an incipient sub-region. An attentuated, estuarine
strip of industrial development is noticeable on both sides of Hull
from Brough in the west to Salt End downstream, and the reclamation
of land for industry as far as Spurn point, proposed in the Feasibility
Study, would accentuate this pattern. Scunthorpe is separated from
its nearest urban neighbours by mile upon mile of fields and it has no
obvious peripheral developments; in this chapter Scunthorpe is
extended to include Trentside, where a number of interesting developments are taking place. Elsewhere in Humberside, manufacturing has
a punctiform distribution at low levels of density, and only Goole,
Selby, Beverley and Gainsborough reach densities as high as those
found in the principal towns. They stand in an intermediate class of
their own, above centres like Louth or Driffield, but less industrialised
than the larger towns. These older market towns preserve the impression of a town-country symbiosis, although in fact they show a
diminishing dependence upon agrarian industry: Gainsborough with
its large engineering factories or Beverley with its motor vehicle components. The character of these towns has been discussed in Chapter
4; the essential division in the present chapter is between the Hull
area on the one hand, and Grimsby with South Humber bank and
Scunthorpe on the other. Some of their industrial characteristics are
summarised below.

DISTRIBUTION OF INDUSTRY IN HULL, GRIMSBY AND SCUNTHORPE

| Sub-region | Number of kilometre squares with manufacturing | Total Employment to nearest 1,000 |
| --- | --- | --- |
| Hull[1] | 70 | 46,000 |
| Grimsby and South Humberside | 35 | 16,000 |
| Scunthorpe | 17 | 22,000 |

[1] Including extensions to Salt End, Brough, also Beverley. The employment is
calculated from HM Factory Inspectorate returns for establishments employing > 10
persons.

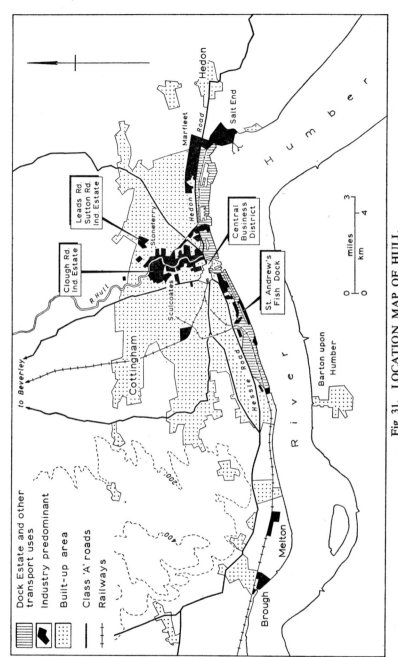

**Fig 31. LOCATION MAP OF HULL**

This map shows the elements of Hull and its immediate region from Brough to Salt End. The principal places referred to in the text are shown, and so is the Central Business District, *CBD*. This map provides a context for the more detailed maps of Fig 32

**North Humberside**

*Hull*

In Hull the densest areas of manufacturing employment and of establishments are aligned along the Humber and the river Hull; the intensity of employment opportunity diminishes rapidly away from this inverted T junction, and the general framework of this industrial pattern is provided by Figure 31. When axes are taken along grid lines, the median centres of employment and establishments occur in central Hull near intersection 10,29 just above the site of the early Queen's dock and near Wincolmlee, the street running along the western bank of the river Hull, whereas the mean centre of employment crosses the river because of the effect of the large factories in east Hull near the newer docks. When industry is expressed as a generalised block in this fashion many interesting facets of locational preference are obscured.

Specialisation Within Hull

There is some evidence of industrial specialisation within different parts of the borough. To illustrate this the concentration of five industries is shown in Figure 32. These maps show the focuses of attraction in Hull for its most distinctive and important industries as well as some interesting features of its industrial development. To facilitate this sense of historical perspective, one map is adapted from some early nineteenth-century plans of Hull. The most immediate impression of these maps is the common pattern of occurrence along the river Hull, on the St. Andrew's fish dock and behind the newer docks to the east of the confluence of the Hull and the Humber. The intensity of allegiance to these three manufacturing areas changes from map to map. Part of the change and indeed part of the pattern depends on the use of a kilometre square grid in assembling the data, but in both there is some approach to the real situation of employment density.

Each industry shows a high degree of concentration in terms of the proportion of total employment found in the proportion of kilometre squares containing that industry. This concentration reflects the persistence of the factors that encouraged the initial location of those firms that survived and grew to become the dominant sources of contemporary employment. The founders of many of these firms were attracted to the area from other regions in the nineteenth century and set up in small businesses using imported raw materials or local resources. They were essentially attracted to the areas flanking the River Hull above the lower reach referred to in the early nineteenth century

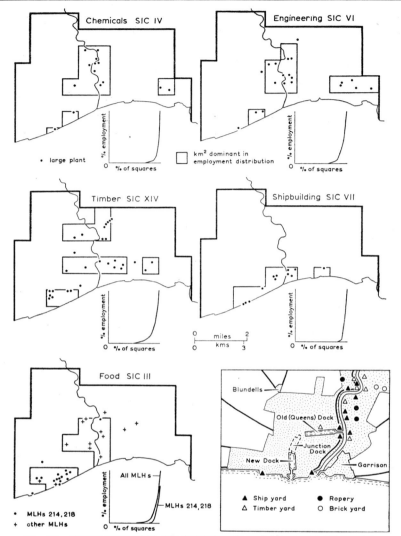

Fig 32.  DISTRIBUTION OF SELECTED INDUSTRIES IN HULL
Over 650 establishments are represented by these maps and graphs. The combination of the important squares, the location of large plants and the graphs showing concentration by area of employment in each *SIC* order characterises the employment pattern of industry in Hull. The map of early nineteenth-century Hull *(bottom right)* is derived from the map published by Scraggs in 1817

as the *old harbour*. The character of this area is seen in the map in Figure 32, and the elements of the present industrial structure are contained in a description of 1796 referring to this riverside as

one of the most busy streets in or near Hull, in which there are three wind oil mills, one . . . worked by a steam engine, besides horse mills

for the same purpose, a wind saw mill . . . ; a steam engine flour mill
. . . This is truly a curious piece of mechanism, consumes about a
chaldron of coals in twelve hours, works four pair of stones and throws
off a vast quantity of flour in a little time. There are likewise in this
neighbourhood dry docks and ship yards, where many hands are constantly employed, a large porter brewery, an iron foundry, greenland
houses, tar houses where pitch is made and a sugar house, so that
business is carried on in this street to a vast extent. (Tickell 1798)

Chemicals

Here, then, are the origins of the modern distribution of chemical
manufacturing establishments bordering both sides of the river Hull.
The industry is more strongly represented on the eastern side, and this
is exemplified by the location of the large chemical plants that employ
ninety or more people. The oil-cake mills lie on this side of the river
on the same reach that, in Scraggs' map of 1817, was the site of the
*Greenland yards* where whale blubber was rendered to oil. This
industry now has a few large firms, dominated by the amalgamation
at the end of the nineteenth century of a number of national firms and
known as the British Oil and Cake Mills. The development of the
seed-crushing factories probably arose from the trade links with north
European countries which were an important source of linseed in the
early nineteenth century. This was a typically small-scale industry,
able to use old corn mills and hired machinery so that a large number
of people felt encouraged to start oil-seed crushing; many firms were
short-lived and few have survived. In fact some figures suggest that
of the more than 140 firms since 1800, 62 were in business for under
5 years and only 8 survived for over 50 years.[2]

Hull has been a principal centre of this industry for over a century
and the development of engineering firms to repair and to make
machinery for crushing seeds may be regarded as an expected adjunct:
particularly as local industrialists experimented with early innovations
such as the steam-engine and Bramah's hydraulic press. Indeed a Hull
paper mill was the first to use steam power and other iron founders
developed steam-powered machinery for seed crushing. One firm,
Rose, Downs and Thompson,[3] emerged during the late nineteenth
century to dominate the production of hydraulic presses for national
and international markets. This firm continues to make an important
contribution to the employment and character of engineering in the
city. A number of firms have been involved in the distillation of tur-
pentine, the processing of smalts and ultramarine and the production
of resins, all related to imported raw materials. The combination of

linseed oil and pigments provided the basis for the early development
of a paint industry in Hull, and the link between oil-seed crushing and
paint manufacture is exemplified by the firm of Blundell-Permoglaze,
whose founder, H. Blundell, applied the principle of Bramah's hydraulic
press to oil-seed processing in the period from 1830 to 1833.[4] His
interest in oil-seed crushing was sold to Barker and Smith in 1837,
and, with his cousin, Blundell concentrated on the manufacture of
paints, first at an old grain mill on the corner of Beverley Road and
Spring Bank and subsequently at the modern site on the west bank
of the river Hull. The region was well placed for the production of
natural resins as the basis for paint-making, and the later development
of artificial resins is consistent with the strong local chemical industry.

The density of employment in the chemical industry increases downstream and is particularly high just south east of the river Hull where
the firm of Reckitt and Colman is sited. This firm was founded in 1840
by I. Reckitt, who moved from Nottingham to Hull, purchased a
starch-making business on the east of the river and laid the basis for
this very large firm.[5] Its development depended on starch and polishes
until the late 1920s, when it entered the pharmaceutical trade and its
subsequent history is one of expansion, of amalgamation with J. & J.
Colman in 1938 and the diversity of trading interests this entailed.
Another branch of the pharmaceutical industry giving even higher
employment densities is near the Princes dock area at the Smith and
Nephew factory, manufacturing bandages, elastoplast and other surgi-
cal dressings. T. J. Smith, the founder, came from Lincolnshire as a
chemist and his first business attempts were in refining cod-liver oil to
make it more palatable. He succeeded, his product was widely
acclaimed and his business expanded. His nephew had been appren-
ticed to a draper and woollen manufacturer but joined his uncle in 1896
and used his knowledge of textiles to develop the production of surgi-
cal dressings; two world wars and developments in hygiene encouraged
the expansion of demand for these products.[6] The firm has grown
substantially, diversifying its interests within pharmaceuticals and is
a most important source of employment in Hull. The extension of
industry along the estuary is seen by the location of Humbrol Ltd at
Marfleet. This firm was founded in 1919 in central Hull to make
bicycle and lamp oils and the manufacture of enamel paint for bicycles
was introduced in the 1930s. The need for cellulose lacquers was
stimulated by the war, the expanded business was moved to the present
large site in 1947, and it continues to grow as the market for model-
ling accessories, adhesives and light oils grows. Further east, beyond

the borough boundary, is the considerable complex of chemical industries provided by British Petroleum at Salt End.

Engineering

A similar pattern of distribution is seen in the engineering trades, but the degree of concentration is rather less. Over a third of the sixty-two kilometre squares included in each map have some engineering establishment, but many of these are rather small, employing less than ten people. This industry is often associated with other trades and this is why it is located along the river Hull and around the docks: reference has been made earlier to businesses making oil-seed crushing and fish-processing machinery. Some of the small engineering firms failed to provide the nucleus for expansion, others expanded but remained as ironmongers; for example S. & H. King were toolmakers who serviced grist-mill machinery and this firm continues today in the general ironmongery trade of supply and repair. East of the river, towards Hedon on the open land behind the large, modern docks, a number of very substantial engineering firms have large factories. W. D. Priestman started as a general engineer in premises in James Street, central Hull, in 1870 and one of his first orders was to install oil-seed presses at the Driffield Linseed Cake Company. But in 1875 he received an order from one Thomas Cristy in London for a winch to work a *clamshell* grab to search for bullion underwater. He made a number of these grabs and the cranes to work them and they were used to discharge such commodities as grain and coal; a number of patents were entered for grapple-buckets and forks and the firm made a grab-dredger for the Hull Dock Company in 1878.[7] This basis for the firm's future expansion was interrupted by the development of an oil engine in 1885 which was widely used until replaced by Diesel's invention. From 1900 the firm concentrated on grabs and excavators to become the large enterprise of today with over 1200 employees and a large export trade.

In Marfleet, but nearer to Hull, is another large and important firm, J. H. Fenner, whose development illustrates the expansion of local firms to national and international stature. The business was established in 1861 in central Hull to make leather belting for power transmission from steam engines. The founder came from London, but his family had a leather business and close family associations with John Holmes and the Hodgson family, who established respectively the large tanneries at Hull and at Beverley. This provided his knowledge of leather and a ready supply of hides, and while leather was the basic raw material the cost of resources represented eighty-eight per cent of the total expenditure.[8] This relatively high cost of materials is a consistent feature of successful industries in this region as noted already in Chapter 4. Steam was adopted by many industries as the prime motive power during the second half of the nineteenth century and Fenner's business expanded; some of the earliest sales were to Marshalls of Gainsborough for belt-drives for threshing machines. In 1890 the firm bought eighteen acres of land at Marfleet, three miles from Hull and well over a mile from its nearest houses, over twenty years before the King George V dock was built, anticipating a trend whose importance is increasingly recognised. The buildings on this site were destroyed during World War II and the business transferred to other factories in northern England, but, attracted by the site's size and good location, the firm returned to redevelop it. This was a happy decision for Hull's prosperity and employment, as the subsequent development of Fenners has been one of very substantial expansion. With the successive changes from leather to textile flat-belting and then to V-section vulcanised and man-made-fibre belting, the firm has become international. This expansion has meant local developments in ancillary branches with an engineering shop making pulleys and variable speed drives, and the manufacture of light conveyor systems at MEC Ltd in the north of Hull. Innovation and expansion continue with the imminent introduction of an electronically-controlled variable-speed drive, and the firm continues to provide a most important source of local employment.

Shipbuilding

Some of the firms concerned with marine engineering are included in the map showing shipbuilding enterprises. Shipbuilding is confined to a very few squares bordering the older docks, although the yards have disappeared from some of their early nineteenth-century locations along the river Hull. These locations, and the rope and rigging works associated with building sailing-ships, can be seen from the 1817 map; until 1778, when the first dock was opened, shipping was confined to the mouth of the river Hull. The conjunction of timber imports and whale fishing encouraged boat-building, and Bellamy has shown that in the early nineteenth century the Port of Hull area, including Gainsborough, Selby and Thorne, had a greater output of vessels registered at Customs Houses than any other major port area and that from 1822–6 the increase was particularly marked. A number of local engineering firms and boilermakers turned to the construction of iron ships, and in 1845 C. & W. Earle were established as engineers, founders and shipwrights in Waterhouse Lane behind Junction dock; they launched their first ship in 1853. Between 1853 and 1931 this firm expanded very substantially and built nearly 700 ships.[9]

The large-scale construction of iron ships was concentrated in other parts of the country, and many local shipyards turned to building fishing boats, tugs and lighters and the modern industry is closely related to the maintenance and repair of fishing vessels. In fact the scattered yards and relatively small establishments have a considerable importance and produce more of the smaller commercial ships than any other area of similar size in the United Kingdom. The yards at Selby, Drypool, Hessle, Beverley, Goole and Thorne launched 12,713 GRT in 1968, with vessels up to 5,000 tons deadweight. The Beverley yard launched five powerful tugs recently, including the second of four for the Bantry Bay Oil Terminal, an order shared with the very substantial yards at Hessle. A cluster of firms specialises in repair on Prince's dock near the town centre, and there are large marine engineering firms and ship-repairing firms towards St Andrew's dock, which is used by the fish trawling fleet. The larger shipyards and marine engineering firms are shown on the map; each one marked employs at least sixty people, and this figure gives some idea of the nature of the business in this area.

Fishing and Food

Fishing has particularly attracted food enterprises to this area, particularly, of course, those trades concerned with processing fish from the traditional curing and smoking of herrings to the post-war quick-freezing of fish. Some of the earliest attempts at freezing fish were made by Smethursts of Grimsby before 1939, but the modern industry developed through C. Birdseye's freezing method, undertaken in this country by Unilever under the trade name of Birds Eye.[10] Birds Eye Foods Ltd began at Yarmouth, but there are now substantial plants in Hull and Grimsby. The tendency is for a few large firms to dominate production and for the establishments in Hull to be a part of a much wider organisation. The control of trawling, processing and marketing by associated companies, whose success depends upon reliable quality, is implied by the use of a brand-name for selling. This, of course, is not peculiar to the food trades or to Hull, although its recognition and emphasis has underpinned the success of many of the large local firms discussed so far. The effect on factories of this amalgamation of enterprises is to reduce the competitiveness and number of small establish-

Page 175: *The Hull factory of Ideal Standard: (above) moulding baths in the foundry; (below) the enamelling stage in the production of porcelain-enamelled baths. The factory produces domestic equipment for central heating and bathrooms. The ceramics section is the largest pottery outside Stoke on Trent*

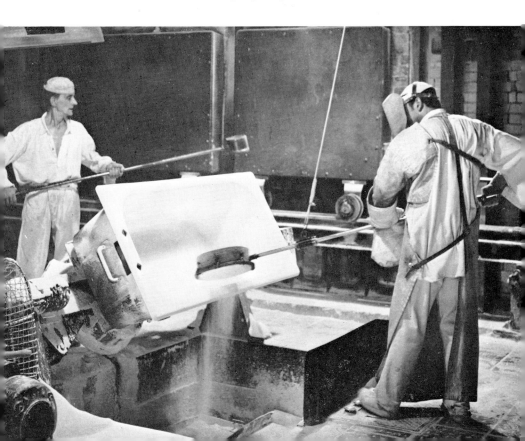

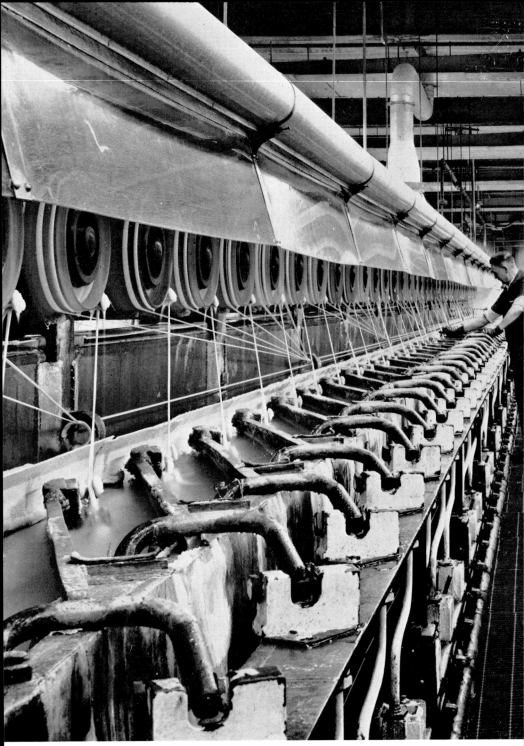

Page 176: *Production of synthetic fibre at the Great Coates plant of Courtaulds Ltd on the south Humber bank*

ments, and this is noticeable in the changes that have occurred around the fish docks in Hull in the few years since the original mapping of *HMFI* data was completed. The increases in the freezer-trawl vessels augments this tendency and many of the smaller factories in the streets at right angles to the fish docks have been replaced by large cold-store warehouses and processing plants.

Curing sheds are fewer, and this important aspect of fish processing is dominated by a very small number of firms; Macrae specialising in kippers and the Ross group laying more emphasis on curing white fish. Factories in *MLHs 214, 218* are distinguished on the map and on the graph showing the concentration of employment. It is not surprising that when the food industries are considered together there is a much greater dispersion of plant and employment than in fish processing. In fact the 180 establishments are distributed among half the kilometre squares, with 95 establishments employing less than 10 people; the 12 largest firms have a minimum employment of 45, whereas there are 16 factories with at least this number of employees in *MLHs 214, 218*. The separation of the two groups is noticeable, as is the concentration of the remainder of *SIC III* in the area near the river Hull. Two of the outlying large plants east of the river are bakeries, while those within half a mile of the river are dominated by grain mills and cocoa and sugar confectionery manufacture.

Timber

Half the squares covered by the map of Hull have at least one firm in the timber trade. There are over 220 establishments and 140 employ less than ten people; there is less concentration of employment than in any other industry, and the 30 largest units employ from 28 to many hundreds of people. It is a long-established industry and the largest firms have considerable histories from the early nineteenth century to 1888 when the largest local timber firm was founded. The concomitance of timber yards and the docks is seen clearly on the early maps, with timber yards lining the river Hull and rail yards along Old Dock on the site of the present Customs House building and east of the river above the Garrison. A line of large sawmilling and wood-using firms stretches along the Hedon road behind the large timber yards of the newer docks east of Hull. It may be fanciful to imagine that dominant plants of the timber industry are aligned parallel to the present docks in three groupings: in fact it is more likely that there is simply an absence of an alignment parallel to the river Hull. There is a marked grouping of firms around the fish dock

L

and most of them make boxes and packing cases; a more recent alignment of timber-using industries is in the north of Hull, and this feature is clearly seen from the map.

These industries shown in Figure 32 have different material needs, varied technologies and diverse histories, but a common pattern of clustering around the St Andrew's dock, following the sinuous line of the river Hull and extending eastwards behind the newer docks. The founders of many of the establishments that grew to dominate Hull's industrial employment structure came to the area from elsewhere and used some local or imported resource. Most of the firms are old; they were established and grew during the nineteenth century, when Hull's population and maritime trade were increasing rapidly, both doubling from 1831–61 and approaching the same rate of growth in the next thirty years. But the old maps show that this development was confined to within 1000 yards of the river Hull's confluence with the Humber; most of the extension was to the west of the river and there was little development on the east by 1834. Trade and manufacture were closely tied to the water's edge; different areas have developed different specialisations and the open sites of a century ago are the congested central areas of today.

### The Development of New Industries

Newer industries imitate the tradition of seeking sites peripheral to contemporary congestion; in Hull the spread has tended to be eastwards, the pattern apparently relentless. Hull needs more new industry. The city has not been particularly successful in attracting new industrial development and the figures showing approved new industrial floorspace since 1951 fluctuate considerably from year to year. They declined steadily from 1959, were at their lowest in 1963, and have shown an encouraging series of increases since then, being above the median value for the seventeen-year period in three of the past four years. But with respect to this overall median or even the median of the past decade there is no evidence to suppose any trend towards an increase above this median or a decrease below it has occurred. Seventeen acres was the mean amount of land developed annually for industrial uses in Hull between 1951–65, and in 1968 nearly 200 acres of land were available for industrial development, and three-quarters of this acreage was privately owned or scheduled to accommodate the expansion of existing firms. Indeed 'much of this demand for land is to cater for the expansion of existing industry . . . A large part of the demand is

for relocating industry moved from redevelopment areas.'[11] Some of
the areas for development are in north Hull along Clough Road,
Leads Road and Sutton Road, picked out earlier for caravan and
timber-working enterprises, but also used by warehouses and transport
firms. Other sites are in the areas of redevelopment, especially on the
west of the river Hull.

Reference has already been made to the development of the area
near St Andrew's dock in connection with large cold-store sheds. The
possibility of developing the site of the former railway sidings at
Springhead has received publicity recently;[12] it has been suggested that
the twenty-acre site could house enough light industry to provide 2,000
jobs at a cost of some £1·5 million. There is an industrial estate at
Marfleet in east Hull, in an area that has been selected by a number
of industrialists in the past seventy years for development, and these
are large firms, as we have seen. Indeed the location of the sites available for industrial expansion tend to perpetuate the existing pattern
of industry in Hull, and the size characteristics of industries moving
into these industrial estates and redeveloped sites in the city's traditional manufacturing areas will probably be consistent with the existing size distribution. We may expect them to be of about the median
size of the particular industry type, and as the largest centre in the
region Hull is likely to attract a greater number of enterprises in the
categories $D$, $E$, $F$, that is industries that are second stage resource
producing for final demand, or that are less directly related to resources,
than the other regional centres.

A desire to attract such industries and especially those that are least
related to resources is shared by the smaller towns in the region. The
addition of new factory floor space has been proportionate to the
existing industrial employment, with Selby and Beverley dominant
and Bridlington, on the coast, expanding substantially since 1945, as
before the war it had little industry. In Selby the expansion reflects
more the growth of the resource-oriented industries of fine chemicals
and papermaking than of final-demand industries, and in Beverley the
expansion of firms established before the war has been the principal
element of the increased factory space. Particular examples of this
are Armstrong Patents Company, Richard Hodgsons and Sons,
tanners, and the Stepney Group of Companies making concrete blocks.
Slightly over half of Beverley's 2,404 acres is common pasture on
which building is prohibited, and the present areas available for industrial development are unlikely to be augmented. Most of the land
scheduled for it lies in the Swinemoor, between the eastern fringe of

the town and the river Hull. The four largest zones constitute some ninety-four acres, but not all of this is ready for development and some is in private ownership. Industrial development has already occurred on the fifteen-acre Swinemoor estate, and the largest site, some ten acres, is owned by Armstrong Patents; other businesses include a fibre-glass company and a pickle factory. Adjacent to this estate is a similar area under private ownership and some sites have been made available to a caravan firm and to Humbrol, a Hull paint firm. Indeed most of the firms are of local origin. The remaining acreage is not developed and its future is speculative, but the area seems well suited to attract 'light' industry and offers a particularly attractive residential environment.[13]

Coastal resorts try to encourage the development of industries compatible with their attractiveness to holiday-makers. Potteries have been established at Withernsea and Hornsea and the output of the latter is sold widely throughout the country. Bridlington, like Hornsea, was a small market town whose growth as a resort coincided with the advent of the railway and whose industrial development really began in 1946 with the establishment of a small industrial estate south of the town adjacent to the railway. There is a firm engraving cylinders for printing, another making soft furnishings, and a shell-fish processing factory. At Lissett, south of Bridlington, a disused wartime aerodrome is used by a caravan firm and in the whole of North Humberside a number of such disused airfield buildings have been taken over by small and medium sized firms as a common element to the scattered development of industry in a rural area. But this is sporadic growth and its contribution to the general industrial framework of the region is comparatively small. The main skeleton of vigorous and large-scale industrial development continues to be provided by the principal rivers, and the Humber will be increasingly the dominant locational factor, different facets of its attraction being preferred by different industries. On the north bank, emphasis is often given to the Salt End section but some important developments have occurred west of Hull. The employment of over 5,000 workpeople in the aircraft factory at Brough is of major importance. The early specialisation was in naval aircraft; expansion occurred from the mid-1930s, and after the war the Brough company absorbed a London firm and moved to Yorkshire; of special importance was the production of a freight-carrying aeroplane. The business was absorbed by Hawker Siddeley Aviation in the late 1950s and production was adjusted nationally so that the local plant lost some manufacturing capacity. But recent orders for

Buccaneer strike aircraft, together with a growth in the sub-assemblies for other plants in the Hawker-Siddeley group, have meant a rapid expansion in work and employment: the pendulum swings under national and international impulse.

A link with a Bristol-based firm is seen at Melton, where the firm of Capper Pass is sited. This firm extracts non-ferrous metals and particularly tin from ore and residue, and uses the port of Hull for the importation of low-grade tin ore from Bolivia and scrap from Europe and the USA. Capper Pass moved to Melton in 1936, has expanded very substantially, employs over 700 people at the present time and has a very considerable capital investment, with much of the new plant and engineering requirements met locally.[14] This sort of firm makes an important contribution to the local economy and illustrates the region's advantages for such industry. The availability of ample flat land for expansion, a large and efficient port with established European trading connections, and adequate water supplies are needs shared by many of the growth industries. These are often members of larger organisations which are increasingly making positive locational decisions within at least a national context and Humberside must hope to be attractive to certain types of such new industrial development. For example, Capper Pass recently became a subsidiary of the Rio Tinto Zinc Corporation, whose international mining interests are widely known. It was announced recently that this firm is to spend over £7 million on doubling its tin refining capacity in the UK, and this major expansion will be concentrated at Capper Pass, doubling its present capacity. Much of this expanded output is likely to be exported. The overall pattern of selection was reviewed in Chapter 4 in terms of costs and value added data, whereas this section has dealt with details of particular firms. In Hull the pattern was residual; outside Hull, along the Humber, it anticipates those elements of locational choice evinced by the recent developments on the south Humber bank.

## South Humberside

Certain problems of definition connected with this linear zone are illustrated by Fig 33. The distribution of factory employment in the mid-1960s indicates that along the length of the deepwater section of South Humberside from Barton-upon-Humber to Tetney, industry was in two separate areas and occupied about half the total Humber frontage. The most important section was from Immingham to

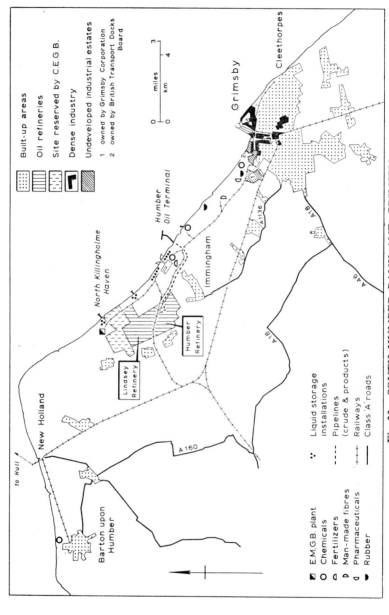

Fig 33. SOUTH HUMBER BANK AND GRIMSBY

The industrial distributions are based on the Development Plan and other publications of Grimsby CB; British Transport Docks Board; Lindsey CC North Lindsey Survey, 1965, and information provided by individual firms

Grimsby, and Barton was a separate, smaller centre at a fairly low level of intensity. But to confine a sub-region of the south Humber bank to those parts in active use in 1967 would be to ignore the very character and potential of the sub-region, since it is still developing and one of its principal advantages had been its relative emptiness. The Feasibility Study considered the entire zone northwards from the margin of industrial development at Killingholme to the bend in the estuary at Skitter Ness and along the bank to New Holland as part of its south Humber bank industrial area, indicating that the whole area possessed good possibilities for industrial growth. It also seems point-less to leave out Barton itself, since many of its industries are linked to the river and use it for transport, although there are no deepwater berths; it is also the centre of the employment area which covers much of the northern part of the south Humber bank. Consequently this sub-region extends from Barton in a narrow band along the southern shore of the Humber to Grimsby and to Cleethorpes. Although certain peripheral industrial sites south of Grimsby are included, since they are related to its suburban expansion, the sub-region has not been taken down to Tetney Haven where the Feasibility Study considered there was scope for industrial expansion if there were a deepwater anchorage off Tetney. At present it has no industrial development at all, and with the concentration of existing efforts further up the estuary its chances of development in the near future presumably rank lower than the empty areas north of Killingholme, although a deep-water oil terminal is now under construction.

Fig. 14 shows that the distribution of employment in manufacturing in the sub-region is very uneven indeed. Of the thirty-five square kilo-metres with industry, most were developed at a low intensity so that half the employment was concentrated in only four square kilometres. Almost a quarter of it was in fact in just one square kilometre, and this intensely concentrated employment distribution is much more pronounced than in the Hull area, where the densest square kilometre only accounted for about eight per cent of the sub-regional employ-ment. The pattern revealed by Fig. 14 summarises the effects of two quite distinct and contrasting distribution patterns within the sub-region: a dense concentration of small and medium plants in one part, and a well-spaced out pattern of large plants in the other. In essence this is a contrast between Grimsby and the remainder of the south Humber bank, but the distribution of grid squares in the highest density category is almost perfectly balanced between the two sections.

The two sections are plain from Fig 14. The distinction of Grimsby

and the south Humber bank industrial development is marked more
by a break in the continuity of the highest density category than a
complete lack of industrial employment. Within Grimsby the high
density squares form a T-shaped pattern in the north of the borough,
with the horizontal axis running along the Humber frontage; an enclosed grid square of lower density denotes that industry is in the
heart of the commercial dock system. Apart from this dense industrial
zone, industry appears to be rather sparsely distributed, only one other
kilometre square reaching a density of 150 per square kilometre and
this is in Cleethorpes. The south Humber bank has a distribution
pattern which is densest at its southern margins and gradually attenu-
ates towards Immingham. Industry clings to the Humber shore, but it
is fragmented, not continuous. The pattern does not include the oil
refineries, which were under construction at the time of data collection,
so that industry ceases at Immingham and does not reappear until
Barton, with the exception of an isolated kilometre square at New
Holland. In essence, it represents a linear axis of industrialisation,
still incompletely developed at the time of survey, between Immingham and Grimsby. The sub-sections are thus rather different in basic
formal terms; Grimsby is a very concentrated block of dense industrial
employment, while on the south bank it is linear and sporadic. In 1967
sixty per cent of the employment was in Grimsby and the rest on the
south bank. But the growth of industry on the south bank has largely
occurred in the postwar period, whereas that in Grimsby is of much
longer standing, and both sub-sections tend to be preferred by different types of industries.

Industrial Land Use Distribution

Figure 33 illustrates some of the major features of the distribution
of industrial land use in the entire sub-region, together with some
major associated distributions. The outline of the two oil refineries is
shown in general terms to give some indication of the areas involved,
but it must not be assumed that the sites have in all cases been completely utilised, since most firms had the foresight to buy land for their
future requirements.

The contrast between the two sections is clear, and expresses the
difference between the tightly-packed industry typical of the town
centre and industry making extensive requirements on land. Within
Grimsby the T-shaped axis that emerged from a previous map is
further emphasised. Industry there is clearly a feature of the inner
urban area, and the distribution of areas predominantly industrial is

remarkable for its strong association with the dock system. This is seen most clearly in the vicinity of the fish docks, where much of the land forms part of the dock estate; however, industrial belts fringe both arms of the Alexandra dock and thus penetrate to the original dock at West Haven, where industry is close to the commercial core of the town. Some industrial concentrations are related to the railway lines in inner Grimsby, but the largest detached block is in the south-east of the town in what was a fringe-belt location but which has since been absorbed by general urban growth; this zone is the location of some of the largest Grimsby plants. An interesting feature is the comparative absence of peripheral 'by-pass' types of industrial estates. The attraction of land near the docks is obviously a principal factor in the development of an industrial policy for the town, and this is reflected in the location of land which has been set aside for major industrial growth. It is situated in the Pyewipe district, and is partly within the perimeter of the dock estate. This forms in effect the beginning of the south Humber bank, possessing ample reserves of cheap, poor quality land. The Corporation of Grimsby has also bought land in the Great Coates area, adjacent to Pyewipe but without direct access to the Humber foreshore. Together these sites provide about 250 acres of vacant industrial land for new industries. Apart from these major industrial areas, a considerable amount of industry is scattered through the nineteenth-century parts of built-up Grimsby; this will be evident in a later map. The Corporation also reserves selected sites for small industries in the inner town, in some cases specifically for industries linked with the docks or fishing. These are in Victoria Street and the district north of the Cleethorpes Road, and both are in close proximity to the docks.

The south Humber bank is essentially the domain of a relatively limited number of plants which cover extensive ground areas and need a great deal of land for ancillary uses, such as railway sidings, storage accommodation, and for projected expansions. Its industries are thus essentially heavy industries in terms of their site requirements, and must seek land as cheaply as possible. All would tend to occupy sites on the outskirts of any urban area, unless inner sites were occupied by reason of industrial inertia. On the south Humber bank the availability of large reserves of land which could be cheaply developed combined with other locational and site advantages to produce a very distinctive industrial complex. Despite the tremendous scale of post-war industrial growth, the available land for industry has by no means been exhausted, even in the most developed section between Immingham and Grimsby. According to the Feasibility Study, in 1966 on the south Humber bank, excluding the Barton-New Holland section, some 590 acres were in industrial use, and a further 660 acres were in process of development, making a total of 1,250 acres.[15] But a further 4,630 acres in the same zone is still undeveloped, although it is covered by planning permission for industrial development, so that there is no shortage of land. However, about sixty per cent of the undeveloped land is owned by existing industries, or by nationalised concerns such as the Central Electricity Generating Board, and these have already pre-empted the choicest riverside sites.

With long-term expansion in mind the Feasibility Study has drawn attention to the section of the south bank lying to the north of the stream known as East Halton Skitter, and outside the current planning conception of the south Humber bank industrial zone. This has most of the advantages of the latter, except direct access to the deepwater channel, and pipelines for liquid raw materials would be a simple expedient. This extra zone contains about 6,500 acres of potential industrial land, almost entirely uncovered by any planning commitments. Moreover it includes two disused airfields to add to its list of advantages. Thus a shortage of land for industry is unlikely in the foreseeable future in the south Humber bank section. This area has attracted a type of industrial development which is quite distinct from that in the Grimsby area, so that it is convenient to consider their growth, structure, and locational characteristics independently. However it must be stressed that the functional links between the two sections are very important, ranging from the supply of labour from Grimsby to the growth of specialist industries such as pipe-fitting, metal fabrication and erection, which have tended to develop there although serving the large plants of the Humber bank.

*South Humber Bank*

This industrial zone is a complex of heavy chemical plants and oil refineries, petroleum product storage and distribution depots, and important transport facilities. It is dominated by the types of industries which planners have termed *Special* because of their particular needs for land, or effluent discharge, or because of the nature of the processes carried out. In the context of the whole Humberside region it forms a heavy-industrial corridor with a familiar repetition of industrial types already found in other estuarine areas in Britain and western Europe.

The concentration of investment in this zone is very considerable, because of the capital intensive nature of the industries involved. The Humber Oil Refinery of Continental Oil alone is costing about £30 million, and while this obviously represents the upper range of investment most projects have been costed in terms of millions of pounds, either for a new plant or for extensions. Because of the high degree of automation associated with modern heavy chemical and allied industries, the employment created in relation to the investment has been relatively low. According to figures quoted in the Feasibility Study, the average employment per acre of industrial land in chemical and allied industries varies between 10 and 20; for general industry, such as engineering, a wider range of 40 to 100 can be expected, and for light and labour intensive industries such as clothing, or light assembly work of such goods as radios, a range of 100 to 200 is normal.[16] In 1967 there were approximately 6,200 people employed in chemical, man-made fibre and rubber production in the Grimsby and Barton areas, which together cover the south Humber bank, and the greater part of this employment was in fact concentrated in the latter zone. The labour intensity of the industries as a whole is low compared with the two densest square kilometres in Hull, which together employ nearly ten thousand industrial workers, but the total work force in the industrial complex is by no means negligible, and has formed an important element in the rising demand for labour in South Humberside generally since the war. Also in 1967, about 1,100 men were engaged in the industrial plant and steelwork industry and over 2,000 in construction in the Barton employment area, most of whom were engaged on contracts associated with new capacity, especially the construction of the oil refineries.

Figure 33 illustrates the distribution of the main plants on the south Humber bank, and aids an appreciation of some of the main motives behind this growth. Perhaps the dominant factor was the abundant flat land which existed, at low prices but easily developed for the extensive heavy machinery and buildings needed in the chemical industries. The Courtaulds plant is set in an estate of 500 acres, and the oil refineries also occupy large areas. Without substantial reserves of land within which plants and processes could be most economically deployed, the operating costs would obviously rise. However, plenty of flat land was not in itself a sufficient attraction for most firms, because heavy chemicals and allied industries tend to use large quantities of water in processing, after which the waste waters must be disposed of as quickly and cheaply as possible. In this respect Humberside added two further site advantages for these industries. The deep tidal estuary offered direct effluent discharge facilities at very low cost along the entire stretch from East Halton Skitter to Pyewipe, visible in the map showing the detailed sites of all the plants. This point is emphasised by the fact that flat land a short distance inland was not developed in the early stages. The chemical industries' needs for water were also easily met in the 1940s and 1950s, since there were no large water-using industries in the area and resources were considerably in excess of demand. Firms needing particularly large quantities of good water, such as the man-made fibres plant of Courtaulds, supplemented their supply from the local water board by boring their own wells into the underlying chalk strata. Water, land and effluent discharge facilities constitute the three dominant attractions for the development of the heavy chemical complex, and so far all have been sufficiently abundant to sustain new additions to capacity and new firms. But the water resources have not proved inexhaustible, and one of the possible checks on industrial growth in the area is the problem of maintaining an adequate supply.

It is perhaps surprising that the deepwater estuary was not considered as a prime locational advantage in the initial growth period, because Immingham was well able to accommodate the import of raw materials and was ideally sited to supply the new chemical plants with only a short road or rail haul in most cases. Rail communications from the south bank to the national markets are excellent for freight, but as the Humberside industrial survey demonstrated, most of the outmovement of goods is by road transport. Road communications from south Humberside are poor and Fig. 1 shows that the road network in the area is essentially rural; a concatenation of lanes serving farms. Yet the region is relatively near to main centres of population and the West Riding, the East and West Midlands and the South-East are all accessible with different degrees of difficulty. The construction of a few modern roads linking the area to the major motorway system would improve this accessibility and augment the existing advantages of the region.

The Humber estuary may have been seen as an ideal sewer for effluent rather than a supply of raw materials at one stage of development. But the tendency towards large vessels bringing vast quantities of raw materials implies the need of some types of industry to be near deepwater estuaries. The two oil refineries illustrate this. In contrast, other technical changes such as container traffic and transferable refrigeration units may reduce the traditional advantages of port locations for a wide variety of industries processing materials at the dock-side. In future, ports may tend to become places where the emphasis is on a change of transport medium for standard packages, not a re-packaging point: the port becomes more than ever a centre of movement. The changes in port function seem to have been anticipated successfully in Humberside, and local authorities and the British Transport Docks Board, with its predecessors, have consistently supported the industrialisation of the south bank since the end of the war. Many firms have benefited from this cooperation.

Chemical and Allied Industries

These plants were established mainly in the late 1940s and 1950s, and mark the first phase of industrial growth. The first to arrive was British Titan Products, which began operating at Pyewipe in 1948, closely followed by Fisons, Laporte, CIBA Chemicals, Courtaulds, John Bull Rubber and Doverstrand. In 1966 ICI opened an ammonia plant on the Immingham Dock estate, while all the plants have at some time or another extended their capacity, and in some cases, such as Laporte or Courtaulds, added a completely new product range. The output of this heavy chemical complex is quite diverse in detail but can be grouped into fertilisers, rubber, titanium pigments which have a very wide range of applications from paint manufacture to plastics, viscose rayon and acrylic fibre, and pharmaceutical bases. Other products include pthalic anhydride and oil hydrocarbon-based ammonia.

The process of expansion for many firms has been continuous. Perhaps the outstanding case is Courtaulds' Humber bank factory, which began as a high-capacity viscose rayon producer with an annual output of about 100 million pounds. In 1957 the acrylic fibre plant was opened to produce all the group's 'Courtelle', with an initial output of 10 million pounds; by 1969 the annual plant capacity was as high as 100 million, and a further expansion scheme announced recently will double this output by 1972.[17] Laporte Industries have also announced recently a scheme to double the output of titanium dioxide at its Stallingborough factory.[18]

These industries belong to the first phase of industrial growth on the Humber bank, in which flat land, water, and effluent discharge were the chief considerations. All rely on the port facilities of Immingham Dock and do not exploit their estuary frontage for transport purposes, although Fisons' fertiliser plant on the dock estate has direct conveyor discharge of phosphate rock and potash. Markets are of course national and international, with road transport dominating the former and sea transport via Immingham the latter.

Oil Refining

The construction of two large oil refineries has inaugurated a new phase in the industrial development of the south Humber bank, particularly in that for the first time the locational advantages of the deepwater estuary have been utilised as well as the site factors, while the possibility of the subsequent growth of a linked petrochemical complex would introduce an entirely new range of products. The location of the refineries is shown in Fig. 33, from which it can be seen that they are not actually adjacent to the Humber shore, which is already occupied by other users, but are in fact served by pipelines bringing in crude oil from the Humber Oil Terminal. The Lindsey Refinery is illustrated on page 70.

In view of the intense regional competition for oil refineries, as one of the major growth points of industrial technology, it is well worth while to examine some of the main reasons behind the choice of Humberside, especially as both Continental Oil (UK) and Total Oil-Fina conducted their own examination of other potential sites.[19] Two factors stand out above all others: suitable land which, according to Total-Fina, was also cheaper than at other locations, and the Humber's potential for taking very large ocean tankers with relatively little dredging expense. While other sites such as Southampton Water or Milford Haven have berthing facilities equal to those of the Humber, a considerable amount of development already in existence left little room for manœuvre, according to Continental Oil. The land requirements are, of course, immense, with the Humber Refinery (Continental) using 380 acres and the Lindsey Refinery (Total-Fina) using 373; a further advantage of Humberside was that drainage or piling operations were not essential for construction to begin. The strategic location of Humberside for distribution to the Midlands and North was also commented on by both groups, as well as its convenience for exporting products to northern European markets.

Both refineries are large by present standards, the Humber refinery having a capacity of about 4·5 million tons per year, and the Lindsey Refinery coming on stream with an initial three million tons, which was doubled by the end of 1969 with the addition of a second stage for Petrofina. In common with all refineries the immense capital investment, amounting to around £30 million in both cases, will generate only low labour requirements; a figure of 250 has been quoted for the Humber refinery. In contrast to existing heavy chemical plants in South Humberside, both refineries will be making extensive use of rail transport for inland distribution, and sidings and loading facilities have been provided on site; the throughput planned for rail loading bays at the Lindsey refinery is 250,000 gallons per hour, as compared with 150,000 gallons per hour for the road bays, which is an indication of the anticipated despatch of products to inland depots. Both refineries will produce the entire range of normal refinery products from liquified petroleum gas and gasolines to heavy fuel oils, but the Humber refinery will have additional plant to produce 110,000 tons of benzene per annum, and 250,000 tons of electrode grade petroleum coke. The former is a vital basic material for manufacturing nylon and polystyrene, as well as a host of other products, and there is a national shortage of it. The petroleum coke plants will be Britain's first, and the capacity involved will result in a substantial export. Its incredible purity and consistent structure physically make it a material in increasing demand in the electric steel industry and aluminium smelting, so that its markets seem assured.

The promise of further expansion into related petrochemical industries is a prime feature of interest in relation to oil refineries; the growth prospects and problems of the south Humber bank industrial complex are treated in the following section.

Growth Prospects

The growth prospects of the south Humber bank complex must be considered promising. One of the major potential sectors of expansion is in the development of petrochemical industries, similar to the developments at Fawley, Teesside (Wilton), Grangemouth or Llandarcy-Baglan Bay. At the last of these a petrochemical complex representing an investment of £13 million began in 1962, and a further expansion costing £60 million is under construction. The final production employment associated with the developments will be around 1,400. The development of petrochemical plants in turn might attract industries which use large quantities of chemical intermediates, or research laboratories.

Certainly Continental Oil operates a substantial petrochemical sector in the United States, particularly in the production of industrial alcohols, vinyl plastic resins, and organic detergent intermediates, and as such might be prepared at some future date to develop similar interests at their Humber refinery, which is the biggest refinery in the entire group's operations. A start in this direction has already been

made at the Humber refinery, with the aromatics plant for the production of benzene which is in effect a petrochemical activity, and the
petroleum coke plant. With three major oil companies committed to
large developments in Humberside, Total-Fina at the Lindsey refinery
as well as Conoco, the prospects for the expansion of petrochemicals
in the region seem bright.

The heavy chemical industry's rate of expansion as a capital intensive sector is affected by government development area policies, which
we shall examine in detail later. In addition the scale of operations in
these industries means that growth is not a gradual process, but rather
a series of major additions in capacity in response to, or in anticipation
of, market trends. The extent of existing investment makes for stability,
and there is, as we have seen, plenty of evidence of massive expansion
under way which will carry the industries into the early 1970s. But
no great employment expansion need be envisaged, since the labour
needs are low and productivity levels very high.

A possible check on the expansion of existing firms or the establishment of new ones lies in the government's development area policy. In
the words of the Hunt Report:

> A fundamental criticism made to us of the financial incentives (to
> Development Areas) is that the package is too heavily weighted on the
> side of capital grants. It was pointed out that the present capital grants
> lower the effective price of fixed capital in the development areas by
> about 25 per cent compared with elsewhere, whereas REP/SET reduce
> labour costs by only 9 per cent.
> (Hunt Report, 1969, para 129)

For capital-intensive industries such an inducement could well be
decisive in a choice between a non-development area such as Humberside and a development area such as Teesside. However the Hunt
Report did stress that factors such as deepwater access, flat sites with
effluent discharge facilities and cheap distribution costs, which it
termed physical location factors, were of critical importance to such
industries, and would be likely to dominate the location decision.
Nevertheless it did produce some evidence to suggest that there was a
tendency for the capital intensive industries to invest disproportion-
ately in the development areas in 1966–67. This is too early to make
any firm judgement; indeed the evidence before us at the moment
would seem to suggest that Humberside's expansion is not threatened,
but this is a situation which needs to be carefully watched, particularly
in relation to prospective new firms.

The water supply position is a further possible limiting factor for future expansion. According to a report of the Lindsey Planning Department in 1965, the abstraction of water from the chalk had already reached the maximum safety limit in the North-East Lincolnshire territory, so that further major expansion of industries with heavy water needs was not possible.[20] The situation in 1965 in the North Lindsey Board area was better, but even so the anticipated demands of the two oil refineries and the gas producing plant were sufficient to abrogate the existing leeway between daily output and safe pumping capacity. Consequently the search for alternative sources continues in the region, and an important additional source for the south Humber bank is the Great Eau scheme, which began sending water into the North-East Lincolnshire area in 1968 and provides a considerable margin of surplus into the early 1970s. The exploitation of the river Ancholme will provide the North Lindsey board with further substantial resources, after which outside resources will be needed, possibly from the Trent, although its heavily polluted state will mean expensive and difficult treatment processes. Thus although some margin exists at present and for a number of years to come, the south Humber bank is no longer an area of abundant and cheap water.

## Grimsby

Although Grimsby is only about one-third the size of Hull it invites comparison with the larger city. It is an important regional centre for shopping, education and other activities in north Lincolnshire, and according to some schemes its general classification as a shopping centre differs from Hull in scale rather than in degree. Both are ports, and have dominant interests in north-European trade. As industrial centres both Hull and Grimsby stand out as concentrations of dense employment in their respective sub-regions, although the Grimsby concentration is smaller and less intense, only four grid squares having employment densities greater than 1,000 per square kilometre compared with seventeen in Hull. The most striking resemblance is in the prominent position of fishing and associated activities, which are proportionally more important to Grimsby.

As the densest concentration of industry on the south Humber bank, Grimsby forms a distinct formal unit with its own characteristic array of industries. Nevertheless there is a strong degree of functional interdependence between the town and the zone of heavy industry along the Humber bank, which is particularly reflected in the movement of workers out of the town. The Corporation of Grimsby has also actively

M

promoted the industrialisation of the south bank, looking upon it as a natural choice for industrial expansion, and is at present developing a large industrial estate in the Great Coates area, as Figure 34 shows; this estate has recently been formally incorporated within Grimsby as a result of boundary extensions. The two units should be seen as com-

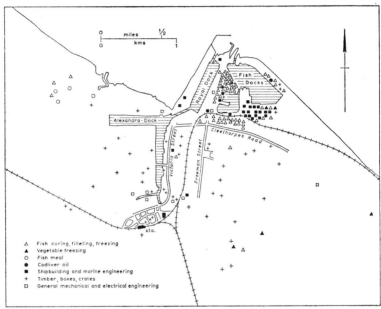

Fig 34.   DISTRIBUTION OF SELECTED INDUSTRIES IN
GRIMSBY

The map is based on HM Factory Inspectors' data; plants are not
differentiated by size

plementary, with sixty per cent of the actual employment in Grimsby according to calculations from Factory Inspectorate data; giving a total employment in industry in Grimsby of about 14,000 in 1967. Grimsby has been gradually transformed from a simple fishing port into an industrial town; at present it still has a narrowly-based industrial structure, but the process of transformation is still continuing, and must be considered as part of the increasing industrialisation of the south Humber bank as a whole.

The Industrial Structure

The industries of Grimsby have mainly developed from its fishing activities, to a much lesser extent from those of its port. The town's association with fishing was due to the active sponsorship of the Manchester, Sheffield and Lincolnshire Railway after the opening of its Grimsby railway and dock in 1848–52.[21] A period of rapid growth in the later nineteenth century secured its position, and today Grimsby ranks a close second to Hull in the tonnage of fish landed; both are far ahead of other fishing ports.

About 3,500 men are directly employed in the Grimsby fishing fleet, and this is the peak of a pyramid which extends into the major part of Grimsby's industry. In 1967 the Food industries *SIC III* employed over 10,000 in the Grimsby employment exchange area, the great majority in Grimsby itself. Over 6,000 worked in the dominant *MLH*, fish processing, and about 2,000 in vegetable preserving, and together these two *MLHs* account for over a third of the industrial employment of this area, and consequently a much higher proportion of the actual town's industry. Over 2,500 work in shipbuilding and ship repairing, whereas other *SIC* orders employ under 1,000, timber, paper and engineering being the most important. The industrial base is, in these terms, narrow, and there is also a close interrelationship between industries of different types, especially in terms of sales, so that industrial development depends to a large degree on food industries.

Figure 34 illustrates the distribution of selected industries in Grimsby, and fish processing is clearly dominant. The fish processing plants are heavily concentrated around the fish docks in the older part of the dock estate, where many of the small plants are sited in the wedge of land between the Royal dock and Fish docks 1 and 2. Many of the larger fish plants are in the newer sections of the dock estate which lie to the south of the Fish docks, in the Wickham Road–Marsden Road area and on the North Wall. A compact group of plants lies just north of Cleethorpes Road close to the Fish docks on an estate developed since the war by Grimsby Corporation to cater for the needs of the fish processing industry. A further isolated concentration of fish-processing factories is in the Pyewipe district, in what was once the western extremity of Grimsby and close to land subsequently developed by chemical plants. These are mainly fish-meal plants. The concentration of fish processing plants around the Fish docks was undoubtedly logical and convenient, particularly in the past, but is now not obligatory for large plants, especially as an increasing part of the catch is landed in a deep-frozen state. Thus the largest single fish processing plant is on the Ladysmith Road estate, some distance away from the docks and the traditional focus of the industry.

Certain processes, such as salting, curing and smoking, are usually associated with fishing ports, and Grimsby was no exception. But the gradual introduction in the inter-war period of fish-filleting prior to sale added a further process to Grimsby's industries; the filleted offal could be processed into fish-meal for animals and poultry. But the real growth has been since the war, as the market demand for fresh fish has been met by quick-freezing. Such fish needs more elaborate packaging, and this has meant more fish factories and more employment. The Grimsby fish processing industry is thus a large collection of different processes, plant sizes, and degrees of integration. Some plants specialise in filleting or freezing and tend to be small, usually employing less than twenty people. Others are fish curers, whilst the larger integrated plants combine filleting and freezing with fish packing. In more recent years the larger plants, operated by firms such as Birds Eye, Fropax-Eskimo, Findus, Ross and Associated Fisheries, have added more elaborate preparation processes in response to market changes, including breadcrumbing and battering, all of which need further additions to the labour force. This forward integration in the fish processing industry has also been accompanied by the creation of ancillary services, particularly the erection of enormous cold-stores which have given Grimsby the largest concentration of sub-zero cold storage capacity in Europe.

Other industries are closely integrated with the fortunes of the fishing industry. This is perhaps most obvious in the case of the many firms engaged in *SIC VII*, ranging from the building and repairing of trawlers to the more specialised aspects of marine engineering such as ships' propellers or boilers. In addition, many industries formally classified in *SIC VI* are in fact making special equipment for the trawlers, such as block and tackle for the trawls. Figure 34 reveals a notable concentration to the south of the new Fish Dock, but other plants are concentrated in the dock estate. Links with the fishing industry are also evident in the numerous plants making wooden boxes and fish baskets, a large number of which are in the older part of the Fish dock estate, although there is also a fairly wide dispersal in the older part of Grimsby. Baskets are being replaced by aluminium casks, so this small-scale basket-weaving industry will probably disappear from the dock areas of Grimsby and Hull. Many plants make nets and rigging, and other services include the repair of radio and navigation equipment for trawlers.

A more recent addition to Grimsby's food industry is the freezing and packing of vegetables. The factories are large and are not tied so closely to the dock area, and two of the largest are on estates in the south of the town, using vegetables from the agricultural hinterland.

This sequence is a reversal of the national development of frozen foods after the last war, when the initial marketing successes were in frozen peas culled from East Anglian fields. The great stimulus to frozen fish marketing came in 1955 from the development of the fish-finger package by Birds Eye Foods. The extension to auxiliary factories providing batter and breadcrumbs is encouraged further by the development of combined packages of fish and chips.[22]

The distribution of industries in Grimsby is closely related to the dock estate—the Alexandra dock for timber and paper, and the Fish docks for the food, shipbuilding and related industries. The progressive elaboration of the fish catch has resulted in increased employment, and has introduced further branches of the frozen-food industry to Grimsby, so widening the economic base. But Grimsby is still overspecialised and linked with the fish industries, consequently every effort is being made to introduce new industries to counter this dependence, and the expansion of employment in chemical and allied industries on the south Humber bank is part of this process, although, as previously mentioned, the period of major growth in employment in these activities is probably finished.

## Scunthorpe

Dependence upon one industry is the outstanding feature of the final sub-region considered in this chapter.

The set-up [at Scunthorpe] reminds the visitor of Wolfsburg, the town 10 miles from the Iron Curtain where the Volkswagen is made; another one-product place set apart on a bleak plain from the rest of the country, seeming to have more in common with foreigners in the same business than with compatriots. (Nicholas Faith, Industrial Editor, *Sunday Times*, 2 Feb 1969)

Scunthorpe, the second largest concentration of industrial employment in Humberside, has usually evoked sentiments like these because it is a classic example of a town dominated by one industry and set in the heart of an environment with which it has little in common. In 1967 almost three-quarters of all manufacturing employment was in the iron and steel industry, and if one adds industries such as chemicals or bricks which are directly tied to the steel industry, this proportion rises to an incredible ninety-two per cent. Scunthorpe's range of retail and other services are of course closely bound up with the fortunes of the steel industry, and this makes the town a very vulnerable asset within Humberside.

This vulnerability has, if anything, been increased as a result of the circumstances of Scunthorpe's industrial growth. As Pocock has shown, the development of the iron, and later of the steel industry there was financed and controlled by companies whose main base of operation was in other industrial districts.[23] The pattern of development was one of exploiting Scunthorpe's ability to produce pig-iron and crude steel very cheaply, and transporting the semi-finished steel elsewhere for finishing. Although finishing capacity was gradually introduced, this process was never carried far enough, or in a sufficiently varied manner. Indeed the most promising development in this direction, the proposed construction of a continuous strip mill and tinplate plant by Richard Thomas in 1935, was diverted by government pressure to Ebbw Vale. Consequently, up to the mid-1960s, the familiar outside dominance continued, with Lysaght's Normanby Park works sending over two-thirds of its output to other GKN companies (mainly billets and rods), and the Richard Thomas & Baldwins' Redbourn works sending about half its output of bars and billets to other RTB works for finishing, especially in South Wales. The Appleby-Frodingham plant had substantial finishing sections, although concentrating on the heavier types of finished products such as plates, but it exported a large surplus of pig-iron to other plants in the United Steel Group. The entire complex was controlled from outside. Since 1965 there has been an autonomous Scunthorpe Division in the British Steel Corporation Midland Group, which unites all the works for the first time and is responsible for ensuring that Scunthorpe develops as a key centre for steel production within the national organisation. Much of this section is thus naturally devoted to the steel industry, but some of the important problems associated with its peculiar industrial structure, and some of the new avenues of industrial development open to the town will also be discussed.

The Steel Industry

The development of the iron and steel industry in Scunthorpe was marked by almost continuous expansion from the opening of the first ironworks in 1864 to the formation of the British Steel Corporation in 1965. Six ironworks were established in the period from 1864 until 1876, and these works, through a complex series of growth phases and acquisitions which continued until 1936, have emerged as the present Redbourn and Appleby-Frodingham plants. The Normanby Park plant was established as an independent entity on a site well removed from the existing concentration of ironworks in 1912. All the works originally made only pig iron, and steel-making was not introduced until 1890; it did not become really important until World War I, for a variety of reasons.

In 1966 the steel plants employed 21,150; some measure of the rapidity of the growth of Scunthorpe in the present century may be gained from the fact that in 1918 about 4,000 were employed, and in 1939 some 12,400. However by 1961 the employment had reached 20,700 so that the really rapid expansion had come to a close by this date. Because of its complex origins, the Appleby-Frodingham works is spread over a very large area, and virtually surrounds the Redbourn works on three sides.

The main locational factor behind the development of the iron and steel industry in Scunthorpe is the Frodingham ironstone. The ore has the leanest iron metallic content worked in Britain—only 21 per cent in 1967, compared to an average of 60 per cent for foreign ores;[24] if this lean ore is to be exploited economically it obviously has to be converted into pig-iron in situ, since it would not stand the costs of transportation. This was the reason for the establishment of the first works, and it has remained a key factor in the prosperous expansion of the Scunthorpe plants until the costs of the much richer imported ores have become increasingly competitive in the 1960s. The lean metallic content has always been balanced by the almost perfect excavating conditions, the enormous reserves and the highly calcareous nature of the ores, which renders a limestone flux superfluous. The consumption of Frodingham ore in Scunthorpe has fallen gradually from a peak of over five million tons in the early 1960s; in 1967 it was 4,656,000 tons. In order to counter the calcareous nature of the ore in the furnace charge, almost three million tons of siliceous Northampton Sands ore was also consumed in 1967; this was rail-hauled from Northants, and has long been a feature of Scunthorpe iron-making practice.

During the inter-war period the Scunthorpe plants developed into major producers of cheap crude steel and semi-finished products. Their cost advantages stemmed from a combination of a cheap and reliable source of ironstone and a high degree of technical efficiency, since the works were fully integrated and large. The basic open-hearth steel furnace used with a molten pig charge has remained the standard steel-making process at Scunthorpe from 1890 to the present day, although there have been many improvements in economy and technique. Important innovations have also kept iron-making costs down, particularly the extensive use of sintering to increase the metallic content of the ore burden. In 1967 over 80 per cent of the charge fed into the steel furnaces was molten pig, the highest proportion of any British steel district; Scunthorpe's crude steel production of 2,820,000 tons represented nearly twelve per cent of the national total.

A summary of the present capacity of the three plants reveals the considerable size differences between them and the dominance of open-hearth practice. The works will in future operate as one integrated system.

Summary of Plant Capacity:

| Plant | Blast Furnaces | Steel Furnaces |
|---|---|---|
| Appleby-Frod. | 2 at 27ft<br>2 at 31ft | 9 open-hearth (basic)<br>6 at 160–99 tons<br>3 at 200–99 tons |
| Lysaght | 1 at 18–20ft<br>1 at 22–24ft<br>1 at 27ft | 4 basic open-hearth at<br>120–49 tons<br>2 LD Converters at 75 tons |
| Redbourn | 2 at 20–22ft<br>1 at 22–24ft | 7 basic open-hearth at 120–149 tons |

The high efficiency of Scunthorpe's iron-making plant is seen in the annual output per furnace of 347,000 tons, compared to a national mean of 275,000 tons.

In recent years Scunthorpe's competitive position has been changed by developments in technology and material supply. Vast overseas finds of rich iron ores have made imported ores correspondingly cheaper and more reliable, and the richer ores are more cheaply smelted, so that optimum location for pig-iron production has shifted from the home ore fields to coastal plants. Moreover, with the introduction of super-ore carriers and the opening of deepwater terminals in South Wales and Teesside, the gap will widen, especially as home ore production costs have been rising. Committed to home ores, Scunthorpe has seen its coastal competitors in the above districts forge ahead, and although it has cut back production of Frodingham ore and substituted imported ores, this has so far been on a limited scale, with 250,000 tons of imported ore in 1967. Secondly, the *LD* Converter steelmaking process has proved itself to be at least twenty-five per cent cheaper than open-hearth steel.[25] However, with the exception of two small converters at Lysaghts, Scunthorpe has remained loyal to the now obsolete open-hearth plants while its competitors, such as Llanwern and Port Talbot, have changed.

The position for Scunthorpe is thus critical. Steel has lost its growth rôle in employment terms, for the major redevelopment scheme put forward by the British Steel Corporation in July 1969 will require a labour force reduction of about 3,500 from its present 20,000. The £150 million plan will increase steel production by 1,800,000 tons, and confirms the place of Scunthorpe in the national steel industry. It also illustrates the immense significance attached to the careful use of all those parts of Scunthorpe's existing plant and infrastructure that are still viable. All the ironmaking capacity will be retained, but will use up to sixty per cent imported rich ores; the additional rail haul on the ores from either Redcar or Immingham deepwater terminal will be offset by the greatly increased outputs possible from existing blast furnace plant. The open hearth steel plants will be replaced by three *LD* converters of 300-ton capacity, and new high capacity bloom, billet and medium section mills will be added, as well as a continuous casting plant. Scunthorpe is fortunate to be chosen as the location of the first major rationalisation scheme of the British Steel Corporation, but the reduced manpower needs can be seen as the final check to a period of very rapid growth, in which the sheer dominance of the steel industry discouraged other types of manufacturing from entering the town.

## Other Industries

Lack of a diversified employment base has been manifested in two ways. In the first place, there is a general shortage of industries employing males which are not bound up with the steel industry. Firms processing the abundant outpourings of slag to make fertilisers or road materials are a familiar part of the Scunthorpe industrial structure, but many of the firms engaged in the engineering industries have also been shown to be very dependent on contracting for the steel works, especially in steel fabrication and structural steel.[26] Employment for females is equally scarce, although knitwear and other similar industries are present. Yet it has been the experience of most of the firms employing female labour in Scunthorpe that full-time labour is scarce. This has been put down to the disincentive of high male wages, but it is more likely to be linked to social factors—a high married proportion geared to male shift work, so that the main demand seems to be for part-time employment.

Scunthorpe's undeveloped Trentside is a possible focus of future growth for industries needing waterborne materials. A major influx of jobs for males in order to diversify the industrial structure, such as in the rather similar case of Port Talbot, is difficult because of Scunthorpe's relatively low labour supply, which cannot easily be rectified in view of its isolation from other towns. Yet, on the basis of population projections made by the planning research unit of Leeds School of Town Planning, the male working age groups in Scunthorpe should increase from 37,700 to 40,200 between 1961 and 1971, without accounting for any migration movement.[27] This increase will occur in a period of static or contracting employment in the steel industry. Scunthorpe has thus a difficult period of adjustment to face, and its ability to attract new industries to employ males must be realistically assessed against two main factors. In the first place, the high wages of the steel industry will command the labour market. Secondly, the granting of *intermediate area* status to Doncaster and district, which has far better communications and a larger labour supply, must act as a very strong counter-attraction to a prospective industrialist considering a site in the region. The strong efforts which are successfully bringing new growth industries to stave off the labour reduction in the steel town of Port Talbot are being made against a labour pool of small conurbation size and full development area status, since Port Talbot, Neath and Swansea, along with smaller urban settlements, form a compact unit from the point of view of labour attraction and mobility. In the light of these considerations, a Humber bridge and related internal road improvements could be of considerable benefit to Scunthorpe.

References to this chapter are on pages 226–7

# 6

# Humberside's Advantages for Industry

SOME FUNDAMENTAL general comparisons of inter-relationships within the industrial structure of Humberside have been made in detail in the previous chapters, and this detail has been referred to the geographical context of selected economic factors. Industries are part of a pattern of considerable duration, and changes in such a pattern occur by attrition and accretion rather than by large-scale and abrupt movements. These slow processes reflect appraisals of an area by industrialists, and in most cases these appraisals have not been made with full information of the local conditions and even less often with a knowledge of comparative advantage with other regions. The resulting industrial mix reflects the successful firms, or the firms whose location decisions have been vindicated by the crucial test of survival in competition. In some cases this is of a local nature, and competition from firms in other areas has little or no effect on their success because they rely on local resources, including industrial links, and local markets. Such firms tend to be small and to constitute a small proportion of the total regional employment. Large firms are rarely initially large and their growth reflects an advantage in a market beyond the local one, for which they have some particular production superiority. A study of the size distribution of firms in the area indicates that the majority are small firms whose market is local and whose employment constitutes a relatively small proportion of the total labour force. The large firms that have evolved show most clearly those features of location that Humberside offers preferentially. Recently, large firms have been created, and they reflect the increasing tendency for industrial managers to make location decisions in a national context. These have received separate treatment because they may represent most clearly those advantages that are considered specific to Humberside and may indicate aspects of the region that have attracted new enterprise and capital, and which may be the basis for continued expansion. The creation of special concessional location features by government legislation is more likely to emphasise these advantages than to create completely new ones.

Business enterprises are complex and much of their complexity stems from organising the assembly of raw materials, developing new production techniques or accepting useful innovations developed by other firms, and pursuing new markets by amalgamation or advertisement. Examples were given of the ways in which local firms have responded to these problems of industrial organisation within a spatial context. The geographer is deeply concerned with problems of spatial interaction, and much geographic literature implies that the location of activities is more readily understood in terms of movement than in terms of place. Industrial growth is closely related to economic circulation, and this puts the arguments about the Humber bridge, the internal road and rail communications and Hull's status as the third-ranking English port into a proper geographic context. Even the region's pivotal position on an estuary has its fullest meaning in terms of the implied opportunity for organising movement.

### Movement, Place, Personnel

Movement is an important consideration and should be prime in the appraisal that industrialists make of the area. The task of collecting data on such appraisals by management was beyond the opportunity of the authors, but the Central Unit for Environmental Planning was able to collect the views of 103, mostly large, firms, employing over 90,000 people in 1966, concerning the advantages and disadvantages of Humberside. The replies from these firms could not be made available to us for clear reasons of confidentiality, but summary tables appeared in the industrial report prepared by the Central Unit, and a copy was kindly given to us. The information in its appendices 5 and 6 was rearranged, so that no data was omitted, to give an assessment of Humberside in terms of movement, place and personnel. Table 26 presents this reconstituted data.

None of the replies was directed because the questionnaire was open, so that the first clear result is that management is concerned most with various aspects of movement. The replies contained references to good access to the Continent, poor road links to the A1, and the lack of facilities for overseas air travel. The distinction between internal and external movement in Table 26 indicates that foreign trade links dominate the advantages, whereas poor accessibility to domestic markets is the basis of most complaint. The difficulties of such contacts are emphasised, and it seems as if the elimination of these would accentuate the advantage of the Humber. Such intrinsically useful

**Table 26**

AN ASSESSMENT OF THE ADVANTAGES AND DISADVANTAGES OF
HUMBERSIDE MADE BY INDUSTRIAL MANAGEMENT AND WEIGHTED
BY THE NUMBER OF EMPLOYEES REPRESENTED BY EACH RESPONSE
AND BY INDUSTRY ORDER

| cts of: | Assessment of the assets and disadvantages of Humberside made by industrialists and weighted by employment involved | | | | | | | | | | | | | |
|---|---|---|---|---|---|---|---|---|---|---|---|---|---|---|
| | *Total* | | *Food* | | *Chemicals* | | *Metals* | | *Eng.* | | *Textiles* | | *Build.* | |
| vement | | | | | | | | | | | | | | |
| xternal | 39·9 | *5·5* | 5·9 | *0·0* | 9·2 | *2·6* | 11·7 | *0·0* | 8·2 | *1·6* | 1·6 | *1·0* | 3·3 | *0·3* |
| nternal | 19·3 | *45·3* | 5·8 | *6·8* | 2·2 | *7·9* | 6·9 | *12·6* | 2·0 | *9·2* | 0·5 | *2·7* | 1·9 | *6·1* |
| otal | 59·2 | *50·8* | 11·7 | *6·8* | 11·4 | *10·5* | 18·6 | *12·6* | 10·2 | *10·8* | 2·1 | *3·7* | 5·2 | *6·4* |
| ce | | | | | | | | | | | | | | |
| ersisting | 8·8 | *2·8* | 0·5 | *1·1* | 2·3 | *1·7* | 4·1 | *0·0* | 0·8 | *0·0* | 0·4 | *0·0* | 0·7 | *0·0* |
| iminishing | 3·4 | *16·5* | 0·0 | *3·2* | 1·4 | *4·3* | 1·2 | *3·6* | 0·0 | *4·2* | 0·3 | *0·5* | 0·5 | *0·7* |
| otal | 12·2 | *19·5* | 0·5 | *4·3* | 3·7 | *6·0* | 5·3 | *3·6* | 0·8 | *4·2* | 0·7 | *0·5* | 1·2 | *0·7* |
| sonnel | | | | | | | | | | | | | | |
| otal | 28·5 | *28.4* | 4·2 | *5·6* | 3·5 | *2·2* | 3·1 | *11·1* | 11·6 | *6·3* | 2·2 | *0·7* | 3·9 | *2·5* |
| al | 99·9 | *98·5* | 16·4 | *16·7* | 18·6 | *18·7* | 27·0 | *27·3* | 22·6 | *21·3* | 5·0 | *4·9* | 10·3 | *9·6* |

*ource:* The data in this table are derived from the information in appendices 5 and 6 in Humberside Industrial Report. Data relating to advantages are taken from Appendix 5; the disadvantages are taken from appendix 6 and are shown in italics. The discrepancy he total in the disadvantages reflects the rounding in the calculations that must have been d by the Central Unit in finding the percentage figures given: our calculations had to be de from these rounded marginal totals expressed as percentages.

assets as the availability of suitable land for development and the relatively easy disposal of effluent were instanced. There is a basic difference: the control of effluent disposal tends to increase with industrial and urban development and these attributes were distinguished as diminishing advantages, whereas the amount of land available for industrial use is unlikely to be an obstacle to development for a very long time and, although it is diminishing, it is classed as a persisting advantage for the period of industrial development covered in this book. The disadvantages of place are greater than the advantages, but the proportion of these disadvantages which is diminishing is dominant. Under this category are the amenities of the area and what was termed the area's 'poor image'. An image reflects an object rather than a supposition, and as more people come to the area the very many excellent attributes will be more widely known and the mental map image will improve as it comes to reflect the reality. The category of persisting disadvantages contains the problem of water supply, but this is not a problem restricted to this area and the solution is not local. Under the category of personnel there is virtually the same proportion of advantage as disadvantage and some replies are incompatible. In some cases the area was praised for its availability of labour, in others for its dearth. The difficulty of recruiting executive and graduate staff is not easily reconciled with the presence of an expanding university, many of whose departments play an active part in local industry. There may, of course, be a strong case for adding new technology departments to the existing faculties. No distinction was made between the diminution or persistence of labour attributes, as these are notoriously variable; for instance the lower costs of labour mentioned by some firms as important may well become more equable as industrial expansion occurs.

In these aggregate terms of industrial opinion there is some evidence, then, that the area's advantages and disadvantages are most strongly focused on aspects of movement, followed by labour and indigenous resources. But a more detailed examination reveals that the area's greatest attraction is seen in terms of its external relations and its strongest disadvantages in terms of its internal accessibility. This is a diminishing disadvantage because improvements are already scheduled and work has already started on trunk road improvements, and, as this accessibility improves, the area's relative position will become an even stronger attraction to industrialists. A similar pattern of diminishing disadvantage is seen with respect to some resources, especially amenities and health or educational facilities, which were cited by some managements. Their views seem opposed to the following opinion expressed in *The Times* of 2 August 1969.

> [The city of Hull] . . . rebuilt the central area shopping centre. Millions of pounds were spent on new schools, slum clearance and welfare facilities. Housing provision for pensioners and recreational and training centres for the handicapped are among the best in the country.
>
> The Queen's Gardens civic centre . . . received high praise from both citizens and tourists.

Many of the positive aspects of the area such as the pleasant environment will persist. These aspects of place are of less importance to industrialists.

## Assessment According to Industry Type

A common misunderstanding concerns the assumption that industry is homogeneous in its location needs. We have noted already that industries may be distinguished in terms of size and of their relation to resource or market or some intermediate position in the industrial sequence. The data available does not permit a partition of the area's appraisal by particular *MLH* categories to match the maps presented earlier, but a more gross division is possible in terms of the *SIC* groups adopted by the Census and also used in part of Chapters 3 and 4. This material can be tabulated to indicate whether the management of separate types of industry shows preference for aspects of movement or of place: each distinguished as persisting/external and as diminishing/internal, (Table 26).

In order to determine whether the different industries attach the same importance to each of the factors, we can attach a rank to each attribute for each of the six industry types for both advantages and disadvantages.* The null hypothesis is that the ranks of the three attributes are similar. An examination of these data, put into ranks to avoid attaching any unwarranted accuracy to the figures, shows that the advantages of the region are assessed differently by the six industrial types. Particularly important are the engineering and textile groups, which attach more importance to labour advantages than to movement or resource in aggregate; whereas in the assessment of the disadvantages each industry accords prime place to movement and, in general, the order of assessments is essentially the same.[1] Each industry gives greater importance to the region's external accessibility than to its relations with domestic trade, and in this respect it is worth noting that the least discrepancy is for the food industry with its reliance on locally produced vegetables, especially in South Humberside. This is an industry whose recent rapid growth has been associated with the proximity and development of the fish freezing industry. Conversely the industries are unanimous about the poor inland routeways. Under the current government proposals these disadvantages are likely to diminish, and the region's attraction as a location for industry will depend even more heavily on good accessibility.

* In this chapter as elsewhere the statements are based on statistical analysis. These are omitted from the text, but the use of 'significant' implies a level of acceptance of a statement at at least a 5 per cent level. The use of unexpected or unusual refers to this same probability level. In this section the tests are all non-parametric and include runs test, the Friedman analysis of variance and Kolmogorov-Smirnov tests.

Similarly, with respect to resources, the greatest emphasis is laid on advantages that are likely to remain and on disadvantages that are likely to diminish: a feature of the comments that is encouraging for industrial development and indicative of the urgent problems. The resource assets of the region ought not to be given an emphasis they apparently do not warrant in the view of most management already in the area, whereas even greater emphasis is due to the trade position of the area; few industries are based on local resources, most on imported resources. The improvement of internal, that is local and domestic, movement facilities will engender regional economic growth in a way that may not be implied by increasing the efficiency of external trading facilities. The lack of particular stress on certain aspects of movement or place by one or two industry types, which is out of sympathy with the general pattern, is surprising; the largest discrepancies are found in the chemical and metal trades. In the former there is an unusually large proportion of persisting disadvantage in terms of external movement and place, whereas in the metal trades the opposite is true, with a greater than expected emphasis on diminishing disadvantages. Again, in the chemical industry, Table 26 shows that the value of 4·3, that is 2·6 + 1·7, is larger than expected and combines a larger than usual external movement disadvantage with a similarly larger persisting disadvantage of place. This negative result from the data indicates that the region is suitable for a wide variety of industry and is not alien to certain types. It also reflects the problems of using this sort of data as the basis for inferences, rather than having particular problems in mind before data is assembled, but we had no such control. It now remains to examine in more detail the types of movement from the area as they affect industry.

### Accessibility to Hinterlands

Value of Materials by Hinterland

The importance of accessibility to different hinterlands for the supply of raw materials can be assessed in a number of ways. The tonnage transported or the frequency of use of particular routes may be seen as less important than the gross value of materials used or the value to the particular industry of materials brought from each area or the number of employees in each industry which is dependent upon materials from each source. Only if there is substantial agreement between these various measures of hinterland importance can it be asserted that, for example, the Humber ports are of greatest significance or that the area is only slightly dependent upon the rest of the country; that it is closely associated with local resources; or that it is not dependent upon the rest of Yorkshire for raw materials. The four hinterland regions used by the Central Unit were the Humber ports, the West Riding of Yorkshire, the local area, and the rest of the country including all other ports.

With respect to the gross value of raw materials assembled in the region, local industry depends on the Humber ports for almost half its supplies, on the rest of the country for nearly a third, and the remaining sixth is split equally between the local area and the West Riding. For those industries that have been established since 1945 the order of priority is retained but the values differ, so that some two-thirds of the raw materials come via the Humber ports, a fifth from the remainder of the country and a tenth from local sources, implying a diminished reliance upon the rest of the Yorkshire and Humberside planning region. This places an interesting emphasis on external accessibility and underlines the diminished reliance on internal, medium and long-haul movement. The proportionate contribution of each industry to the total value of materials derived from each of the four hinterlands is given in Table 27.

### Table 27

THE ORIGIN BY HINTERLAND OF RAW MATERIALS USED BY
INDUSTRIES IN HUMBERSIDE AND ASSESSED BY VALUE AS A
PERCENTAGE OF TOTAL VALUE

| SIC | Per cent of total value | | Hinterland Humber | | Rest of Country | | West Riding | | Local | |
|---|---|---|---|---|---|---|---|---|---|---|
| | % value | Rank | % value | Rank | % value | Rank | % value | Rank | % value | Rank |
| IV | 39·4 | 1 | 30·42 | 1 | 7·29 | 2 | 0·75 | 4 | 0·95 | 3 |
| V | 25·7 | 2 | 3·24 | 4 | 10·18 | 1 | 9·02 | 2 | 3·26 | 3 |
| III | 14·4 | 3 | 4·22 | 2 | 3·79 | 3 | 0·37 | 4 | 6·03 | 1 |
| XIV | 3·9 | 4 | 3·39 | 1 | 0·28 | 2 | 0·08 | 4 | 0·14 | 3 |
| X | 3·7 | 5 | 1·38 | 2 | 2·03 | 1 | 0·13 | 4 | 0·17 | 3 |
| VIII | 2·8 | 6 | 0·01 | 4 | 2·56 | 1 | 0·16 | 2 | 0·07 | 3 |
| XI | 2·3 | 7 | 0·40 | 2 | 1·58 | 1 | 0·24 | 3 | 0·09 | 4 |
| XV | 2·2 | 8 | 1·74 | 1 | 0·25 | 2 | 0·17 | 3 | 0·04 | 4 |
| IX | 1·3 | 9 | 0·05 | 4 | 1·11 | 1 | 0·06 | 3 | 0·08 | 2 |
| VI | 1·2 | 10 | 0·12 | 4 | 0·62 | 1 | 0·31 | 2 | 0·15 | 3 |
| VII | 1·1 | 11 | 0·12 | 3 | 0·65 | 1 | 0·08 | 4 | 0·24 | 2 |
| XII | 0·9 | 12 | 0·00 | 3.5 | 0·39 | 2 | 0·51 | 1 | 0·00 | 3.5 |
| XIII | 0·5 | 13 | 0·00 | 4 | 0·18 | 2 | 0·23 | 1 | 0·09 | 3 |
| XVI | 0·6 | | 0·00 | | 0·60 | | 0·00 | | 0·00 | |
| Total | 100·00 | | 45·0 | 1 | 31·5 | 2 | 12·1 | 3 | 11·3 | 4 |

*Source:* Derived from marginal totals of Table 13 in Humberside Report Industrial Survey. 77·2 per cent of the chemical industry's imports come via the Humber ports. The value of 30·42=39·4 (77·2)/100

N

This table shows two facets of the value of trade. In the first place it indicates the importance of each hinterland as a supplier of raw materials to each industry group; there are important and significant variations from the overall pattern of priorities. The three classifications most heavily dependent on imports are, in order, timber with 87 per cent, paper and printing with 79, and chemicals with 77. It must be recalled that this figure of 87 per cent reflects the dependence of the timber industry on the Humber ports; it does not necessarily imply that this imported timber constitutes a large proportion of all materials for all industry: in fact it is less than 4 per cent. For the paper industry the raw materials coming to the Humber ports constitute less than two per cent of the area's total imports by value. The case of the chemical industry is quite different. It depends very much, 77 per cent, on the Humber ports and these materials constitute practically one-third of the value of all materials assembled in the region. In contrast to this set of industries, the clothing, building materials, vehicles and other manufacturing industries each have less than 1 per cent of their raw materials by value supplied via the Humber ports. Chemicals, metal manufactures and food industries, with eighty per cent of the total value of imported materials, dominate the area's trade to such an extent that comparison between industries can become distorted. For example, while paper and printing relies for 79 per cent of its materials on the Humber ports, the food industries import 29 per cent, yet in terms of value these imports are 6·5 times greater.

The data in Table 27 do indicate the *relative* importance to each industry group of the four source hinterlands, but when this set of priorities is referred to the overall set of priorities to determine whether industry groups tend to show the same pattern of hinterland preference it must be remembered that these overall preferences are heavily affected by the values of materials imported by the three largest industry groups. Therefore it would be unrealistic to use the value of 45 per cent in column 3; but it is appropriate to assert what the least or most important hinterlands are for each industry, and to compare this with the general *order* of importance. If each industry tended to express the same hinterland preference as the general one, then we should expect a preponderance of *ones* in column 3 and of *fours* in the final column. In fact there are more *fours* in the third column than in the last, and the overall pattern of priorities shows considerable variation between industry groups. The most persistent feature is the high priority given to the value of materials coming from the rest of the country and the slight difference between the other three sources. There is no reason to believe that even this distinction exists between the hinterlands of the six categories of industry established since 1945 when it is assessed in terms of priority of preference.

Secondly we can note the extent of the discrepancy between the value of the materials supplied from each hinterland and the value expected for that industry under the assumption that it follows the overall pattern of value of materials derived from each source. An unexpected result is one showing a significant departure from the value that would occur if the industry followed the general pattern; it does not mean necessarily that such a departure is unexpected on other criteria.[2] There are important departures from the expected pattern in the chemicals, paper and, to a less marked extent, in the timber industries in terms of dependence upon the Humber. In contrast there is a marked independence of the port for metal manufactures, and to a smaller but still significant extent this is found with engineering and vehicles. Both food and metal manufacture show an unexpectedly large dependence on local sources, in contrast with chemicals. Textiles, leather and clothing, combined for reasons relating to the test statistics used, and engineering and vehicles, also combined, have a marked dependence on the rest of the country and this tendency is seen to a slighter extent in the metal goods industry. These results are refreshingly consistent with the findings and their explanations offered in Chapter 4, because the data sources are so different and to get similar conclusions from two sets of measurements is a test of validity. The departures from the expected pattern for all industries are imitated by the values for the industries established since 1945, with chemicals intensifying its dependence upon imported materials and food increasing the value of raw materials drawn from the local area.

Number of Employees dependent on Materials by Hinterland

When the industries are considered in terms of their numbers of employees there is a change of emphasis in the importance of hinterlands for raw materials. Two-fifths of the region's employment depends on imports from the rest of the country, and one-fifth on imports from each of the other three hinterlands, implying a reduction in importance of the Humber ports and illustrating the difference between labour intensive and material intensive industries. In fact the importance of the Humber ports in terms of value of materials supplied depends to a great extent on the chemical industry which ranks first in value of materials, and whose materials constitute 67 per cent of the total value of imports. But the metal manufacturing category and the vehicles and the metal goods categories, ranking first and fourth in terms of employment, depend for the bulk of their employment on supplies from the rest of the country. This ambivalent allegiance of hinterland preference between value and employment is more readily understood if the use each industry makes of materials from the four sources is assessed in its ranked importance, when the ranks are taken in terms of either the actual value or of employment, or in terms of the relative importance of each source to each industry, as shown in table 28.

These ranks are closely associated in all cases except the supply of local materials. The important anomalies are seen in building

**Table 28**

THE RANK IMPORTANCE OF HINTERLANDS BY INDUSTRY ORDER
IN TERMS OF THE ACTUAL VALUE OF RAW MATERIALS AND THE
ACTUAL NUMBERS OF EMPLOYEES INVOLVED IN THE FIRMS
RESPONDING

| SIC | Total | | The rank importance of hinterlands by industry order in terms of actual value and actual employment involved | | | | | | | |
| | | | Humber | | Rest of Country | | West Riding | | Local | |
| | Value | Employ-ment | Value | Employ-ment | Value | Employ-ment | Value | Employ-ment | Value | Employ-ment |
| | R | R | R | R | R | R | R | R | R | R |
| IV | 1 | 2 | 1 | 1 | 2 | 3 | 2 | 5 | 3 | 5 |
| V | 2 | 1 | 4 | 5 | 1 | 2 | 1 | 1 | 2 | 2 |
| III | 3 | 3 | 2 | 4 | 3 | 4 | 4·5 | 7 | 1 | 1 |
| X, XI | 4 | 8 | 5 | 6 | 5 | 6 | 4·5 | 9 | 5 | 9 |
| VIII, IX | 5 | 4 | 9 | 9 | 4 | 1 | 8 | 6 | 7·5 | 7 |
| XIV | 6 | 7 | 3 | 2 | 8 | 11 | 10·5 | 11 | 9 | 10 |
| XV | 7 | 9 | 6 | 3 | 9 | 8 | 9 | 10 | 11 | 8 |
| XII, XVI | 8 | 11 | 10·5 | 10·5 | 11 | 9 | 3 | 4 | 4 | 11 |
| VI | 9 | 5 | 7·5 | 7 | 7 | 5 | 6 | 2 | 7·5 | 6 |
| VII | 10 | 6 | 7·5 | 8 | 6 | 7 | 10·5 | 8 | 6 | 3 |
| XIII | 11 | 10 | 10·5 | 10·5 | 10 | 10 | 7 | 3 | 10 | 4 |

*Source:* Values derived from data in Table 13 and Appendix 7b in the Humberside Report Industrial Survey.

*rho* (value, employment) = 0·7000
*rho* (Humber)                = 0·9205
*rho* (Rest of country)       = 0·8545
*rho* (West Riding)           = 0·6364
*rho* (Local)                 = 0·4250 (not significant)

The general level of accord between employment and value of materials is not in itself remarkable, but it needed establishing once the reduction in overall importance of the Humber ports as a basis of employment as compared to their prime importance in terms of value of materials was noted. It largely reflects the shift in emphasis between the chemical industry and the metal manufacturing industry, metal goods and Vehicles.

materials, with a low value of materials but high employment, and for paper the same is true to a slighter extent. This is not surprising in view of the conjunction in this category of papermaking and printing, which have quite different locational requirements. The other anomalies of clothing plus other manufacturing industries and textiles plus leather, may be anomalous because they are grouped together. This generally very close relationship between the ranked value and ranked employment dependency on imported materials from each hinterland is useful because it makes more general any results that arise from comparisons of either value or employment; it gives some basis for comparability between the criteria.

It may well be that industries assemble their raw materials from one region and sell their product in another; thus the Humber ports may be of greater locational significance for imports than for exports when the rest of the country may dominate. In fact industries in general show no preference for an import function over an export function when all values are considered as one series. If there were a preference we should expect a significantly lower sum of ranks for the import values.[3] But when we examine Table 29 for the priority accorded to

**Table 29**
THE RANK IMPORTANCE OF EACH HINTERLAND FOR IMPORTS
AND EXPORTS TO EACH INDUSTRY ORDER

| SIC Order | Humber | | Local area | | West Riding | | Rest of Country | |
|---|---|---|---|---|---|---|---|---|
| | import | export | import | export | import | export | import | export |
| III | 3 | 4 | 1 | 2 | 4 | 3 | 2 | 1 |
| IV | 1 | 2 | 3 | 3 | 4 | 4 | 2 | 1 |
| V | 4 | 3 | 3 | 4 | 1 | 2 | 2 | 1 |
| VI | 4 | 2 | 3 | 4 | 2 | 3 | 1 | 1 |
| VII | 4 | 4 | 2 | 1 | 3 | 3 | 1 | 2 |
| VIII, IX | 4 | 4 | 3 | 2 | 2 | 3 | 1 | 1 |
| X, XI | 2 | 4 | 4 | 3 | 3 | 2 | 1 | 1 |
| XII, XVI | 3·5 | 4 | 3·5 | 3 | 2 | 2 | 1 | 1 |
| XIII | 4 | 4 | 1 | 1 | 2 | 2 | 3 | 3 |
| XIV | 1 | 4 | 3 | 3 | 4 | 2 | 2 | 1 |
| XV | 2 | 4 | 3 | 2 | 4 | 3 | 1 | 1 |
| Total | 32·5 | 39 | 29·5 | 28 | 31 | 29 | 17 | 14 |

*Source:* Adapted from figures stated in the Humberside Industrial Survey.

each hinterland for import and export by industry type we note that the rest of the country seems to be placed high very often.[4] This is not complete; for example, chemicals and timber place their import priority on Humber ports, food and building materials on the local region and metal manufactures on the West Riding. In fact five *SIC* categories import more raw materials from some specific region than from the rest of the country. The impression remains that the non-specific areas, that is the heading 'rest of country' in Table 29, are important. In terms of market, only shipbuilding and building materials —including pottery—place a priority that is not in the rest of the country: both are local and this result may be expected in terms of the cost of transporting the bulky materials.

We can also see from Table 29 that the export category through the Humber ports is least important in the majority of cases cited, chemicals, metal manufactures and engineering being the exceptions. If there were no preference for certain areas by industry we should expect the sum of ranks of preference to be similar. For exports and imports there is a significant departure from such a value, and this gives some ground for believing that a preference is shown for a certain region or regions. In fact from the sum of ranks we conclude that it is the rest of the country that is exceptional for imports and exports. The portmanteau nature of the rest of the country as a region perhaps makes it less interesting than if we were able to isolate a more specific region or quality as being exceptional. Nevertheless this result, together with a similar appraisal of the ranks of the relative importance to employment of each hinterland, indicates that the remainder of the country is more important as a market function than as a supplier of raw materials. In fact, three-quarters of the employment dependent upon sales to each hinterland is associated with goods destined for the rest of the country, a tenth is consumed locally, just less than this is sent to the West Riding and only five per cent is exported from the Humber ports. There is no important difference between the ranked assessment for imports of the other three areas, although the Humber ports seem anomalous in their low export priorities. This provides an interesting adjunct to the assessments of industrialists that was considered earlier. The rank attached to the *actual* distribution of material sources and markets indicates that greatest dependence is placed upon the rest of the country for a market and least upon the Humber ports, while the earlier assessments emphasised the value of the ports. These are complementary, not incompatible; increased efficiency in road links to the domestic hinterlands would seem to entail substantial improvements to local industry.

Road and Rail Transport

Most industry categories seem to move most of their products by road: the overall pattern of movement is shown in Figure 35. The only

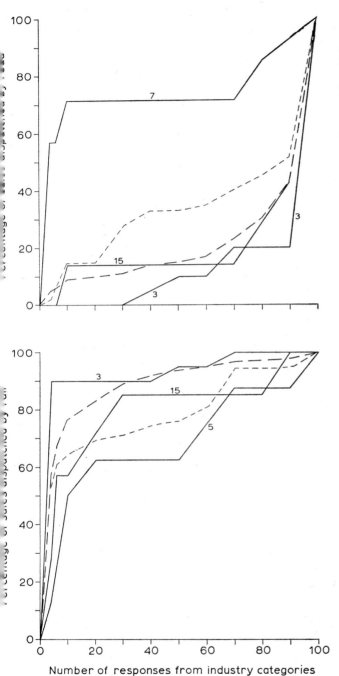

Number of responses from industry categories
as a percentage

Fig 35.
DISTRIBUTION OF
SALES BY ROAD
AND RAIL

(a) ROAD. This graph is derived from data contained in the *Industrial Survey* carried out for the *Humberside Report*. In this report, information was tabulated for each of the *SIC* categories *III* to *XVI*, in terms of the number of responses from each industry sending a given range of its sales by road. The general pattern is shown in the graph, together with *SIC III* with 20 responses, *SIC VII* with 7 responses, *SIC XV* with 7 responses. The total number of responses was 102. Each cumulative frequency was compared with the overall distribution, and only *SIC VII* departed significantly from it

(b) RAIL. The general pattern is again shown in the graph. It is quite different from the pattern of road traffic: indeed the two are necessarily complementary. *SIC III* is anomalous, *SIC V* with 8 responses is anomalous at very nearly the *p* 0·05 level. *SIC XV* is essentially similar to this general pattern, as is every other order

*Source:* Humberside Report, The Industrial Survey, Appendices 9 and 10. The employment represented by the responses is distinguished: in both cases it differs significantly from the graph of responses. The finer breakdown of employment by response from individual orders cannot be derived from the published data

significant departure from the overall pattern, on the evidence contained in the number of responses from industry, is the shipbuilding
industry whose pattern of movement is the inverse of the general
pattern. As the majority of domestic sales is dispatched by road or
rail, it follows that the pattern of rail movement is complementary and
this can be seen from the graph. The food industry is anomalous, in
that an even greater majority of its rail movement is in very small
consignments, whereas the metal manufacture trades very nearly show
a significantly greater proportion of the larger consignments sent by
rail. Doubtless more insight would be gained in this sort of situation
if we had access to figures for separate *MLH* categories and for the
size of firm making particular responses. The overall patterns of
responses are significantly different from those responses when
weighted by employment and this pattern is shown on the graphs.
Nevertheless it seems reasonably clear that substantial improvements
in road communication are required.

**Circulation and Industrial Location**

The purpose of this chapter has been to examine the difficulties and the assets of the region for industrial location as they were
implicit in the evidence collected from the management of large local
firms. To give some framework to the various replies, the first distinction concerned the importance attached to three basic aspects of
locational advantage; movement, place attributes and labour supply.
Overwhelming importance was given to various aspects of movement,
because the efficient control of movement is fundamental to business
success. We then distinguished internal from external movement and
found that the weight of evidence was directed towards dissatisfaction
with the access to domestic hinterlands; this emphasised the attractiveness of the Humber ports. The collection of materials from these
hinterlands and the movement of finished products to them was then
considered in two ways; first by reference to the value of goods, and
secondly by reference to the employment dependent upon each hinterland. There was a difference in weighting, caused by the different
structures of industry, contrasting, for example, chemicals or food with
engineering or metal goods. The region is attractive to industries
dependent on resources, especially imported resources, and has been
preferred in particular by such industries with a high value added.
Only Hull shows any consistent attractiveness to later-stage industry
categories; this reflects more the existence of inter-industry links than

good transport links to other non-local markets. This chapter contains strong evidence that the rest of the country provides the most important market, and it may be assumed that this region will continue to depend more and more heavily on the domestic market. Finally, contact with the rest of the country is primarily by road traffic and there is wide agreement that the roads linking this area with all other places are inadequate. Any improvements will augment the very real advantages offered to industry by the deepwater estuary. A link across it will promote movement between North and South Humberside and thus make the attributes of Hull more widely felt. This seems essential in order to encourage those industries least dependent on resources and most dependent on the characteristics of large towns, such industries being integral to a balanced industrial structure. Bridge and improved roads will engender movement, and movement engenders industrial location.

References to this chapter are on page 227

# Acknowledgements

WE WISH TO thank the following people and organisations for their help in the preparation of this book:

Tables 6, 7, 15, 17, 26, 27 and 28, and Fig 7 are based on material first published in *Humberside—a Feasibility Study* (1969) and the accompanying *Humberside Report: the Industrial Survey*, both prepared by the Central Unit for Environmental Planning for the Department of Economic Affairs. The material is reproduced here with the permission of the Controller of HM Stationery Office. No responsibility can be accepted by any government department or body for the uses to which it has been put.

Her Majesty's Factory Inspectorate for permission to view the records at various regional offices; the Central Unit for Environmental Planning for giving us a copy of their report on the Industrial Survey conducted for the Feasibility Study; Mr G. E. Skipworth for his very considerable help in the collection of the data, its tabulation and its mapping, especially in Kingston upon Hull: we also benefited from discussions with him; Dr E. Evans, Department of Economics, University of Hull, for making available Employment Exchange data collected by his staff as part of the Humberside Manpower project; Miss Brenda Myers for collating the data used in the preparation of some of the maps; Mr R. Dean, Mr K. Scurr and Miss W. Wilkinson, of the Department of Geography drawing office, for preparing the final maps and diagrams; Mrs J. Dealtry and Mrs B. Smith, of the Department of Geography, University of Hull, and Mrs S. Leigh, of the Department of Geography, Gainesville, Florida, for typing the manuscript; various firms for information and photographs, and the British Transport Docks Board at Hull, Grimsby and Goole.

We should particularly like to thank our wives, Rosemary and Jean, for all their help in the collection of the data and for their constant help and encouragement in the preparation of the book at all stages.

219

# References and Bibliography

## CHAPTER 1

*Background to Humberside* pages 11–47

1 Attention was drawn to these trends in two pioneer analyses of the inter-war period:
PEP. *The Location of Industry in Britain* (1939)
Report of the Royal Commission on the Distribution of the Industrial Population (1940. Cmd 6153). Also called the Barlow Report

2 See for example:
Smith, D. M. 'Recent changes in the regional pattern of British industry' *Tijdschrift voor Economische en Sociale Geografie* 1965, 133–145

3 Central Unit for Environmental Planning. *Humberside: a Feasibility Study* (1969) and the Industrial Survey, mimeographed

4 James, J., Scott, S. F., and Willats, E. C. 'Land use and the changing power industry in England & Wales' *Geographical Journal* 127 (1961), 286–309

5 Rostow, W. W. 'The Take-off into self-sustained growth', *Economic Journal*, 66 (1956), 25–48

6 *Feasibility Study*, 88

7 For a detailed definition of North and South Humberside see below p. 21, also Figures 3, and 8

8 *Feasibility Study*, Chapter 1, fits Humberside into the context of national planning strategy in the later decades of the century. It has this to say about the anticipated role of Humberside:
A large population increase—estimated at nearly 15 million—is expected to take place between now and the end of the century. These extra people will need houses, schools, shops and roads . . . part of the new population could be housed in large new urban areas in relatively underpopulated parts of the country. Such a policy would have its problems, but also its advantages. In effect what we had to do was to assess the costs and benefits of this course in the particular circumstances of Humberside. (*Feasibility Study*, para 1.2)

9 Needleman, L. *Regional Analysis* (1968)
Income differences are not always insignificant, however; Perloff and

associates have shown that per capita income in New York State in 1951 was approximately three times as high as in Mississippi

10    Peter Shore, Secretary of State for Economic Affairs, writing in *The Times*, 3 July 1969 ('Policy to keep pace with industrial change')

11    Report of a Committee under the chairmanship of Sir Joseph Hunt. *The Intermediate Areas* (1969)

12    The measures of assistance to the seven new intermediate areas were announced in Parliament by Peter Shore on 25 June 1969. Apart from North Humberside, these areas are the Yorkshire coalfield, part of the Notts-Derby coalfield, NE Lancashire, SE Wales, and Plymouth, with Leith in Scotland. The aid, estimated at about £20 million per annum, includes building grants, industrial development certificates available as freely as in development areas, full development area labour training grants, assistance with derelict land clearance, and job transfer benefits

13    Yorkshire and Humberside Economic Planning Council. *A Review of Yorkshire and Humberside* (1966)

14    Blumenfeld, H. *The Modern Metropolis* (MIT 1967)
      The interested reader is also referred to:
      Fortune (Editors of) *The Exploding Metropolis* (1958)

15    For a discussion of the problems arising out of the use of irregular areal units in work-journey studies, see:
      Chisholm, M. C. 'The geography of commuting', *Annals of the Association of American Geographers*, 50 (1960), 187–8, 491–2

16    *Report of the Royal Commission on Local Government in England* (Maud Report) in three volumes (1969)

17    This axis of uplift is generally known as the Market Weighton axis, after the small East Riding town. For a detailed description of Humberside's geology the reader is referred to:
      British Regional Geology, *East Yorkshire and Lincolnshire* (1948)

18    *Feasibility Study*, p 63

19    Ibid p 65. CEGB announced, in July 1970, its intention to build Britain's biggest power station at South Killingholme, costing some £250m, oil-fired with a 4,000mw capacity

20    For further details on the water supply position in relation to the development of South Humberside see Chapter 5 p 187–8

21    British Road Federation. *Yorkshire and Humberside's Needs* (1968), 5

22    New boundary extensions for the city of Hull came into effect on 1 April 1967, and these have incorporated a considerable acreage on the north-east periphery of the city, including the large Bransholme Estate which is still in the construction stage

23    The 1961–66 figures are estimates based on the census material and the Annual Abstracts of the Registrar General, and because of the slight difference in date of collecting the statistics they are not precisely comparable, although the order of magnitude is not likely to be affected. The authors wish to thank their colleague Mr D. G. Symes for making available these calculations, which form part of his own joint work on

population in Yorkshire and Humberside, qv Symes D. G. and Thomas J. G. with Dean R. R. *The Yorkshire and Humberside Planning Region: An Atlas of Population 1951–66* (University of Hull, Department of Geography Misc. Series No 8, 1968)

24  *Feasibility Study*, Table 2d, p 7


## CHAPTER 2

*The Humberside Estuary and its Ports* pages 48–63

1  *The Times*, 28 September 1966
2  *Feasibility Study*, Ch 9, p 62
3  British Waterways Board. *The Facts about the Waterways* (1965)
4  Bird, J. H. *The Major Seaports of the United Kingdom* (1963)
5  *The Times*, 28 January 1969
6  British Transport Docks Board and Grimsby Corporation. *Grimsby—a Place for industry to expand* (1968)
7  Bird, J. H. *The Major Seaports*
8  On 11 July 1969 the British Steel Corporation announced that it was considering the feasibility of importing iron ore for a reconstructed Scunthorpe steel complex through such a deepwater jetty. But a firm commitment for a terminal at Redcar might have meant that a 100 mile rail haul for ores from Redcar to Scunthorpe would have been preferred
9  It should also be noted that some oil companies, including Shell, Regent and Petrofina, have their own private jetties and storage installations which lie outside the Dock Estate


## CHAPTER 3

*The Economic Structure of Humberside* pages 64–99

1  Perloff, H. S., Dunn, E. S. Jr., Lampard, E. E., and Muth, R. F., *Regions, Resources and Economic Growth* (1961)
2  This and all other employment figures in this chapter are based on the Ministry of Employment and Productivity returns for the Humberside Exchange areas, and the Annual Abstracts of Statistics for national figures
3  Leeds School of Town Planning, Planning Research Unit. *Scunthorpe: a study in Potential Growth* (Scunthorpe, 1966)
4  See Davies, G. 'Getting the regions off the dole', *Sunday Times*, 8 October 1967
5  *Feasibility Study*, Ch 10, 85–87
6  The literature of urban hierarchy and central place studies is vast, but an introduction is provided by:
Smailes, A. E. 'The analysis and delimitation of urban fields'. *Geography* 32 (1947), 151–161

Berry, B. J. L. and Garrison, W. 'Functional bases of the central place hierarchy', *Economic Geography*, 34 (1958), 145–154

7  Among the more important grading schemes of British urban centres are:
Smailes, A. E. 'The urban mesh of England and Wales'. *Transactions of the Institute of British Geographers*, 11 (1946), 87–101
Green, F. H. W. 'Urban Hinterlands in England and Wales: an analysis of bus services', *Geographical Journal*, 116 (1950), 65–88
Carruthers, W. I. 'The main shopping centres of England and Wales', *Regional Studies* 1 (1967) 65–81

8  Residential development since 1961 has been particularly rapid in the area covered by Hessle exchange, which includes much of Haltemprice and Beverley RD (see also Chapter 1)

9  See, for example:
Hall, P. G. *The World Cities* (1966)
Humphreys, G. 'Services in Growth centres and the Implications for regional planning with special reference to South Wales. *Advancement of Science*, 22 (1965), 181–2

10  Perloff, H. S. and others. *Regions, Resources*, Ch 4, 60–62

11  Blumenfeld, H. 'The economic base of the metropolis', *Journal of the American Institute of Planners*, 21 (1955), 114–32

12  Duncan, O. D., Scott, W. R. and others. *Metropolis and Region* (1960)

13  Florence, P. S. *Location, Investment and Size of Plant* (1948). Florence actually uses two methods of calculation in this work, qv pp 41 and 60 which refer to the method adopted in this chapter, and which Florence used for regional calculations; and page 63 which outlines an alternative method which Florence tended to use for sub-regional calculations for small units

14  Central Unit for Environmental Planning. *Humberside Industrial Survey* (1969)

15  Ibid

16  Duncan, O. D. and others. *Metropolis and Region*. The scheme used by Duncan and his associates is based upon a table of 'Important Input-Output Relationships for Primary Resource Extractors and First and Second Stage Resource Users, 1947', prepared by the Regional Studies Unit of Resources for the Future Inc. (Baltimore)

17  Weber, A. Translated C. J. Friedrich. *Theory of the Location of Industries* (Chicago, 1929)

18  Florence, P. S. *The Logic of British and American Industries* (Revised Edition, 1961)

19  The term 'weight-losing' is used to describe the loss of weight of materials through wastage and other causes as they are manufactured. With raw materials the proportionate loss is usually high, but this rapidly diminishes as the materials themselves assume a semi-manufactured state. See also:
Weber, A. *Theory of the Location of Industries*

Smith, W. 'The location of industry', *Transactions of the Institute of British Geographers*, 21 (1955), 7–18

20 On the strength and significance of such linkages in an established industrial region see:
Florence, P. S. *The Logic of British and American Industries*

21 *Feasibility Study*, Ch 3, 37–39

22 Maud Commission, 1969. The Report stated that '. . . neither [Grimsby nor Scunthorpe] would be strong enough, and that joining them would make a much more effective unit. We also recognize that a single unit would better fit the future facts as industry grows on South Humberside and communications improve'

23 For a general discussion of the sector theory of economic growth see Perloff, H. S. and others. *Regions, Resources*, pp 60–62

24 For further information on growth industries see:
Humphreys, G. 'Growth industries and the Regional Economies of Britain', *District Bank Review*, 144 (1962), 35–56
Humphreys, G. 'The growth industries in Britain', *Geography*, 49 (1964), 288–293

25 Perloff, H. S. and others. *Regions, Resources*, Ch 4, pp 55–62

26 *Feasibility Study*, Ch 10, p 97

27 British Steel Corporation Press Information Office. News Release 23 (January 1969)

28 Creamer, D. S. U.S. National Resources Planning Board. *Industrial Location and National Resources* (Washington, 1943)

29 For further details see Chapter 5, page 201

30 A firm of cycle manufacturers moved from Smethwick to take up vacant space in part of the Elswick Hopper cycle factory in 1968; this may inaugurate a renewed phase of expansion

CHAPTER 4

*Industrial Distribution in Humberside* pages 100–164

1 The tests used for the Humberside data are those developed by Clark and Evans, 'Distance to Nearest Neighbour as a measure of spatial relationships in populations', *Ecology* (35) (1959) 445–453. The minimum level of acceptance used in this chapter is p0·05; that is a chance of being right 95 times in every hundred; this is an acceptably rigorous level of acceptance, but more details can be found in any elementary statistics text, and the word significant is used only when this level is reached

2 Lewis, P. W. 'A Numerical Approach to the Location of Industry', Hull University Press, Occasional Papers in Geography No 13 (1969)

3 Watts, H. D. 'The Industrial Geography of Rural East Yorkshire', M.A. thesis, Hull University (1966) p 64

o

4 The median proportion of total costs spent on raw materials + fuel, labour, and transport by each category, A to F, varies, and so does the median value added. The proportion of MLHs in each category with a value greater than the median for all categories changes from A to F for raw material cost, transport costs and value added. There is a significant trend in these changing proportions, and the pattern of change in them was analysed by partitioning the overall chi-square value. This partition was done in two ways: first by collecting the MLHs into A + C + E and B + D + F and comparing their variability, secondly by seeing how much of the total chi-square value was accounted for by a linear trend in the proportions. Details of this technique can be seen in (2)

5 Watts, H. D. 'The Industrial Geography . . .'

## CHAPTER 5

*Industrial Patterns within the Region* pages 165–202

1 Johnson, B. L. C. 'The distribution of factory population in the West Midlands Conurbation', *Transactions of the Institute of British Geographers*, 25 (1958), 209–223
The figures for Humberside and for the West Midlands conurbation are derived from HMFI records

2 Bellamy, J. M. 'Some aspects of the economy of Hull in the nineteenth century, with special reference to business history'. Unpub. Ph.D. thesis, University of Hull, 1965

3 Rose, Downs & Thompson Ltd. *At the Tail of two Centuries*

4 Blundell, Spence & Co Ltd. *The Blundell Book, 1811–1951, A Short History* (1951)

5 Reckitt, B. N. The History of Reckitt and Sons Ltd (1951)

6 Bennett, R. Smith and Nephew 1856–1956 (1956)

7 Bellamy, J. M. 'Some aspects of the economy of Hull . . .'

8 Davis, R. *Twenty One and a Half Bishop Lane* (1961)

9 Bellamy, J. M. 'Some aspects of the economy of Hull . . .'

10 Reader, W. J. *Birds Eye, The Early Years* (1963)

11 Alston, H. F. *Annual Report 1967–68 Kingston upon Hull* (Hull, 1968)

12 *Hull Daily Mail*, 8 July 1969

13 Information provided by the Beverley Borough Council, 1969

14 Little, B. *The First Hundred and Fifty Years* (1963)

15 *Feasibility Study*, p 70

16 *Feasibility Study*, p 69

17 Courtaulds Annual General Meeting, July 1969. Chairman's statement

18 *The Times*, 25 April 1969

19 The authors are grateful to Total Oil (GB) and Continental Oil (UK) for providing technical data on the Lindsey and Humber oil refineries,

20 County of Lincoln, Parts of Lindsey. First Development Plan Review *Report of the Survey on North Lindsey* (Lincoln CC, 1965)

21 Gillet, E. 'The history of Grimsby' in Grimsby Official Guide (1967), 35–50

22 Reader, W. J. *Birds Eye*

23 Pocock, D. C. D. 'Iron and steel at Scunthorpe', *East Midland Geographers*, 3 (1963), 124–138

24 The statistical material relating to the Scunthorpe steel industry is based on British Steel Corporation: Iron and Steel Statistics Bureau. *Iron and Steel Annual Statistics 1967* (1968)

25 British Iron and Steel Federation. Stage I Report of the Development Co-ordinating Committee—Benson Report (1966)

26 Leeds School of Town Planning: Planning Research Unit. *Scunthorpe —a study in Potential Growth* (Scunthorpe Corporation, 1966) Ch 6, 35–47

27 Leeds School of Town Planning: (Scunthorpe Corporation, 1966) Ch 4, 19–23

## CHAPTER 6

*Humberside's Advantages for Industry* pages 203–217

1 For the Food Industry the greatest importance is attached to *Movement* which is given *rank 1*; the least to *Place*, given *rank 3*, and *rank 2* goes to personnel. When this is done for each of the six orders the sum of ranks is 8, for place is 16, for personnel is 12. A Friedman $X^2_r = 5.33 = p0.072$ is not significant. Thus the sums of ranks are not significantly different. For disadvantages, the sum of ranks for movement is 6, for place is 17, for personnel is 13. $X^2_r = 10.33 = p0.0017$. Thus the sums of ranks are significantly different

2 A table for this is not required. The values can be derived from Table 27, and the chemical industry, *SIC IV* can be used to illustrate the derivation of these values. For all industry 45 per cent of raw material costs are derived via the *Humber Ports*, thus for *SIC IV* we should expect 45 per cent of 39·4 (the contribution of the chemical industry to all imports from all sources for all industries) to come from the *Humber Ports*. That is 17·73 per cent. With $12.45 = 31.6$ per cent of 39·4 from *Rest of Country*; $4.71 = 12.1$ per cent of 39·4 from *West Riding*; and $4.45 = 11.3$ per cent of 39·4 from *Local*. These values are different from the actual ones and statistical tests were made of the discrepancy for each *SIC*

3 Again a table would be cumbersome as it involves ranking each value of goods moved. Eleven orders are used for 4 hinterlands for both imports and exports, giving 88 possible positions of the actual value of goods moved. The largest value is for the export of chemicals and this

has rank 1. The smallest is for no exports or imports; there are 5 such occurrences, each having rank 86. The sums of these ranks for each hinterland are, Humber = 545; Local = 545·5; West Riding = 550; Rest of Country = 279. The Mann-Whitney 'U' = 929·5 giving a $Z_u$ = 0·321, not significant. And it is the similarity of 3 hinterland sum of ranks and the low value for the *Rest of Country* category which are important

4    In fact Friedman $X^2_r$ = 17·28 > p0·001
     A statistics text usually includes an explanation of these methods. One elementary text is Siegel S. *Non-parametric statistics for the behavioural Sciences* (1956)

# Index